HERBERT HOOVER AND THE REPUBLICAN ERA

A Reconsideration

Edited by
Carl E. Krog
William R. Tanner

**UNIVERSITY
PRESS OF
AMERICA**

LANHAM • NEW YORK • LONDON

Copyright © 1984 by

University Press of America,™ Inc.

4720 Boston Way
Lanham, MD 20706

3 Henrietta Street
London WC2E 8LU England

Library of Congress Cataloging in Publication Data
Main entry under title:
87-1524
Herbert Hoover and the Republican Era.

Includes bibliographies.
1. Hoover, Herbert, 1874-1964—Addresses, essays,
lectures. 2. United States—Politics and government—
1919-1933—Addresses, essays, lectures. 3. Agriculture
and state—United States—History—20th century—
Addresses, essays, lectures. I. Krog, Carl E., 1936-
II. Tanner, William R., 1933-   .
E802.H38   1984   973.916'092'4   84-17317
ISBN 0-8191-4288-3 (alk. paper)
ISBN 0-8191-4289-1 (pbk. : alk. paper)

All University Press of America books are produced on acid-free
paper which exceeds the minimum standards set by the National
Historical Publications and Records Commission.

This volume is dedicated to Martin L. Fausold, who
exhibited enthusiasm for the pursuit of knowledge.

TABLE OF CONTENTS

INTRODUCTION

This book describes a man, an age, and their interaction. Herbert Hoover lived a long life. He was born in the home of a village blacksmith in the small eastern Iowa farming village of West Branch in 1874, and died ninety years later in New York City's Waldorf-Astoria.

To varying degrees we are all prisoners of time and place. What makes life and history interesting is how people respond and adapt to different circumstances. The first three essays discuss Hoover's successful career as Secretary of Commerce in the Warren Harding and Calvin Coolidge Administrations. The remaining essays, deal with Hoover's presidency from 1929-1933. To Americans of the New Era, Hoover reflected and epitomized the myths and ideals of an earlier America. Although a majority of Americans lived in cities by the 1920s, adult Americans, like Hoover typically were born in nineteenth century rural America. Although not born in a log cabin, Hoover resembled Henry Ford and Thomas Edison, and other famous contemporaries in beginning life in rural community. Unlike many contemporaries, however, Hoover was orphaned at ten and lived in a Quaker community. Hard work, mutual help, and self-reliance comprised Quaker tradition and practice.

Like many other Americans, Hoover left the Middle West for the West Coast. Hoover spent his teenage years in Oregon, graduated from Stanford University, and began a very successful career as a mining engineer. While Hoover worked in Australia, China, and Siberia, America continued its rapid transformation from a rural to an urban, industrial society. Before returning to America, Hoover earned his reputation as a humanitarian by administrating a relief program during World War I.

As the first three essays suggest, Hoover's quest for efficiency, reliance of specialized expertise, and calls for volunteerism and limited government, fit well within the dominant political, social and economic world of the 1920s.

The 1920s, however, were not only the world of increased industrial production, consumerism, and automobiles. It was also the world of the Harlem Renaissance, Black Nationalism, Mahatma Ghandi's

Nationalism. This non-white world of rising
expectations and awareness, added a new dimension to
the 1920s. As the two essays on Hoover's relations
with Blacks and American Indians make clear, he seemed
unaware of these changes. Hoover's racial views
undoubtedly fit well within the world he
knew--American society of the 1920s. Moreover, these
two essays reveal Hoover the politician rather than
Hoover the humanitarian.

The next two essays highlighting Hoover's farm
policies and the paradox of "want in the midst of
plenty" during the Great Depression, reveal Hoover the
rigid ideologue rather than the politician or the
humanitarian. The portrayal of a rigid, unfeeling,
doctrinaire man is the picture embedded in the memory
of a generation of Americans after 1929. A generation
of Democratic office-seekers reminded voters if their
memories faltered. Hoover's emphasis on self-help and
self-reliance for individual achievement of the
"American dream" did not work in an urban-industrial
society of mass unemployment and an agrarian
environment of overproduction and rural poverty.
Workers and farmers did not share in the Hooverian
vision, nor in the "prosperity" of the 1920s. One
spokesman for disgruntled farmers was North Dakota's
Senator, Gerald P. Nye. Nye's views and the voting
patterns of the Iowa Congressional delegation,
featured in the last two essays, suggest that by the
end of his presidential term, America's agricultural
heartland believed that Hoover had not done enough to
meet the national emergency where traditional values
were found wanting.

Until recently, most historians, along with large
segments of the American public, have shared a
critical view of Hoover and the Republican Era. John
D. Hicks' book, Republican Ascedancy, 1921-1933,
published in 1960, pilloried Republicans and the
Republicans associated with Presidents Warren Harding,
Calvin Coolidge, and Herbert Hoover. In it, Secretary
of Commerce Hoover, is characterized as "an
understanding friend at court" of business. As
President, Hoover is portrayed as the friend of "great
business corporations" willing to dole out federal
monies to rehabilitate industrial giants while
refusing to relieve "distressed individuals" during
the Great Depression. This occured, according to

Hicks, because (pp. 279-280) the American people had
"turned their backs" on reform and reformers, and
handed the country over to the hard-boiled
conservatives who controlled the Republican Party
after Theodore Roosevelt led the progressives into the
wilderness and left them there. . . . /and/ business
leaders led straight to the Panic of 1929, then on
deeper and deeper into the worst depression the
western world had ever known in modern times."

Subsequent scholarship--Joan Hoff Wilson and
Ellis W. Hawley readily come to mind* --attempted to
redress that view of the Republican Era with
particular attention to the role of Herbert Hoover.
Wilson attempted to cast Hoover in the role of a
"forgotten Progressive" while Hawley portrayed the
Great Engineer as the architect of a New Era and New
Day vision of future America. This vision was
primarily a business-government-labor partnership
which smacked not only of a "liberal vision" for
American society, but became a reality of the postwar
1940s and 1950s political economy.

The present collection of essays portray no such
unity. Indeed, they are a diverse lot which focus
upon some of each of the aforementioned
interpretations. Some emphasize Hoover's
"progressive", reformist and forward-looking
tendencies; others see him in the traditional mold of
the aloof, cold President, unwilling to accomplish
needed changes in human relationships during the Great
Depression. Thus, while all deal with Hoover and all
are based upon extensive research at the Herbert
Hoover Library in West Branch, Iowa, each author
retains his own interpretation of Herbert Hoover's
role during the "Republican Era"

Herbert Hoover is representative of those who
attempt to build a bridge between the past and the
future.   The era between the World Wars was a
continuation of that effort and the Great Engineer
played a major role. It was a time of America's
"coming of age". According to Donald R. McCoy,*

In effect, the United States of the 1920s
and 1930s was an island of time somewhat
separated from the past and the future by
the titanic storms of the two world wars.
It was an island of diverse people

ix

and forces struggling both to escape and
preserve the past and to find and evade the
future, in a time and place sufficiently
isolated so that none of these desires could
be accomplished effectively.

After Hoover left power, ending the Republican
Era, the American government and society moved in new
directions to face the national emergencies of the
1930s and 1940s. During these years, Hoover continued
to warn of big government, excessive spending,
expansive foreign policies and generally to defend his
philosophy of "rugged individualism". Within a decade
after his death in 1964, some of his worst fears
seemed realized. By 1974, Americans were having
sobering second thoughts about getting mired down in
spending programs. Americans were also increasingly
aware of being too dependent upon government
bureaucracies over which they had little or no control
as the facts of the Watergate scandals unfolded.

What Hoover tried to do as Secretary of Commerce,
and as President, was to find a middle ground between
the cooperative, simple, interdependent society of his
early youth and the impersonal, complex, industrial
society with its prerequisites for a stronger guiding
hand from government. As these essays make clear--in
the end, Hoover failed. Americans still have not
resolved the dilemma between needing a strong
government to help and protect the weak on the one
hand, and on the other, protecting the individual from
the overwhelming power of the state.

The authors of these essays came from different
parts of the country: William R. Tanner, Humboldt
State University, Arcata, California; David D. Lee,
Western Kentucky University, Bowling Green, Kentucky;
Carl E. Krog, University of Wisconsin Center,
Marinette, Wisconsin; William G. Robbins, Oregon State
University, Corvallis, Oregon; Larry Grothaus,
Concordia College, Seward, Nebraska; C. Roger Lambert,
Arkansas State University, State University, Arkansas;
Bernard M. Klass, Pierce College, Woodland Hills,
California; David A. Horowitz, Portland State
University, Portland, Oregon; and David L. Porter,
William Penn College, Oskaloosa, Iowa.

Many of these essays have been published
previously in historical journals. "Herbert Hoover
and the Development of Commercial Aviation,

1921-1926", appeared in Business History Review, 58
(Spring, 1984) 2:78-102." 'Organizing the Production
of Leisure': Herbert Hoover, Fishing, and Outdoor
Recreation in the 1920s" was published in a slightly
modified form in the Wisconsin Magazine of History, 67
(Spring, 1984) :199-218 as " 'Organizing the
Production of Leisure': Herbert Hoover, Fishing, and
Outdoor Recreation in the 1920s". "Herbert Hoover's
Indian Reformers Under Attack: The Failure of
Administrative Reform" appeared in Mid-American, An
Historical Review, 63, (Oct., 1981), :155-168. "The
Federal Farm Board and the Antecedents of the
Agricultural Act, 1929-1933" was previously published
in Readings in Historical and Contemporary Economic
Issues. "The Perils of Western Farm Politics: Herbert
Hoover, Gerald Nye, and Agricultural Reform,
1926-1932" appeared in the North Dakota Quarterly, 52,
(Summer, 1984), and "The Iowa Congressional Delegation
and the Great Economic Issues, 1929-1933" first
appeared in the Annals of Iowa, 46, (Summer, 1982),
:337-345.

     Collectively, the authors of the foregoing essays
are indebted to the following people and institutions.
Robert McGown and the staff of the University of Iowa
Libraries; Peter T. Harstad, former Director of the
State Historical Society of Iowa; Larry Angove of the
Herbert Hoover Institute; Director Thomas T. Thalken
and his staff of the Herbert Hoover Presidential
Library, and the National Endowment for the Humanities
Summer Seminar Fellowship Program. These sources
provided support and services enabling the seminar
participants to conduct research in pleasant
surroundings in east central Iowa. The writers are
indebted to Marge Burley, Typing Plus; Susan Polzin,
and Violet DeWilde, who prepared the manuscript for
publication. For stimulating ideas and questions,
thanks go to George H. Nash, Richard Kottman, Susan E.
Kennedy, Richard Lowitt, and Donald R. McCoy,
consultants at the NEH Summer Seminar in 1979.
Special thanks go to Lawrence E. Gelfand and Ellis W.
Hawley, who attended nearly all seminar sessions and
contributed much to the success of the research.
Above all, we are grateful to Martin L. Fausold, of
the State University College of Arts and Science,
Geneseo, New York, and Director of the 1979 NEH Summer

Seminar in Iowa. His kindly personal manner and
competent professionalism promoted a scholarly,
productive atmosphere in sultry, summertime Iowa.
This volume is dedicated to Martin, who exhibited
enthusiasm for the pursuit of knowledge.

Carl E. Krog
William R. Tanner

* Joan Hoff Wilson, Herbert Hoover: Forgotton
Progressive. Little, Brown, 1975; Ellis W. Hawley,
The Great War and the Search for Modern Order. St.
Martin's Press, 1978

Donald R. McCoy, Coming of Age. Penquin Books, 1973

SECRETARY OF COMMERCE HOOVER'S WAR ON WASTE 1921-1928

by William R. Tanner

Historians have always recognized the important role played by Herbert Hoover in the development of Federal economic policies during the 1920s. Secretary of Commerce Hoover and his associates, among other things, waged a highly-publicized campaign against waste in industry. They championed efficiency, standardization, simplification and other programs designed to increase production of goods and services. Until recently, histories lumped Hoover's economic policies with a general interpretation of the Harding-Coolidge years as an Era of a Second Great Barbecue, wherein the federal government resumed the Gilded Age practice of dispensing large favors to business interests. This interpretation cast the 1920s as rejecting progressive reform ideas so prominent in the Pre-World War I era. New works have challenged such a simplistic view and suggest more continuity between pre- and post-World War I America.(1)

Although legislative progressivism (i.e.) New Nationalism and New Freedom withered on the vine after the Republican Ascendancy in 1921, administrative progressivism (i.e., elite decision-making and centralization) was alive and well. The sources for the "New Era" relationship between business and government lay in the era of Theodore Roosevelt and Woodrow Wilson. Guided by Secretary of Commerce Hoover, 1921-1928, the quest for the elimination of waste in industry was a continuation of similar ideas advocated earlier by what Otis Graham labels "Order" progressives. Hornell Hart, a member of President Hoover's Research Committee on Social Trends in 1933, characterized the transition as one from "combative reform psychology to cooperative efficiency psychology."(2)

This paper will analyze one aspect of Hoover's War on Waste, simplification and standardization, with special emphasis upon the Division of Simplified Practice, 1921-1928. The origins and activities of the simplification and standardization movement and Secretary Hoover's close association with it manifest that administrative progressivism did not end with World War I. The New Era political economy constituted a continuation of the American search for

order in a society experiencing the pangs of
urban-industrial change.

One thread of continuity which suggests a close
connection between the Progressive Era and the New Era
was the "efficiency craze." Theodore Roosevelt was a
prototype of the administrative progressive, who
reflected disdain for the legislative, insisting that
"good" men and experts be appointed to commissions,
and generally, sought to place more power in the hands
of nonelected bureaucratic agencies. He linked
morality, efficiency, and good government through the
wielding of executive power. Other people in this
connecting link were Louis Brandeis, who popularized
the term "scientific management"--the synonym for
efficiency in production--in 1910,(3) the "father"of
Scientific Management, Frederick Winslow Taylor, and a
corps of professional engineers and experts, Morris L.
Cooke, Archibald W. Shaw, L. W. Wallace, E. W.
McCullough, men who thought of themselves as a
technical elite with social responsibilities. Many of
these engineers--like Hoover--voluntarily served in
administrative agencies under Woodrow Wilson during
World War I and later served Hoover when he was
Secretary of Commerce. One close associate, Edward E
Hunt, pressed for Hoover's candidacy for president in
1920 because he thought of him as a "Roosevelt
Progressive."(4)

While Hoover was not as politically charismatic
as Roosevelt, he did vigorously pursue government by
expert-staffed commissions and conferences as Commerce
Secretary, and rarely called on Congress for support.
One difference between Roosevelt and Hoover may have
been the latter's persistent emphasis on economics as
the epitome of "social creativity," and his consistent
offers of advice and service to private leaders of
commerce and industry, which he believed were in the
public interest.(5)

Another important similarity between the two men,
understanding Hoover's fetish for efficiency in
commerce and industry, was that both came to accept
large scale combination. Roosevelt and the
progressive organization, the National Civic
Federation, had early denounced small-scale,
competitive enterprise as wasteful and inefficient.
Large-scale business enterprise was acceptable, even
preferable, so long as it behaved responsibly. This
idea came to be gospel for Herbert Hoover in the 1920s
and was manifested by his continued promotion of

cooperation, ethical standards and trade associations.(6) The Sherman Act lost its appeal as a trust-busting weapon not only to New Nationalist progressives, but to most political leaders throughout the Twentieth Century--including Hoover.

Secretary of Commerce Hoover's ideas were also similar to those of Frederick W. Taylor outlined in his Principles of Scientific Management (1911). The Great Engineer would have largely agreed with Taylor's stress on science, as opposed to "rule of thumb" in production, harmony in employer-employee relationships, cooperation as opposed to individualism, and maximum productivity in industry.(7) Hoover was not a simon-pure Taylorite, but he had close associations with followers of Taylor, both before and after World War I, appointed a majority of them to the important Committee on the Elimination of Waste in Industry in 1921, wrote at least two articles for Taylorite publications and, in 1924, appointed a member of the Taylor Society, Ray M. Hudson, to head up the Division of Simplified Practice.(8)

The concept of simplification as a part of the elimination of waste program was established during World War I. A simplification program was conducted by Archibald W. Shaw as head of the Conservation Division of the War Industries Board. That work resulted in the reduction of styles and sizes of such items as solid rubber tires, steel pins, china, crockery and rubber footwear. For example, the number of styles of pneumatic tires was reduced from 232 to nine. Those achievements were highly praised in both popular and professional publications after the war and popularized ideas for a peacetime application of the principle.(9)

One of the more puzzling semantic problems of the age was the confusion over the meaning of the two terms, simplification and standardization. Indeed the phrase "standardization and simplification" was used with such abandon, by both Government officials and publicizers, that special pains were taken to distinguish between them. In 1923 Bureau of Standards Director George K. Burgess asserted that standardization applied to "materials, practice and performance," and simplification to "type, design, and dimensions" of commodities. This did not entirely clear up the matter, but it was accepted that simplification was a part of the broader movement

toward standardization. Essentially, simplification
meant the reduction of sizes, varieties, types and
colors of products and services for the purpose of
eliminating waste, or at least reducing waste,
duplication and "superfluous variety" in production
and product in commerce and industry.(10)

Shaw continued to work for the idea of
simplification after the war and, as a close friend of
Hoover, helped to organize the Division of Simplified
Practice in late 1921. As a private publisher of the
business journals, System and Factory, he continued to
promote the activities of the DSP. Also instrumental
in the workings of the program were E. W. McCullough,
officer in the United States Chamber of Commerce, who
sponsored "simplification conferences," and A. A.
Stevenson, President of the American Engineering
Standards Committee. The AESC lent technical
expertise to the simplification effort and established
its relationship to the general standardization
movement. These and other members of engineering,
business and government organizations were also
members of the DSP Planning Committee throughout the
1920s.(11)

The most immediate impetus for establishing the
DSP was the much heralded investigation of waste in
industry of 1921. The study was conducted between
January and July by the Committee on Elimination of
Waste in Industry, seventeen members of engineering
societies affiliated with the newly-formed Federated
American Engineering Council. This investigation was
important for at least three reasons: [1] it was the
first major effort to press engineers into public
service during peacetime; [2] the Committee was
appointed by Herbert Hoover, first president of the
AEC, executive body the Federated American Engineering
Societies (FAES); and [3] it officially launched
Herbert Hoover's War on Waste as Secretary of
Commerce.(12)

The Committee investigated six industries to
determine where wastes occurred in "material, time,
and human effort" and to recommend how these could be
eliminated. The four principal causes of waste, the
final report concluded, were inefficient management,
idleness, and both intentional and physical ailments.
In other words, any factor which impeded the
productivity of a given industry was waste.
Furthermore, nearly all the criticisms were directly
linked with inadequate standardization and

4.

simplification of materials, design, quality control, costs, research, personnel relations, training of workmen, health and safety standards.(13)

Nearly everyone shared in the responsibility for elimination of waste--management, labor, owners, the public, government and engineers. But the lion's share--more than 50 percent--was assigned to management for planning and controls in eliminating waste. Labor was to cooperate, the public, owners and government were to support increased productivity and a special role was assigned to the engineering profession. They had a "part of all the responsibilities," because they possessed "an intimate and peculiar understanding of intricate industrial problems" and because they were "in a position to render disinterested service and expert judgment." It was "peculiarly the duty of engineers to use their influence individually and collectively to eliminate waste in industry." The chief service of scientific management--thus placing the heaviest responsibility on management of industry--in eliminating waste was "the removal of the unexpected through the standardization of all elements in the manufacturing process."(14)

Waste in Industry, the final Committee Report, was published in July, 1921, several months after Hoover took over his duties as Secretary of Commerce and it set the tone and laid the basis for the New Era economic philosophy and programs. The "domestic dynamo"(15) gathered about him professional experts, mostly engineers and businessmen, began to establish committees and conferences, initiated a publicity campaign that would reach major proportions, and reorganized the Department of Commerce. In his first report to President Warren Harding, Hoover said Commerce would become a "service" department and a kind of "general staff to American business." This did not mean interference, but only to find out what American businessmen wanted and then perform that service for them. The report's major thrust was on how to eliminate waste, which he said was caused primarily by inadequate "collective capacity." Thus Commerce would do all it could to "assist trade associations," promote cooperation, minimize labor conflicts, "maximize" production, and coordinate a program of standardization which would look toward the elimination of waste.(16)

In both his overall reorganization plans and

5.

establishment of the DSP, Hoover relied heavily on two
men outside the Department, Frederick M. Feiker and
Archibald W. Shaw. Both strongly supported
simplification and after the establishment of the
Division, remained as members of the DSP Planning
Committee. Feiker was an electrical engineer and
vice-president of McGraw-Hill in charge of publishing
journals on the electrical industry and electrical
engineering. He was granted a temporary leave of
absence to work with Hoover during 1921 as Assistant
to the Secretary. He not only contributed to the
reorganization plans and initiated the first
simplification conference with the brick industry, but
later used his publications to promote the elimination
of waste program.(17)

     Archibald W. Shaw was an old acquaintance and, as
noted earlier, former head of the Conservation
Division of the War Industries Board. He, too, was a
publisher, in this case, of business magazines, and
was probably most valuable to Hoover as a propagandist
for simplification in the business community. A
constant stream of articles on the benefits of
simplification appeared both in his own and other
journals. In addition, he played an important role in
publishing the first DSP "textbook," Simplified
Practice: What It Is and What It Offers (1924), to be
used for college courses in industrial management.(18)
Indeed, next to Hoover, Shaw could be dubbed the
Sultan of Simplification! However, upon the
recommendation of Feiker, Hoover appointed William A.
Durgin as Chief of the DSP in December, 1921. Durgin,
top-level corporate executive in Samuel Insull's
Commonwealth Edison, served until June 21, 1924, when
he was replaced with Ray M. Hudson.(19)

     Ideally, simplified practice was to improve
production and distribution of goods and services
through the elimination of waste. More efficient
production, it was argued by Commerce, would promote a
higher standard of living, better relations among the
citizenry, and generally, national progress. Through
a triad of representation from industry and commerce,
engineering societies, and government, the DSP brought
these people together and coordinated efforts to
reduce sizes, varieties, types and colors of goods.
All this was to be done voluntarily, in a cooperative
spirit, in an effort to promote an industry-wide
agreement to follow certain Simplified Practice
Recommendations (SPRs).

DSP was, then, to "simply" be the coordinator and
publicizer. Engineers provided technical expertise,
and "manufacturers, distributors, and users" were to
make the final decisions and agree to abide by the
SPRs. Hoover or a representative of the DSP addressed
trade associations and other organizations on the
advantages of simplification. The DSP then authorized
representatives of trade associations to make a
preliminary survey to determine the existing state of
simplification in a particular industry. The next
step would be to arrange a conference for
manufacturers, distributors and users to consider the
findings, make recommendations and establish a
simplification committee within that industry.

After at least two of these conferences and
agreements were made, the DSP advertised or "sold" the
proposals through a publicity campaign to all segments
of the industry, whether they were a part of the
conference proceedings or not. The Simplified
Practice Recommendations were given official sanction
through publication by Commerce and circulated in
order to solicit a "pledge" by each member of the
industry to adhere to the SPR. However, the process
did not end there, because simplification (and
standardization) committees, in cooperation with DSP,
continued to meet periodically to take stock and
engage in a continual updating of the SPRs. The
purpose of this procedure was to promote
"self-government in industry," another goal of
Hoover's, in order to avoid regulations and controls
of industry by government.(20)

It was readily perceived that total compliance
was impossible because not all businesses were engaged
in mass production. As A. W. Shaw put it, there were
two major groups of business, "custom" and
"utilitarian." Simplification was most adaptable to
the latter or "relatively large-scale, repetitive,
machine process enterprise." The more purposeless
motion and complexity of production that could be
eliminated, the fewer the costs. Thus, if
manufacturers increased their profits through reducing
costs, the savings could be passed on to the buyer,
seller, middleman, and the ultimate customer.

The philosophy of simplification meant the
questioning of each function of business enterprise:
record-keeping, inventory, purchasing, marketing and
other costs of production or distribution. It
entailed asking the question,

7.

What is the lowest expenditure, the smallest
number of clerks, the least equipment, the
minimum degree of complexity with which a
given task may be performed, and to how
great an extent are standard practices and
repetitive performances possible in its
execution?

In other words, what is the "simplest way" to
accomplish a given task in production?(21)

However, effective cooperation was necessary to
achieve maximum efficiency in simplification. Trade
associations, individual manufacturers, wholesalers
and retailers, Hoover insisted, must cooperate with
each other. For example, although a manufacturer of
steel plate might agree to produce a restricted number
of dimensions or thicknesses, the makers, sellers and
buyers of say, refrigerators also had to agree to the
same specifications. In addition, the Bureau of
Standards and other agencies--government and
non-government--were required to coordinate their
activities. The DSP had limited powers of enforcement
and only served as a clearinghouse for experts in
trade associations, engineering societies, and
government agencies with their varied interests and
sensitivities. And, to add to the complexities, all
of these activities were to be coordinated and
rationalized with other standardization programs and
practices at all levels of government and in the
private sector of commmerce and industry. These are
just some of the reasons why simplification was not
simple!

One illustration of jurisdictional conflict
within the government was an early dispute between the
Departments of Commerce and Agriculture over which
agency would coordinate a simplification and
standardization program for the wood products
industry. Secretary Hoover insisted the DSP, because
of its close contacts with manufacturers and
distributors, "would accomplish much better results."
Agriculture Secretary Henry C. Wallace argued that
since the Forest Products Laboratory was lodged in his
Department, that it should coordinate simplification
activities. Although this minor "feud" endured until
Wallace's death in late 1924, Hoover won out with his
insistence that all simplification and standardization
activities were "entirely within the province of the
Department of Commerce."(22)

The activities of the DSP centered on sponsoring simplification conferences, publicity for the program, and giving "official" recognition of the Simplified Practice Recommendations adopted by various industries. Between 1921 and 1924, more than one hundred such conferences were held and DSP officials, or Hoover, gave 193 formal addresses and attended 177 additional meetings where simplified practice was a subject for discussion. The public relations effort included publication of hundreds of articles in trade and technical magazines and newspapers nationwide. The DSP publicity campaign appeared to stimulate interest in, and knowledge about, simplified practice, at least among government officials at all levels, professional technicians, and businessmen.(23)

The tangible result of this activity by 1924 was the acceptance of 25 SPRs. Manufacturers of the brick paving industry, for example, reduced the varieties of their product from sixty-six to six, or a 92 percent reduction. The finished lumber products industry reduced the dimensions of lumber by 60 percent. Other significant reductions were achieved in the varieties of milk bottle caps, brass lavatory and sink traps, hospital bed heights, automobile parts, elevated steel tanks and towers, grocery bags, manhole frames and covers, rubber heels, screw drivers, and wood handles for tools!(24)

Secretary Hoover and members of the DSP were very proud of the simplified practice program, particularly because cooperation was achieved voluntarily, with a minimum of rancor, and because producers, distributors and users had made decisions by themselves--only with the "help" of government. Or, as DSP Chief William A Durgin said, the Hoover policy was to put government "behind business rather than in business." While simplification was accepted by more and more industries, there were still some skeptics, of course, who failed "to appreciate its true value. There seems to be little or no reason for fear on the part of anyone."(25)

The U.S. Chamber of Commerce, commenting on the program, cited numerous benefits to the manufacturer, wholesaler, retailer, and the consumer. For the manufacturer it meant, among many things, less capital tie-ups in raw materials and storage space, "happier" and more permanent employees, "better quality," fewer factory shut-downs, and "intensified sales momentum."

9.

For the wholesalers and retailers simplification meant
"elimination of slow-moving stock," decreased
overhead, less clerical work, better services, and
lower prices. The consumer would benefit by "better
prices," (not lower?) "better quality product," and
"better service."(26)

Engineers played a crucial role in the
simplificataion program, as well as, in Hoover's
overall war on waste. They were the technicians and
experts, many of whom were part of a generation of
engineers with a sense of social responsibility. Many
were industrial engineers employed by large-scale
enterprise. The main consulting group for the DSP was
the American Engineering Standards Committee. The
AESC received and passed judgment upon recommendations
for standards and specifications in commerce and
industry. In 1922, an arrangement was worked out
whereby the AESC became the official technical advisor
for accepted SPRs, as well as, other standards and
specifications established by the Department of
Commerce. The liaison man between the AESC and the
DSP was A. A. Stevenson, whom Hoover also appointed to
the DSP Planning Committee. Like Hoover and the DSP,
the AESC had an elitist orientation, defining
"producers" as manufacturers and distributors of
commodities, "consumers" as "the representatives of a
firm or corporation that uses the commodity," and
"general interests" as including such peple as an
"independent engineer, educators, and persons wh are
neither consumers nor producers as defined above."(27)

Because so many groups were involved in the
program, DSP Chief Durgin and the man who would
replace him, Ray M. Hudson, realized that there was a
need to eliminate "waste" in the standardization
movement itself. Efforts to standardize (which
included simplification), were overlapping and
ill-coordinated. Simplification and standardization
programs were being led by a variety of public and
private groups, including the AESC with its 29
associated bodies, and nearly 100 cooperating bodies,
the U.S. Chamber of Commerce, hundreds of trade
associations, the Federal Specifications Board, the
Bureau of Commerce, several other agencies in the
government, and the Division of Simplified Practice.
This "multiplicity of uncoordinated agencies,"
therefore, was itself in need of streamlining with a
view to eliminating the wasted effort in promoting
simplification and standardization.(28)

A series of meetings were held, after Hoover officially named the DSP as "clearinghouse" for work on all questions related to "simplification and commercial standardization" in the government. Noncommercial applications would be outside its bailiwick. This left the DSP with four major areas of responsibility which required: (a) the interest and support of producers, distributors and consumers to insure effective development and adoption; (b) the appointment of committees or consultants by or from any of these economic groups; (c) the survey of industry or business, by mail or by representation of the Department; and (d) the arrangement of conferences to modify or ratify proposed recommendations.(29) The DSP not only acquired greater decision-making responsibilities, but its areas of responsibility went beyond merely simplified practice. In other words, the DSP became a more comprehensive agency.

If there were problems of duplication and overlapping, difficulties also arose with getting some industries to cooperate. While it is true that some industries were enjoying the benefits of simplification,(30) many were skeptical early for three primary reasons. The first may be categorized as "foot-dragging" or a natural skepticism over trying out a new program. Was simplification profitable? Could cooperation be worked out in all phases of an industry? Would customers be happy with the elimination of certain varieties, sizes and colors of commodities? Hoover's answer was to promote more favorable publicity on the benefits of simplification, place more pressure on trade associations to make them realize this was to their benefit--profit-wise--and motivate the Chief of the DSP to be more of an "evangelist, educator and salesman." The most important of these "foot-draggers" were the electrical, hardware and paint, oil and varnish industries.(31) It was critical to get these important areas into simplification programs because of the widespread and common use of their products.

A second and persistent problem was the fear that collusion among trade associations and industry-wide adoption of simplification and standardization practices might be interpreted as in violation of the Sherman Antitrust Act. In 1922, for example, the Justice Department brought suit against the Associated Tile Manufacturers for violating laws against price fixing. Associated Tile had adopted a simplification program which had received the blessing of Hoover,

although it had not been arranged officially through
the auspices of the DSP. This had led to a charge
that standardization, endorsed by the Commerce
Department, promoted violations in restraint of trade.
Hoover objected, arguing there would always be a
minority of trade associations who would not follow
the rules--whether they adopted simplification and
standardization or not. He strongly supported trade
associationalism which manifested a code of ethics,
cooperation, and even competition within certain
guidelines. Cooperative trade associationalism, he
was convinced, was the only way to eliminate waste,
increase production, and elevate the standard of
liing.(32)

     Finally, there was a fear of excessive
interference by government in private industry. A
special example of this fear surfaced in 1922 with the
lumber industry, particularly the National Hardwood
Lumber Association (NHLA). The heart of the
controversy revolved around defining the dimensions of
a one-inch board! Prio to a Simplified Practice
Recommendation in 1923, there were approximately 32
different dimensions for a one-inch board in the
industry, and the DSP was especially interested in
getting the lumber trade associations to adopt
simplification. The principle reason was to promote
and standardize the building and housing construction
program that Secretary Hoover had in mind.

     The controversy heated up in the summer of 1923,
when members of the NHLA charged Durgin with secret
dealings and a disingenuous relationship with them.
They objected to his recommendations to inspect and
control the lumber industry, which stirred up a minor
revolt against the simplification and standardization
program by the South Pine Association along with the
hardwood people. Durgin's thin skin got the best of
him in an encounter with a New York Lumber Company
which insisted that "An Inch is Still an Inch at
Tonowanda!" Despite this flap, as noted earlier, the
lumber industry did adopt a simplification
program.(33)

     Two other related concerns reared their ugly
heads and continued to plague Commerce during Hoover's
term of office. One of the arguments continually
stressed by supporters of simplification (and
standardization) was that it would increase production
through the elimination of waste, and benefit not only
the producers, but others down the buying and selling

12.

line--"immediately" for the producer, and "ultimately" for the consumer by lowering prices. If this were so, then why did installment buying accelerate during the 1920's? This concerned officers of the National Association of Credit Men as early as December, 1923. Secretary-Treasurer J. H. Tregol warned Hoover that individual credit was "the most dangerous kind of credit" because it presented a false sense of prosperity.(34) One might account for the increased incidence of installment buying, because, whatever the wage-price ratio at this time, the prices of goods were not low enough to thwart widespread credit purchases by individuals.

Another and even more politically sensitive issue related to the simplification and standarization movement was an effort to put the United States on the metric system through compulsory legislation. It was politically sensitive because it smacked of "internationalism" and was viewed as a coercive measure by government. The metric system also had implications for international trade and competition. The Bureau of Standards and Hoover worked behind the scenes throughout the 1920s for its adoption, but refrained from making public statements in support of Congressional bills calling for implementation of the system.(35) Going metric through legislative fiat did not fit into Hoover's voluntary cooperation scheme but it might have encouraged even more acceptance of simplification and standardization for purposes of capturing new foreign markets.

Although Hoover often made much of his concept of "associational activities," and cooperation and voluntarism in matters relating to the elimination of waste, he used at least one method that bordered on coercion. In the spring of 1923, Hoover arranged for a "specification" conference for purposes of coordinating the standardization of purchasing specifications by government agencies. In attendance, besides members of the Bureau of Standards, including the DSP, were members of the National State Purchasing Agents Association and representatives of the United States Chamber of Commerce, National Association of Manufacturers, Society of Automotive Engineers, American Engineering Standards Committee, War Department and Bureau of the Budget. Hoover's address to the gathering stressed the importance of government-suggested simplification, standardization and specifications. When adopted by manufacturers, he pointed out, this would not only eliminate waste in production, but would benefit business, the taxpayer, and the consumer.(36). Soon the federal government was fast becoming the standard setter for commodities, which meant that those in private commerce and industry interested in government contracts were virtually forced to adopt simplification and standardization in order to meet government specifications.(37)

Despite these ripples of discontent, by 1924, the simplification and standardization programs were supported by the vast majority of business and, it seemed, nearly everyone else. This support was garnered in a number of "Hooverian" ways. One was by convincing and influencing certain key leaders of business, like Owen D. Young of General Electric and E. W. McCullough of the U.S. Chamber of Commerce on the value of the programs. They were among the many business leaders and managerial elites who possessed a sense of social responsibility, headed up or called special conferences and committees, and welcomed Hoover's policies, assumptions and direction. Another important method was through a continuing public relations campaign for simplification and standardization. Not only did Hoover and members of Commerce write glowing articles in professional and popular periodicals, but people like Shaw, Feiker, E. E. Hunt and, for a while, Morris L. Cooke, wrote such pieces. Shaw would even send drafts of his articles to the Chief to scrutinize for "errors" before sending them to publishers.(38)

The work of Hoover and the Commerce Department was given particular attention in 1924 for political purposes. Although Hoover was not as influential with Calvin Coolidge as he had been with Warren Harding, he did command respect for his achievements as Secretary of Commerce. And despite the fact that 1924 was a good year economically, there was still the shadow of Teapot Dome, other Harding scandals and the Progressive Party split to worry about in an election year. Therefore, a special effort was made to publicize the "good works" of Commerce and Herbert Hoover.(39)

Between 1925 and 1928, more problems, old ones and new ones, plagued the simplification and standardization movement. For one, and it was the supreme irony, there was continued duplication and overlapping of the work in the movement. Hoover and DSP Chief Ray Hudson were in the unique position of having to devise methods to eliminate waste in their program to eliminate waste in the industry! There were disagreements among professional engineering societies over who had jurisdiction over what and between industrialists and the engineers they worked with in the program. In addition, there wre increased murmurings of discontent by labor leaders, economists and critics-at-large, who were suspicious over who, exactly, was benefiting from the simplification and standardization program. Many concluded that it was not a majority of the working families of the nation. Hoover, Burgess and Hudson confronted these issues through reorganization and efficiency moves, more special conferences, a renewed publicity campaign and, for the first time, modest efforts to involve organizations and representatives of groups other than strictly the business and professional engineering societies.

In early March of 1925, Hudson reported a declining interest in the simplification program by businessmen, since requests for simplification conferences had declined. He attributed this to economic "good times" for industry, which, in turn, deflected their concern for the elimination of waste. On the other hand, statistics indicated that the cost of living had risen by five points since August of 1924. Thus "waste elimination is needed more now than ever before." He recommended two tactics for improving the atmosphere: 1. To stop "indirect selling" of the simplification program and take direct initiative with business. They should "act as leaders, guides or coaches, rather than 'cooperators.' We should be salesmen, not consultants or doctors." 2. In addition, he suggested that the Coordinating Committee be expanded to include groups like the American Farm Bureau, American Federation of Labor and the National Consumers League for purposes of broadening the input and perspective of the programs.(40)

Secretary Hoover apparently approved these suggestions, for a renewed publicity campaign was initiated to promote simplification. This included appeals to trade associations to participate, efforts to defend the program against critics that were "rather mean," and to emphasize the monetary benefits from the program.(41) These efforts continued throughout Hoover's Commerce years and with concrete results, in terms of numbers of simplification conferences held, meetings addressed, publications,

and participants in the programs. Publicity events
such as "Thrift Week" and "Elimination of Waste Week"
were established in order to draw the attention of the
general public. As a part of the education process,
Hudson and E. L. Priest of DSP published an article,
"Saving Through Simplified Practice," in the official
publication of the American Home Economics Association
during "Thrift Week" in 1926. Through this medium
they hoped to encourage home economics teachers across
the land to inculcate in future homemakers the
"science" of budgeting: "And shall we not then say
that a capable home manager, i.e., a wife, means a
better home life, a happier wage earner, and that such
capabilities may be stimulated by common sense
adoption of the elimination of waste programs in the
home?"(42)

Statistics by mid-1928 verified the success of
the rejuvenation campaign. Between 1925 and 1928 the
DSP put sixty-two Simplified Practice Recommendations
into operation,making a total of eighty-six since
1921. It was also emphasized that these SPRs were
accomplished "only on definite requests from
manufacturers, distributors or consumers of a
commodity for assistance in eliminating avoidable
waste," guided--not dictated--by DSP and its advisors.
Monitoring of sales indicated that approximately 80
percent of some 815 trade associations and 7,731
individual firms in commerce and industry had accepted
these SPRs. What was the result in terms of monetary
savings? The lack of reliable statistics made it
"difficult to interpret their benefits in terms of
money," but a general estimate was that the program
saved an overall $600 million annually.(43)

On the surface then, it seemed that the
simplified practice program was broadly accepted by
commerce and industry and a monument to the
achievements of Hoover's overall War on Waste. But
disagreements arose within the leadership of the
simplification movement and dissent and conflict
escalated among the rank and file. During 1926-1927
serious grumblings surfaced among those most
responsible for coordinating simplification and
standardization.

One dimension of the rift involved the failure of
the DSP and the American Engineering Standards
Committee (AESC) to establish good relations. AESC
complained that the DSP usurped too much power and was
insensitive to the prestige of their organization.

The two groups also disagreed over certain technical questions related to simplification. AESC, as well as some industrialists, feared "the possibility of the Government assuming full control of the standardization movement." On the other hand, Commerce charged that the work of the AESC was too slow and lacked systematic follow-up on simplication and standardization matters. Not only was the engineering group's prestige over-blown, but it was uncooperative on the international level and with other branches of the government and engineering societies. As an example of the confusion over jurisdiction and duplication of work, it was pointed out that the AESC and the National Committee on Metal Utilization were duplicating efforts in forty-three areas. Hoover feared the program was not only in chaos, but "seems in many particulars to be losing ground." Therefore, he called a special group of "leading men" to iron out some of these difficulties.(44)

Hoover held his meeting with sixteen men including industrialists Charles M. Schwab, E. M. Herr and Gerald Swope; presidents of engineering societies, John H. Gibboney of the American Society for Testing Measurements, C. E. Skinner of the AESC, L. W. Wallace of the American Engineering Council, and George K. Burgess of the Bureau of Standards. As a result of this preliminary meeting, Hoover decided to establish a committee "to make a comprehensive survey of the standardization movement."(45) But, apparently, the subsequent meetings between industrialists and engineers did not promote harmony. By early spring of 1927 Hoover became displeased over the haggling and delay tactics, which he blamed on representatives of the AESC. In mid-March he wrote industrialists John W. Lieb: "I am convinced that advancement and coordination of standardization work in the country is a question of money and of industrial support." He was disposed, he wrote, to call a meeting "composed solely of industrial executives" to determine the path to take and eliminate engineering representatives. He asked these industrial executives to coordinate and to finance the program, at a cost of one million dollars over a five year period.(46)

Available evidence suggests the tactic did not work, that is, the idea of a non-governmental body virtually taking over the entire work of simplification and standardization. The effort may have been as close as Hoover came to achieving--at

least in one area--his ultimate goal of
self-government in industry. However, he did initiate
a significant reorganization plan in the Commerce
Department, which created an umbrella agency within
the Bureau of Standards to coordinate all activities
related to the simplication and standardization
movement. The former Scientific and Technical branch
of the Bureau (where the DSP had been placed) was
divided into two divisions, Research and Testing and
Commercial Standards. The latter division,
established on July 1, 1927, included Simplified
Practice, Building and Housing, Commercial
Specifications, Commercial Standards, the Federal
Specifications Board, and others. Ray M. Hudson
retained his position as head of Simpified Practice
and also became Assistant Director of the Bureau and
head of Commercial Standards. This remained the
organization pattern until May of 1929.(47) Despite
their reservations, then, it appeared that
industrialists were more than willing to let the
government coordinate and fund programs in commercial
simplification, as well as standardization and
specification.

In the public arena, until 1926, the principles
of simplication and standardization were generally
supported. Simplification and standardization was
accepted as beneficial to society at large; it was on
the details that disagreements arose. Labor union
representatives--especially the AF of L--supported the
movement, even though they did not participate in the
decision-making or deliberations. There was much talk
of cooperation between business, engineers, and labor,
in a striving for "a new economic system," increased
production, high employment rates, high wages and
better working conditions as a result of applying
simplification and standardization. It was taken
more-or-less on faith that elimination of waste would
"increase the purchasing power of the dollar and
likewise advance the American standard of living."(48)

Although concern was expressed within the
Commerce Department over the distributive benefits of
simplification,(49) form 1926 until after Hoover left
Commerce, public criticism of simplification and
standardization steadily mounted. Using questionable
statistics, Hoover and his supporters defended the
movement just as critics charged that it was causing
underconsumption, underemployment, overproduction and
maldistribution. William T. Foster and Waddill
Catchings, two early critics, and unlike most

18.

economists, detected a trend of underconsumption in the nation. The problem was not necessarily overproduction, they wrote, but that industry was reaping more than its share of the profits and thus, the people could not buy the commodities produced. This, they illustrated, by the increased incidence of installment buying.(50)

Increasingly the Chief became unhappy with "popular treatments" of simplification, harsh criticism, and claims--even by his own people--that overproduction was a problem. In May of 1927 he became clearly upset over criticisms of the economy and the workings of Commerce, and asked Archibald W. Shaw to write a rebuttal in one of his publications.(51)

Shaw's response to critics claiming overproduction, published in September, 1927, is instructive for at least two reasons: (1) it probably reflects the insistence by Herbert Hoover that nothing could go wrong, and (2) it manifests how statistics can be used to support almost any position. For example, Shaw pointed to the low prices of 1920-1922, which afterwards made a "modest advance," without mentioning the severe depression of the earlier years. He also indicated that the "union-wage rates" index was 199 for 1920 and 238 for 1925. From this he argued that lower prices and higher wages had produced a better purchasing power for the consumer. However, he failed to mention that only a small percentage of workers in the nation earned "union-wage rates," or that figures which worked for 1920-1925, did not necessarily work for 1927.

His overall argument was that the combination of restricted immigration, a widespread domestic market, and business innovation had produced a great self-contained, consumptive and productive "fortuitous circle," all of which had brought prosperity to the United States. Furthermore, to critics of the "machine" he noted that technology had increased output-per-man-hour by forty percent, and that the number of workers on the payroll had increased some 27 percent between 1914 and 1923. The machine had "improved management" and American business had "answered the call" by having "the nerve to pay high wages." He concluded: "Have we not more pressing problems to worry about than overproduction?"(52) Not only was Shaw's use of statistics faulty (or manipulated?) but there may not have been reliable

19.

statistics available. The main point to be made,
regardless of the validity of his arguments, is that
Shaw--and presumably Hoover--was unwilling to admit
that there <u>might</u> be some "clinkers" in the system.

The problem of increased unemployment was
recognized in 1928, again, both within and outside the
Department of Commerce. Some charged that
unemployment and maldistribution of income were due to
the simplification and standardization movement and
mass production technology. Hoover believed it was
caused by temporary shifts in employment and DSP Chief
Ray Hudson attributed it to "faulty management <u>within</u>
and lack of coordination <u>between</u> groups. "An
editorial in <u>Saturday Evening Post</u>, avoiding reference
to the unemployment problem, merely reinforced the
official position that the savings from simplification
was divided "among manufacturers, security holders,
wage earners and ultimate consumers."(53)

Labor leader William Green attributed the problem
of "serious unemployment" to simplification and mass
production. The key to increased employment, he
wrote, was shorter working hours, wage increases, and
more education for workers. Others charged that
simplification and standardization were not so much
the problem, but that employers and stockholders were
reaping huge benefits and not passing them on to the
workers. In other words, wages were not keeping pace
with production efficiency and the purchasing power of
the mass consumer was drying up.(54)

In May, 1929, critic T. Swann Harding wrote that
Bureau of Labor statistics suggested an unequal
distribution of wealth, caused by "overstimulated
production" and a faulty, enforced and artificial
consumption through advertising and installment
buying. The American economic system, he charged, was
"absurd" and "a menace." How can the nation's economy
be sound, he asked, when there were 23,146 industrial
failures in 1927, the second largest number of
business failures in one year, historically?
Something had to be done, "for men died of starvation
on the streets of Baltimore in the fall of 1928, while
politicians shouted about an unprecedented prosperity
to audiences that were themselves existing on unstable
economic grounds."(55)

During 1928, as the presidential campaign
mounted, it is improbable that these voices in the
wilderness had much impact. There were the Great

Engineer and the urban-immigrant politician Al Smith
to make the headlines. Prohibition and religion were
issues of more interest that "dry and dust" economic
questions. Besides, Hoover and his supporters for
years had touted his formula for economic prosperity
as infallible--so long, of course, as everyone
voluntarily cooperated. A central feature of that
formula was elimination of waste, a part of which was
the simplification and standardization movement.

Did businessmen cooperate in this program?
Probably, and most assuredly they did in simplified
practice. It was in their interests to do so, which
Hoover recognized and exploited in his appeals for
cooperation. This does not mean that businessmen and
managers had no social conscience. It appears certain
that many businessmen believed in the Hooverian
dream--dare one say reform?--of voluntarism,
cooperation, ethical standards, self-regulated
industry, service, and responsibility to the
community.(56)   Owen D. Young and Gerald Swope were
prime examples of reform minded professional business
managers. But, were there enough of them? There were
also businessmen like Samuel Insull, who, in response
to the question of efficiency and a humane labor
policy said: "My experience is that the greatest aid
to efficiency of labor is a long line of men waiting
at the gate."(57)

In any case, Herbert Hoover strongly believed his
system was working, or at least refused to believe
that it was not, and that it would work even better in
the future. He entered the presidency with his mind
unchanged and ignored the warning signs. Two days
after he took office a Nation editorial issued a
prophecy. After citing Hoover's difficulties in
getting along with the press and Congress, and
impatience with challenges to his views, the writer
suggested: "It is this which is making competent
observers say that Mr. Hoover's Administration will
either be, on the purely executive side, one of the
most memorable in our history, or that he will be one
of the greatest failures in the Presidency."(58)

The simplification and standardization movement
was clearly consistent with the Hooverian effort to
avoid blatant statism, promote voluntarism and
cooperation, and self-government in industry for
purposes of eliminating waste and increasing
production. But it was not a partnership of
government, management and labor; it was restricted to

business and engineering elites and guided by a bureaucratic government elite. In this respect, it was consistent with what this writer chooses to call "administrative progressivism," reform imposed from above, that harkens back to the days of Theodore Roosevelt.

In this respect, the simplification and standardization movement fits what Ellis Hawley suggests was a search for a middle way or a third alternative toward a "new liberalism," one chanelled between the New Nationalism and the New Freedom. There is no question about it: Herbert Hoover was a reformer, a conservative reformer to be sure, attempting to change the system by imposing a framework within which society chould adjust to the consequences of an urban-industrial political economy.

The simplification and standardization movement appeared to achieve results. Those who adhered, undoubtedly, did save time, materials and costs--and profits probably were increased in many industries.(60) Beyond that, the waters are muddied, since most of the work was designed to promote increased profits and production in industry; hardly any concerted effort was made to see whether the Hooverian formula was working. It was only assumed. In other words, profits and production were on the increase, but it was difficult to determine whether these were being passed on down the line to the worker in the form of higher wages, and to the ultimate consumer in the form of lower prices. One important reason for the lack of statistics in these matters was because leaders of commerce and industry were not eager to share their profit and loss statistics with agencies like the DSP.(61)

Simplification and standardization also encouraged the increased use of new technologies for mass production. This had the effect of displacing--both temporarily and permanently--many workers in a given industry. Combined with the massive number of business failures--especially in 1927--it makes one confident that unemployment was a problem, at least after 1926, and that this was partly due to the simplification and standardization movement.

Perhaps those people who did retain steady employment, particularly if unionized, did share in the increased production and profits. But even here

22.

the evidence is weak. Contemporary assessments
estimated that while workers' incomes rose 27.5
percent, 1919-1929, the power to produce rose by 50
percent. Furthermore, while some people had
respectable--even spectacular--incomes the vast
majority were living below acceptable standards of
subsistence by 1928. Historian Irving Bernstein
suggests that while production sky-rocketed between
1923-1929, real wages "moved gently upward," leading
him to conclude that "the vaunted high-wage philosophy
of American industry . . . appears to have activitated
employers' vocal chords more than their purse
strings."(62)

If Populism was in response to the "embattled
farmer," and Progressivism was in response to the
"embattled consumer," then "Hooverism" was a quiet and
cloistered reform movement orchestrated by one man and
his ideas. While most reforms have been imposed by an
elite group, there appears to be some important
differences between the era of reform which preceded
and proceeded from the elevation of Herbert Hoover to
the Secretaryship of the Department of Commerce. The
twenties does fit the "elite-led" pattern, but
Hooverism is different in other respects.

First of all, Hooverism was preconceived, based
upon a successful program during World War I, and was
initiated from above, rather than in response to a
demand or outcry. There was no demand for reform;
indeed, most of the history of the 1920s suggests the
opposite. In the second place, Hooverism was a
movement to rehabilitate and uplift, not the lower,
less fortunate, or even the middle classes, but the
economically privileged classes--the leaders of
commerce and industry who for nearly three decades had
been the target, rather than the object of reform.(63)

Nor was it a case of demanding action on the part
of government, especially the federal government, to
regulate or control or to negate the economic
concentration of power of a new corporate plutocracy.
Rather it was a more positive and persuasive set of
reform ideals in response to which the former
"enemies" were to reform themselves--without coercion.
The elite were different also. They were engineers
and technicians, rather than traditional politicians,
social workers and journalists. They were
semi-private managerial elite, led by Herbert Hoover,
who carried on a reform crusade--quietly and without
using the familiar reform rhetoric, creating an

ideology of reform that would appeal to the good
senses and self-interest of the object of that reform:
Big Business. While the first premise of that
ideology was a payoff for this group, it was also
perceived that ultimately it would be a payoff for the
entire nation.

Hoover's activities and directorship while
Secretary of Commerce, 1921-1928 can be viewed as a
genuine "era of reform." His use of old World War I
and engineerng chums, engineering and technical
societies, his stress on elimination of waste,
simplification, standardization, conferences,
publicity and the like, fit into the scenario of a
reform movement. Production, trade associationlism,
higher profits, higher wages, and lower prices--all
were appealing to not only reformers and labor unions,
but the object of Hooverism: commercial and
industrial leaders in the country. And it would be
accomplished, so the line went, without government
coercion and with cooperation.

Even his American Individualism (1922) fits into
this view. Thus while progress toward perfection
demanded that individualism be preserved, it was not
the laissez-faire "devil take the hindmost" kind, but
a new individualism which conformed to the
urban-industrial society. This individualism would
stimulate liberty, production, initiative,
responsibility, efficiency, service, cooperation and
the ideal of equality of opportunity. Hoover's
individualism rejected a concentration of power in
either government or an oligarchy; it rejected
radicalism and reactionary nonprogressives; it
rejected socialism and autocracy. Indvidualism would
be preserved by retaining the spirit of
individualism--constructive, responsible, purposeful
and cooperative, with capable leadership from those
persons given the opportunity to rise to leadership
positions because of their intelligence and
competence.(64) In all of this can be discerned an
appeal to both conservatives and progressives: A
formula for rationalizing the past with the future, no
appeals to extremism, and yet a promise of progress
and prosperity for posterity. Who were to be those
leaders? Listen to Hoover speaking to the United
States Chamber of Commerce in May of 1924:

>I am one of those who believe in the
>substratum of inherent honesty, the fine
>vein of service and kindness in our

citizenship . . . And our homemade
Bolshevist-minded critics to the contrary,
the whole economic structure of our nation
and the survival of our general levels of
comfort are dependent upon the maintenance
and development of leadership in the world
of industry and commerce. Any contribution
to larger production, the wider diffusion of
things consumable and enjoyable, is a
service to the community and the men who
honestly accomplish it deserve high public
esteem.(65)

Here we have the Chosen People--honest,
productive, service and community-minded realist? But
that is sniping. Hoover should not be criticized for
failing to achieve his vision, for many reformers have
failed, and fewer had the capabilities of the Great
Engineer. His major weakness was his unwillingness to
make the adjustments in his vision when faced with the
realities that not all of society was cooperating in
an effort to achieve his vision.

FOOTNOTES

*In addition to those associated with
the 1979 NEH Summer Seminar in Iowa,
the author thanks the following who
read and critiqued this manuscript:
Homer P. Balabanis, Barton J.
Bernsteid, Michael J. Brodhead, Stephen
C. Fox, John Gimbel, John C. Hennessy,
Jerrald Krause, Rodney M. Sievers, and
Frank Stricker.

1. Most influential for revising this author's
    thinking about both progressivism and the 1920s
    were: Samuel P. Hays, Conservation and the
    Gospel of Efficiency: The Progressive
    COnservation Movement, 1890:1920 (Cambridge:
    Harvard University Press, 1959); Robert H. Wiebe,
    The Search for Order, 1877-1920 (New York: Hill
    and Wang, 1967); William L O'Neill, The
    Progressive Years: America Comes of Age (New
    York: Dodd, Mead and Company, 1975); John Hoff
    Wilson, Herbert Hoover: Forgotten Progresive
    (Boston: Little Brown and Company, 1975); and
    most recently, the significant work by Ellis W.
    Hawley, The Great War and the Search for Modern
    Order: A History of the American People and
    Their Institutions, 1917-1933 (New York: St
    Martin's Press, 1979). But see also Herbert
    Hoover, The Memoirs of Herbert Hoover: The
    Cabinet and the Presidency, 1920-1933 (New York:
    The Macmillan Company, 1952), especially Chapter
    6.

2. Otis L Graham, Jr., The Great Campaigns: Reform
    and War in America, 1900-1928 Englewood Cliffs:
    Prentice-Hall, Inc., 1971); Report of the
    President's Research Committee on Social Trends,
    Recent Social Trends in the United States, Vol.
    I (New York: McGraw-Hill Book Company, 1933),
    429.

3. See John Blum, The Republican Roosevelt
    (Cambridge: Harvard University Press, 1954);
    Edwin T. Layton, Jr., The Revolt of the Engineers
    Cleveland: The Press of Case Western Reserve
    University, 1971); Samuel Haber, Efficiency and
    Uplift: Scientific Management in the Progressive
    Era, 1890-1920 (Chicago: University of Chicago
    Press, 1964), xi; Paul W. Glad, "Progressives and
    the Business Culture of the 1920s," Journal of

American History, 53 ()June, 1966), 75-89;
Richard L. Watson, Jr., "Theodore Roosevelt and
Herbert Hoover," South Atlantic Quarterly, 53
(January, 1954), 109-129; Oscar Kraines,
"Brandeis' Philosophy of Scientific Management,"
Western Political Quarterly, 13 (March, 1960),
191-201.

4. "Herbert Hoover," March 25, 1920, E. E. Hunt
    Papers, Individuals, Herbert Hoover, 1917-1929,
    Herbert Hoover Presidential Library (Hereafter,
    HHPL).

5. See Peri Ethan Arnold, "Herbert Hoover and the
    Department of Commerce: A Study of Ideology and
    Policy," Ph.D. Dissertation (University of
    Chicago, 1972), 15, 21, 215-222. Hoover may have
    also inherited Woodrow Wilson's concept of
    voluntarism: see Robert D. Cuff, "Herbert
    Hoover: The Ideology of Voluntarism and War
    Organization During the Great War," Journal of
    American History, 64 (September, 1977), 358-372.

6. Arthur M. Johnson, "Antitrust Policy in
    Transition, 1908: Ideal and Reality,"
    Mississippi Valley Historical Review, 48
    (December, 1961), 415-434.

7. Frederick Winslow Taylor, Principles of
    Scientific Management (New York: Harper and
    Brothers, 1911), 140.

8. Edwin Layton, while characterizing Hoover as
    "clearly in the tradition of engineering
    progressivism" questions his devotion to
    Taylorism: Revolt, 189-195. But see Haber,
    Efficiency, 156-167. See also Edward Eyre Hunt
    (ed.,), Scientific Management Since Taylor: A
    Collection of Authoritative Papers (New York:
    McGraw-Hill Book Company, 1924), especially the
    introduction and Hoover's contribution
    "Industrial Standardization," 189-196; Ray M.
    Hudson to W. C. Mullendore, February 7, 1923,
    Commerce Papers (Hereafter COM), Simplified
    Commercial Practice (Hereafter SCP), 1923, HHPL;
    "Herbert Hoover Emphasizes Duty of Engineer in
    Reestablishing Economic Balance," Mechanical
    Engineering March, 1922), 206-207.

9. "Order Out of Chaos by Standardization," Literary
    Digest, 62 (August 15, 1919), 77-84; Homer Hoyt,

"Standardization and Its Relations to Industrial
Concentration," Annals, 82 (March, 1919),
271-277. See also, U.S. Department of Commerce,
SImplified Practice: What It Is and What It
Offers (Washington: United States Government
Printing Office, 1924).

10. F. C. Brown, "Standardization of Prosperity,"
American Review, 2 (July, 1924), 396-397; G. K.
Burgess, Address to American Society for Testing
Materials, June 26, 1923, COM, Bureau of
Standards, 1923, HHPL; Commerce, Simplified,
2-3; U. S. Department of Commerce, A Primer of
Simplified Practice, Ernst L. Priest
(Washington: United States Government Printing
Office, 1926), 1.

11. Ibid., 1-2; editorial clipping, System (November,
1921), COM, A. W. Shaw, 1921. There is also
evidence that Hugh Johnson, member of the War
Industries Board and later New Deal figure, was
affiliated with this program. See A. W. Shaw to
R. S. Emmet, January 13, 1922, COM, A. W. Shaw,
1922; H. Johnson to H. Hoover, January 16, 1922,
COM, Hugh Johnson, 1921-1928, HHPL.

12. Committee on Elimination of Waste in Industry of
the Federated American Engineering Council, Waste
in Industry (New York: McGraw-Hill Book Company,
1921), introduction.

13. The industries were: building trades, men's
clothing, boot and shoe, printing, metal trades
and textile manufacturing. Ibid., 8-23.

14. Ibid., 24-33, 266.

15. Wilson, Herbert Hoover, provides best concise
description in Chapter IV.

16. Hoover to President Harding, November 1921
(draft), COM, Assistant to Secretary (Feiker),
1921, HHPL. See also Herbert Hoover, "The
Crusade for Standards," in National Standards in
a Modern Economy, ed. by Dickson Reck (New York:
Harper and Brothers, 1956), 3-4. As things
turned out, Commerce came more near telling
business what they ought to "volunteer" to do for
their own good, than merely finding out what
business wanted from government.

17. Hoover's fetish for reorganization extended beyond the Commerce Department; Wilson, _Herbert Hoover_, 83:85. For a special case of resistance by the Agriculture Department and resultant conflict, see correspondence, 1922-1925, between Commerce and Agriculture, COM, Boxes 11 and 145; A. W. Shaw to F. M. Feiker, May 9, 1921; J. H. McGraw to Staff, May 27, 1921, Feiker Papers, 1921; L. W. Wallace to F. M. Feiker, July 14, 1921, COM, Assistant to Secretary, 1921, HHPL.

18. A. W. Shaw to Hoover, March 26, 1921; Hoover to Shaw, August 3, 1922; Shaw to Hoover, November 24, 1922; Hoover to Shaw, March 12, 1923; Hoover to Shaw, June 7, 1923, COM, Shaw, 1921-1923, HHPL.

19. Hoover to E. H. Goodwin, August 5, 1921, COM, E. W. McCullough, 1921-1922; Hoover to S. Insull, March 2, 1923, COM, SCP, 1923, HHPL.

20. Commerce, _Simplified_, 3-5.

21. A. W. Shaw, "Simplification: A Philosophy of Business Management," _Harvard Business Review_, 1 (July, 1923), 417-427.

22. Hoover to H. C. Wallace, February 8, 1922; Hoover to Wallace, February 25, 1922 and March 7, 1922; R. S. Emmet to W. C. Mullendore, March 23, 1922, COM, Agriculture, H. C. Wallace, 1922; Wallace to Hoover, March 23, 1922, COM, SCP, 1921-1922. Later, a more congenial relationship developed between Commerce and Agriculture. See Hoover to H. M. Gore, November 24, 1924; Hoover to Gore, December 24, 1924, COM, Agriculture, Gore, 1924-1925, HHPL.

23. Ray M. Hudson to Hoover, August 13, 1924; E. L. Priestly to Hudson, January, 1925, COM, SCP, 1924 and 1925-1926; Hoover to Shaw, January 13, 1925, COM, Shaw, 1925-1928, HHPL.

24. U. S. Department of Commerce, _Elimination of Waste: Simplified Practice, Paving Bricks_, 2nd Revision (Washington: USGPO, 1923); E. L. Belles, "Economic Effect of Simplification in the Paving Brick Industry," _Annals_, 89 (September, 1928), 438-441; Commerce, _Elimination of Waste: Lumber_ (Washington: USGPO, 1924); Commerce, _Simplified_, 5-7.

25. Ibid., 7-9. See also, William A. Durgin, "Alice in Modernland," Nation's Business, 11 (June, 1923), 13-15.

26. Commerce, Simplified, 19-21.

27. P. G. Agnew to Hoover, March 21, 1921; Minutes, AESC, March 9, 1922; G. S. Boudinot to AESC, June 23, 1922; COM, AESC, 1921; AESC, "Rules of Procedure for the Development of Standard to be Approved," (Revised, October, 1920), COM, Standardization, 1927, HHPL.

28. Hudson to W. A. Durgin, November 16, 1922; Durgin to Hoover, November 27, 1922, COM, SCP, 1922, HHPL.

29. Hoover to Durgin, J. Klein, and G. K. Burgess, May 23, 1923, COM, SCP, 1923, HHPL.

30. Press Release, AESC, October 7, 1922, COM, AESC, 1922; Ray M. Hudson, "How the 'Hoover Process' Reduces Mining Costs," The Mining Congress Journal (April, 1923), 129-130 (copy), COM, SCP, 1923; Durgin to Hoover, January 1, 1924, COM, SCP, 1924, HHPL.

31. Press Release, February 14, 1922, COM, Unemployment, Building Materials Simplification, 1922; F. M. Feiker to C. Herter, September 23, 1922; Hoover to O. D. Young, September 27, 1922; Durgin to Hoover, September 25, 1922; Hoover to H. Williams, September 22, 1923; R. M. Hudson, November 22, 1923, COM, SCP, 1922 and 1923, HHPL.

32. Durgin to Hoover, October 5, 1922, COM, SCP, 1922. For the best articulation of Hoover's economic philosophy, see Address by Herbert Hoover (U.S. Chamber of Commerce), May 7, 1924, COM, Achievements, 1924, HPL.

33. Memorandum, Durgin, June 18, 1923, COM, National Council-National Research, 1923-1926; "Hoover and the Lumber Industry," Southern Lumberman, 109, (March 24, 1923), 1; R. T. Jones Lumber to Durgin, December 13,1923; Durgin to R. T. Jones Lumber, February 18, 1924; R. T. Jones Lumber to Hoover, February 20, 1924, COM, SCP, 1924, HHPL.

34. Irving Bernstein, The Lean Years, 1920-1933

(Boston : Houghton-Mifflin), 1960; G. K. Burgess
to Hoover, May 15, 1923, COM, SCP, 1923; J. H.
Tregol to Hoover, December 17, 1923; J. Goldman
to Hoover, January 27, 1928, Installment Buying,
1920-1928, HHPL. For criticism on the
distribution of goods, see F. J. Sclink and R. A.
Brady, "Standardization and Specification from
the Standpoint of the Ulimate Consumer," Annals,
89 (May, 1928), 231-239.

35. Unsigned Memorandum to Hoover, April 8, 1922; A.
Drury to Hoover, May 22, 1923, COM, Metric
System, 1919-1923; Address by Hoover, May 26,
1924, Metric System, 1924; Notes by John
Marrinan, May 22, 1926, COM, Metric System,
1925-1926; Letter by W. R. Ingalls, June 27,
1927, COM, Metric System, 1927-1928; Burgess to
E. M. Herr, July 12, 1927, COM, Metric System,
1926-1927; L. Richey to A. R. Hall, February 8,
1928, COM, Metric System, 1927-1928, HHPL.

36. Hoover to Burgess, May 26, 1923, COM, Bureau of
Standards, 1921-1923; Address by Hoover, May 26,
1923, COM, Achievements, 1921-1923, HHPL.

37. Burgess to Hoover, October 25, 1923; unsigned and
undated Memorandum, COM, Conferences, 1923-1925,
HHPL.

38. Fletcher H. Montgomery, "We Turn Stocks Seven
Times As Fast Through Simplification," System
(June, 1923), 745-750 (copy), COM, A. W. Shaw,
1923; Shaw to Hoover, January 19, 1923, COM, A.
W. Shaw, 1923; Burgess to Hoover, May 21, 1923,
COM, Bureau of Standards, 1921-1923; Press
Release, June 11, 1923, COM, 1923-1925; H. P.
Stokes to E. E. Hunt, September 23, 1924, COM, E.
E. Hunt, 1923-1925; Address by F. M. Feiker, May
3, 1928, Feiker Papers, Speeches and Articles,
1928, HHPL.

39. Donald R. McCoy, Coming of Age (Baltimore:
Penguin Books, 1972), 89. See especialy Address
by Hoover (U. S. Chamber of Commerce), May 7,
1924, COM, Achievements, 1924; Chester M. Wright,
"Can We Trust Industry to Govern Itself?"
Nation's Business, 12 (July, 1924), 13-15;
Burgess to H. P. Stokes, July 11, 1924; "Summary
of the Achievements of the Department of Commerce
Under Secretary Hoover," July 25, 1924; P. Wooton
to Stokes, October 11, 1924, COM, Achievements,

1924, HHPL.

40. Hudson to Hoover, March 9, 1925, COM SCP, 1925-1926, HHPL.

41. Hudson to Hoover, April 30, 1925, COM, SCP, 1925-1926; Stokes to Wallis, July 8, 1925, COM, Bureau of Standards, 1925; Croghan to Stokes, July 17, 1925; Hudson to Hoover, November 5, 1925; Division of Simplified Practice Monthly News Bulletin, November 15, 1925, COM, Elimination of Waste in Industry, 1925, HHPL.

42. "Progress in the Elimination of Waste," November 8, 1926, COM Elimnation of Waste in Industry, 1926; U. S. Department of Commerce, A Primer of Simplified Practice, by Ernst L Priest (Washington: USGPO, 1926); Hudson to Hoover, July 15, 1927, COM, SCP, 1927-1928; Address by E. E. Hunt (copy), "Waste Week," December 5, 1927, E. E. Hunt Papers, 1927-1928; Hudson to Hoover, February 6, 1928, COM, SCP, 1927-1928; "Hoover's Waste-Elimination Campaign," (Spring, 1928?), COM Elimination of Waste of Industry, 1927-1928, HHPL; Burt Struthers, "The Standardized United States," Saturday Evening Post, 201 (May 11, 1929), 10-11+; R. M. Hudson and E. L. Priest, "Saving Through Simplified Practice," Journal of Home Economics, 18 (January, 1926), 6-12.

43. "Division of Simplified Practice," (July, 1928?), COM, Accomplishments of the Department, 1921-1928 (1), HHPL.

44. W. C. Wetherhill to Hoover, December 27, 1926, Conferences, 1923-1927, HHPL.

45. Hoover to C. M. Schwab, January 22, 1927, COM, Conferences, 1923-1927; "Main and Executive Committees," February 3, 1927, COM, AESC, 1927-1928; I. J. Fairchild to Burgess, February 10, 1927, COM, Standardization, 1921-1926. HHPL.

46. Hoover to J. W. Lieb, March 15, 1927, COM, Conferences, 1923-1927. HHPL.

47. Hudson to Hoover, April 6, 1927, COM, Standardization, 1927; Burgess to Hoover, July 13, 1927, COM, Bureau of Standards--Commercial Standards, 1927; Hoover to Burgess, July 14, 1927, COM, Commercial Standards, Hudson, 1927,

HHPL. See also ANnual Reports, 1927-1929.

48.   Horace B. Drury, "Labor and Production," American
      Federationist, 27 (March, 1920), 237-244; Samuel
      Gompers, "Organized Labor and Industrial
      Engineers," American Federationist, 28 (January,
      1921), 33-35; Herbert Hoover, "A Plea for
      Cooperation," American Federationist, 28
      (January, 1921), 35-40; Waste in Industry"
      American Federationist, 32 (January, 1925),
      470-472; Ray M. Hudson, "Simplified Practice and
      Labor," American Federationist, 33 (February,
      1926, 158-162. However, shortly before he died,
      Gompers expressed some skepticism about Hoover's
      interests in labor's welfare. See Samuel
      Gompers, "A Splendid Man Gone Wrong," American
      Federationist, 31 (November, 1924), 889-893.

49.   "Questions for the Secretary's Saturday Morning
      Conference," February 23, 1924, COM,
      Conferences-Secretary's, 1924; National
      Distribution Conference, 1925, Collection of
      Business Figures (copy), COM, Committee on
      Distribution Statistics, 1925; Hoover to E.
      Stewart, May 23, 1925; COM, Committee on
      Distribution Statistics, 1925; Hoover to O'Leary,
      December 29, 1925, COM Conferences-Distribution,
      1924-1926, HHPL.

50.   Foster and Catchings were "unconventional
      economists" who advocated spending in the public
      sector to correct imbalance in the private
      sector. See Ellis Hawley, The Great War,
      119-120, 200-201; William T. Foster and Waddill
      Catchings, "More Pay and Less Work--Is This a
      Futile Aim?" American Federationist, 33 (January,
      1926), 35-44.

51.   Marrinan to Croghan, March 20, 1926, COM, Foreign
      and Domestic Commerce, Croghan, P. J., 1926-1927;
      Gregg to Hoover, May 3, 1927, Bureau of
      Standards, 1926-1928; Monthly News Bulletin, May
      15, 1927, COM, SCP, 1927-1928; Hoover to Shaw,
      May 3,1927, COM, A. W. Shaw, 1925-1928, HHPL.

52.   A. W. Shaw, "The Underlying Trend of Business,"
      (clipping), System (September, 1927), 285-289+,
      COM, Shaw, 1925-1928, HHPL.

53.   C, J. Henderson to Hoover, March 2, 1928; Hudson
      to Hoover, April 10, 1928, COM, Unemployment,

1926-1928, HHPL; "Mr. Hoover's Savings Accounts,"
Saturday Evening Post, 200 (June 23, 1928), 24.

54. William Green, "The Effect on Labor of the New
     Standardization Program of American Industry,"
     Annals, 39 (May, 1928), 43-46; Lawrence B. Mann,
     "Occupational Shifts in the United States,
     1920-1927," American Federationist, 35 (July,
     1928), 667-669; Colston E. Warne, "Is Technical
     Efficiency Responsible for Unemployment?"
     American Federationist, 35 (December, 1928),
     1495-1498; F. J. Schilnk and R. A. Brady,
     "Standardization and Specification from the
     Standpoint of the Ultimate Consumer," Annals, 89
     (May, 1928), 231-239.

55. T. Swann Harding, "Those Menacing Machines,"
     Christian Century, 46 (May 29, 1929), 708, 711.
     See also a 1920s version of "small is beautiful:"
     Walter Burr, "Overdone America," American
     Federationist, 36 (April, 1929), 439-444.

56. Morrell Heald, "Business Thought in the Twenties:
     Social Responsibility, American Quarterly, 12
     (Summer, 1961), 126-139.

57. O. S. Beyer, "Unemployment and the Morale of
     Industry," American Federationist, 40 (August,
     1933), 859-863.

58. "The Thirty-First President," Nation, 28 (March
     6, 1929), 272.

59. Hawley, The Great War, 6-11.

60. David F. Noble, America By Design (Oxford:
     Oxford University Press, 1977), 81-82.

61. Although the Committee on Recent Economic Changes
     issued a lengthy report on many aspects of
     economic activity, 1922-1929, they recognized the
     absence of unreliable statistics. Report of the
     Committee on Recent Economic Changes of the
     President's Conference on Unemployment, Recent
     Economic Changes in the United States, Textbook
     Edition (New York: McGraw-Hill Book Company,
     1929), xxiii-xxv.

62. Harding, Christian Century, 708-711; "Prosperity
     and a Rising Standard of Living," American
     Federationist, 38 (February, 1931), 192-198;

Bernstein, <u>Lean Years</u>, 66-70.

63. By this I mean they were targets for destruction
    in the anti-trust tradition, as opposed to the
    more regenerative and positive approach of
    Herbert Hoover.

64. Herbert Hoover <u>American Individualism</u> (New York:
    Doubleday, 1922).

65. Address by Herbert Hoover (U.S. Chamber of
    Commerece), May 7, 1924 (copy), COM,
    Achievements, 1924, May-June, HHPL.

HERBERT HOOVER AND THE
DEVELOPMENT OF COMMERCIAL AVIATION, 1921-1926

by David D. Lee

On March 4, 1921, Herbert Hoover took office as
secretary of commerce in the newly-formed Warren
Harding administration. The commerce secretariat
seemed a strange position for the hard-driving
engineer-turned-public servant. Since its creation in
1903, the post had been an extremely minor one that
made few demands on its generally mediocre incumbents,
one of whom, assured the incoming secretary, his job
would require only two hours of work a day. "Putting
the fish to bed at night and turning on the lights
around the coast were possibly the major concepts of
the office," Hoover later recalled. Despite this
meager precedent, Hoover had ambitious plans for his
department. Temperamentally unsuited for a passive
role, he was determined to forge a dynamic Department
of Commerce deeply involved with the major economic
forces shaping American society.(1)

Hoover entered the Harding cabinet with very firm
ideas about nurturing economic progress through
positive but restrained government action. As Ellis
Hawley has demonstrated, Hoover envisioned an
"associative state" in which the government,
particularly the Department of Commerce, fostered the
growth of cooperative institutions working together to
provide a voluntary network of self-regulation. In
this way, Hoover intended to avoid the growth of
monopoly capitalism on the one hand and the appearance
of a strong, interventionist state bureaucracy on the
other. Either of those, he believed, would destroy
the national heritage he called "American
individualism." Hoover assigned the federal
government a definite role in this system. Besides
encouraging the growth of these associations, it
should prod them to put aside selfish impulses, resist
efforts to enhance economic power with political
power, and act to preserve opportunity and initiative.
The government's authority to coerce these units,
however, should be carefully limited. It should work
toward its ends by avoiding direct regulation and
concentrating on promotional conferences, expert
inquiries, and publicity designed to stimulate private
solutions to problems.(2)

The area of commercial aviation posed a test for
this philosophy because flying had a certain public

dimension almost unique among private businesses. Aircraft manufacturers relied heavily on the government as the major consumer of their wares, while the planes themselves crisscrossed the nation's airspace like commercial ships travelled its navigable waterways. Essentially, Hoover had to devise a policy for aviation that fit with his understanding of the proper relationship between government and business but at the same time took into account the distinctive obstacles that aviation faced. His efforts to do this, help to elucidate his concept of the associative state and define the circumstances under which Hoover felt government action was appropriate. Furthermore, Hoover's involvement with aviation provides an example of the ways Hoover used the resources of the Department of Commerce to foster economic growth.(3)

During his first five years in office, Hoover was left to his own devices regarding commercial aviation. No federal agencies dealt with civilian flying, and no federal laws existed to regulate it. Instead of ignoring the industry, Hoover sketched a hybrid policy to encourage its development through private initiative within a broad framework of federal supervision. It would be up to the industry to organize itself, define its problems, and propose solutions, but the government would support this process by encouraging industry cooperation, providing expert information, and mobilizing public support through publicity. Beyond this, the government would provide an infrastructure - airways, navigational aids, emergency landing fields - and underwrite the safety of the system by licensing pilots and certifying the reliability of aircraft. In this fashion, Hoover intended to reconcile the special needs of aviation with his views on cooperative interaction between business and government.

This concern for rational economic progress places Hoover squarely within one of the main trends of twentieth century American reform. As Robert Wiebe and others have pointed out, an important part of the Progressive movement was the attempt to restore order and predictability to a society where the old verities were being shattered by the pace of industrial change. Hoover's aviation policy represents an attempt to bring stability to a chaos-ridden industry through typically Hooverian mechanisms of voluntary associations and minimal government involvement. By implementing these procedures while flying was still in its infancy, Hoover hoped to avoid the problems railroads had faced in the late 1800s and early 1900s. Thus Hoover's action in this area represents a carryover into the 1920s of an important part of the Progressive impulse.(4)

The new secretary of commerce found an aviation industry hard hit by the post-World War I slump. Prior to April, 1917, aircraft manufacturing had been virtually non-existent in the United States. A handful of factories had produced only some two hundred planes in the decade and a half since the Wright brothers' flight at Kitty Hawk, but during the nineteen months of America's involvement in the war, the nation's factories produced 13,894 aircraft and 41,953 engines. By the time the Armistice was signed in November, 1918, the production rate had reached 21,000 planes yearly, and the industry employed 175,000 people. A 1925 government report declared, "A colossal effort was made, and a colossol industrial machine created from practically nothing." Of the country's twenty-four aircraft plants, only six had made as many as ten planes before the war began, and most of the others had not even existed. Peace brought an abrupt end to this prosperity. Within days of the Armistice, one hundred million dollars in contracts were cancelled and the industry shriveled to roughly ten per cent of its wartime size in just a few months. By 1922, aircraft production in the United States was down to 263 planes a year. Most businesses, established to exploit the wartime boom, retooled for other kinds of manufacturing or simply collapsed.(5)

In the wake of this sudden contraction, aviation in the early 1920s faced several serious problems. To begin with, because there was little commercial flying in the United States, there was no civilian market for planes. The government's decision to sell its surplus aircraft to civilians at cheap rates made an impossible situation even worse. The availability of inexpensive planes did lure many people into the air transport business but those enterprises proved too precarious either to provide reliable transport service or to serve as a market for planes. For example, in 1921 there were eighty-eight airline operators in the United States and 129 in 1923, yet the latter figure included only seventeen of the original eighty-eight. While some concerns managed to eke out a thin existence with a plane or two, as late as 1924 the nation still did not have a single regularly scheduled air transport line. As Hoover summarized the situation, "We have had, from time to time, sporadic service . . . but without financial success." Similarly, few passenger airlines existed, although the Aeromarine line did a small albeit brisk business hauling thirsty Americans from their prohibition battered homeland to Caribbean resort area. With the meager civilian market satiated, the manufacturers competed desperately for the thin trickle of government contracts, a competition that only heightened antagonism in an industry that had a history of bitter quarrels stretching back to the patent battles between the Wrights and Glenn Curtiss in the early days of flying.(6)

Such instability seriously damaged the already tarnished public image of aviation. Besides a transient prosperity, the rapid expansion of the war years had also brought charges of excess profits due to fraudulent misdealings by industry and government officials. President Woodrow Wilson named the distinguished republican, attorney Charles Evans Hughes, Wilson's opponent for the presidency in 1916, to head an investigation of the industry's transactions with the government. The Hughes Committee uncovered conduct of a "reprehensible nature" and spoke of "obvious impropriety" in dealings between the government and aircraft manufacturers. Congressman John M. Nelson of Wisconsin accused the manufacturers of forming an "air trust" to capitalize on the nation's defense needs. Despite the fact that no one was ever convicted of criminal activity, the findings were a serious blow to the credibility of the aircraft manufacturers.(7)

A spotty safety record also hurt aviation in the eyes of the public. Flying was a dangerous occupation even in the best of circumstances. Thirty-one of the first forty pilots hired by the government to haul the mail died in crashes, many occurring along the treacherous routes across the Appalachians. But the irresponsible actions of stunt fliers made aviation's safety record seem worse than it really was. Often, these pilots had only minimal training and were performing their sensational acrobatics in planes the government had sold as surplus because they were considered unsafe for military use. Moreover, the basic services necessary to safe flying did not as yet exist in the United States. Aeromarine began its operation flying all-water routes because emergency landings at sea were easier and safer than on land. Orville Wright warned a government board that the lack of suitable airports and emergency landing fields was the greatest handicap aviation had to face. Few air lanes had been laid out, and even those that had been, were not properly marked. Consequently, fatal crashes were frequent and well-publicized, so the general public, conditioned by the war, continued to see the airplane as another dangerous military toy that had little practical commercial application.(8)

Instability and low public standing bred other problems, specifically, a dearth of investment capital and high insurance rates. As New York Congressman Frederick Hicks pointed out, aviation would not attract investment until financiers were confident that they were "entering a business project instead of a romantic adventure . . . ." The Aircraft Yearbook of 1922 underscored the congressman's view noting, "The financial powers of the nation are notably unwilling to take cognizance of, much less interest themselves in, new commercial activities until such activities have demonstrated security and utility." Grover Loening, an aircraft manufacturer, complained, "We cannot borrow money in the banks, because there is no confidence in aviation." Likewise, insurance presented serious problems. A 1925 study of commercial flying reported that "coverage is not easily obtained and premiums for many types of insurance are practically prohibitive." Aeromarine Airways, which had had only one fatal crash in four years of operation, still paid 17.25 per cent of its total operating costs for insurance in 1923.(9)

These frustrations were compounded by the fact that aviation had no definite legal status. The idea of government supervision of flying was nearly as old as the airplane itself, but by 1921 sponsors of such laws had made little headway. In 1911, Judge Simeon E. Baldwin of the Connecticut Supreme Court urged the American Bar Association to begin work on laws to regulate the new enterprise, and a few months later, the Aero Club of America called for federal regulation of aircraft and the licensing of airmen. Neither the government nor the ABA responded, so the Aero Club tried to fill the void. Holding its charter from the French based Federation Aeronautique Internationale, an international organization that sponsored aviation meets and certified world records, the Aero Club now began to require that pilots who entered its meets be licensed and their planes inspected by the club. These efforts were largely ineffective, so individual states, led by Connecticut in 1912 under newly-elected

Governor Baldwin, began to pass their own laws, but over the next decade only four states took such action.(10)

By 1921, a broad concensus of the aviation industry favored federal regulation as the surest answer to its problems. Howard Mingos spoke for many of his colleagues when he wrote, ". . . officials and civilian experts agree . . . that unless Congress takes definite and affirmative action . . . , what there is left of American aviation will likely disappear." After holding hearings on proposed air legislation, the Senate Commerce Committee reported, "No one appeared or asked to appear in opposition to it. Representatives of the industry urged its passage and letters were received from many who could not come urging its passage . . ." The committee found it "startling, to say the least, to have an industry . . . asking and urging legislation putting the business completely under federal control." Later that same year, Secretary Hoover observed, ". . . this is the only industry that favors having itself regulated by the government."(11)

Confronted with this situation, the new Secretary of Commerce took a cautious attitude toward aviation. The brutal infighting among the manufacturers was a far cry from the voluntary cooperation Hoover so prized in the economic sector. From his perspective, aviation was making no effort to police itself or confront its problems. Until the industry took a first step, Hoover believed the government should do nothing. Writing to Maurice Cleary, a director of the Aero Club of America, Hoover said bluntly, "There is no reason why those interested in civil aviation should not form an association for promotion of their views . . . ." If that happened, Hoover said he would be willing to meet with a delegation from such an organization.(12)

Beyond this, the legalistic Hoover was well aware he had absolutely no statutory authority over any aspect of the aviation industry. With regard to radio, another new industry in the 1920s, the Radio Act of 1912 had given the Secretary of Commerce limited authority to regulate broadcasting, but no federal law concerning flying had ever been passed. Without such statutory backing, Hoover realized any action he took would have to be based solely on voluntary cooperation, a rare commodity in the aviation industry. By taking action in the area of

aviation, Hoover would not only be exceeding his legal
authority but also would be inviting embarrassment by
having his efforts ignored. His usual practice,
therefore, was to refer aviation inquiries to Congress
explaining he had no jurisdiction in such matters.(13)

Hoover began to relax his aloofness only after
the president endorsed giving him legal authority over
aviation, and the industry itself was able to generate
the outline of a policy it would accept. Intrigued by
the controversial ideas of air power advocate General
Billy Mitchell, Harding directed Secretary of War John
Weeks, Postmaster General Will Hays, Assistant
Secretary of the Navy Theodore Roosevelt,Jr., and
Hoover, to devise an administration position on aerial
matters. The committee suggested Harding ask the
recommendation of the National Advisory Committee on
Aeronautics, an independent government agency created
in 1915 to research the scientific aspects of flight.
By April 9, 1921, just eight days after the
president's request, a report was on his desk calling
for federal regulation of air navigation and the
creation of a bureau of aeronautics in the Department
of Commerce to plan airways and build landing fields.
Three days later, Harding incorporated these NACA
proposals in his address to the opening session of the
67th Congress putting the administration on record in
favor of a proposal to add aviation to Hoover's
domain.(14)

Hoover now found himself eagerly courted by
industry leaders who felt the secretary personally was
very important to their cause. As the most dynamnic
figure in the administration, they felt he had the
stature to secure congressional approval of an air
law, while his impeccable reputation could help
refurbish their own and increase public confidence in
flying. In June, a group of fifty executives
representing civil aviation petitioned Harding to name
Hoover chairman of an aviation consulting committee to
formulate "a policy for the advancement of aeronautics
in this country." As one of the petitioners explained
to Hoover, "Civil aviation has never been asked by
anyone to express its views and it is felt that
someone in the Administration should hear its opinions
. . . . I believe that if you and a committee . . .
would confer informally . . ., all of you would agree
on the main policy to be proposed." It is a measure
of their eagerness to involve Hoover that the
petitioners specifically requested him as chairman
even though three other cabinet officers, Weeks, Hays,

and Secretary of the Navy Edwin Denby, all headed
departments more directly involved in aviation than
the Departmentof Commerce.(15)

Hoover's first general meeting with the aviation
industry took place on July 18 in the secretary's
office. Arranged by Luther Bell, director of
information for the Manufacturers Aircraft
Association, it also included men from the Aero Club,
the National Aircraft Underwriters Association, and
the Society of Automotive Engineers. The conference
explained to Hoover specifically what the industry had
in mind when it called for regulation and provided him
with tangible proof that the industry was now agreeing
within itself on the nature of its problems and was
formulating solutions. His visitors insisted that the
future of civil aviation depended on the creation of a
federal agency to rationalize flying by mapping out
airways, licensing pilots, and inspecting planes. If
the Department of Commerce would exert leadership
along these lines, aviation could be made
substantially safer. The question of safety was an
extremely important one for Hoover, with regard to all
industries. He asked the Manufacturers Aircraft
Association to supply him with accident statistics and
created a committee chaired by Howard Coffin of the
Hudson Motor Car Company to prepare a bill
encompassing the recommendations of the meeting
concerning an air law. The committee's completed
draft was introduced in the Senate by Senator James
Wadsworth, Jr. of New York.(16)

With the legislative process initiated, Hoover
moved to promote his position by gathering and
publicizing information on flying. He directed the
Department of Commerce to make a brief study of
commercial aviation so it would be ready to act if the
Wadsworth bill passed, but because he had no funds for
research that was tangential to department concerns,
Hoover relied heavily on the industry itself for data.
The material was then incorporated into Hoover's
public statements or issued as a press release. For
example, the MAA accident statistics Hoover requested
at the industry meeting subsequently appeared in
sixty-three newspapers. In a November progress report
on public attitudes, Luther Bell informed the
department that sixty-six newspapers had editorially
endorsed the Wadsworth bill with "practically no
adverse comment."(17)

It is not surprising, given his sources of

information that Hoover's views on air legislation were largely those of the industry itself. This reliance on the industry for ideas on how it should be regulated was partly dictated by the fact that there were very few aviation experts in 1921, and Hoover freely confessed he was not one of them. As one congressman put it, "The subject is new from the ground up, or from the air down, whichever way you choose to look at it." More importantly, the essence of Hoover's conduct of the Commerce Department was to assist industry in solving its problems, not to devise and impose government solutions. Normally, Hoover worked through voluntary associations in the industry, but since the few aviation organizations were fragmented, discredited, or ineffective, Hoover seized on the July 18 conference as the expression of the will of the industry and adopted its suggestions.(18)

Unfortunately, the Wadsworth bill encountered turbulent weather over Capital Hill. The idea of federal regulation of aviation was generally accepted, but the advocates of such legislation were divided on the form it should take. A small but vocal minority, led in Congress by Charles Curry of California, insisted on the creation of a separate Department of Air, either to exist independently, or as part of a newly structured Department of Defense. Introduced in Congress several times, such a bill never had a serious chance of passage. Most observers agreed that responsibility for civil aviation should be vested in the Department of Commerce, but the debate went beyond questions of government structure. States rights advocates and some constitutional experts believed the federal government did not have the authority to regulate intra-state flying. Their opponents argued that the safety of all traffic required that no aircraft escape federal supervision. Another disagreement was over how specifically the legislation should be written. Broadly speaking, air law advocates wanted a very detailed bill that carefully explained regulation procedures, but some felt the law should simply provide guidelines for the secretary of commerce and permit him the flexibility to formulate and modify rules in the light of experience.(19)

Wadsworth, whose bill provided for regulation of intra-state flying, soon found his proposal attacked as unconstitutional. Despite the bill's endorsement by President Harding and Hoover and the widespread newspaper backing it enjoyed, states rights senators on the Commerce Committee attacked it harshly.

Fearful the bill would not reach the floor, Wadsworth submitted a new measure in January, 1922, that dropped the provisions concerning intra-state commerce. Wadsworth's action alarmed aviation leaders who felt the new draft was too weak. A fretful Howard Coffin, who had chaired the industry committee responsible for the original Wadsworth bill, wrote to Hoover, "I trust that the teeth are not being extracted from this Bill, and that the counsels of our timid friends who fear the States Rights and other bugaboos, may not be given too much weight . . . ." Moreover, the Wadsworth bill was not the elaborate bill many wanted but a very general one intended, as Wadsworth put it,"to be as simple as possible and to be used, if enacted, to break the ground as it were in the development of comprehensive legislation based on experience." The industry would accept a broad bill if intra-state flying was regulated but not if that feature was eliminated. By the time the revised Wadsworth bill passed the Senate on February 14, 1922, NACA, the Society of Automotive Engineers, the National Aircraft Underwriters Association, and the recently formed Aeronautical Chamber of Commerce were all urging substitute bills be prepared.(20)

Responsive to the air industry's unhappiness with the altered Wadsworth bill, as early as December, 1921, Hoover had department solicitor William Lamb at work on a more satisfactory proposal. Besides Lamb, two other men who played an important part in shaping the bill were Massachusetts Congressmman Samuel Winslow, chairman of the House Committee on Interstate and Foreign Commerce, and William P. MacCracken, a former World War I pilot, chairman of the ABA committee on aviation law, and advocate of a comprehensive air measure. When the Wadsworth bill reached the House, it was referred to Winslow's committee. MacCracken visited the congressman to suggest revisions but found Winslow more interested in harness racing than airplanes. The pragmatic MacCracken shrewdly played to his subject's interest and finally secured a promise from Winslow to sponsor any new bill MacCracken recommended.(21)

Unfortunately, this auspicious beginning evolved into a fiasco. Winslow became infatuated with the idea put forward by Congressman Charles Curry to create a Department of Air with complete control of military as well as civilian flying. Industry spokesmen like Samuel Bradley of the Manufacturers Aircraft Association were appalled because they feared

a completely new aviation bill, especially one
containing such a controversial provision, would delay
congressional action indefinitely. Then Lamb and
MacCracken offended everyone with their slowness in
drafting the bill. By late May, 1922, Winslow was
making pointed complaints about the "efficiency" of
the department solicitor and indicating his interest
in the whole matter was rapidly dwindling. When
Hoover prodded Lamb, the latter pleaded problems with
the intra-state flying section but assured his chief
the final draft, although late, would encounter
virtually no opposition. A week later, an irritated
Hoover told Lamb the House committee was "becoming
indignant over the delay" and ordered him to "send it
along immediately in whatever shape it may be." Only
as an afterthought did the secretary insert the word
"kindly" at the beginning of the sentence. Even then
Hoover waited another week and a half before the bill
reached his desk.(22)

        Hoover's worst embarrassment was yet to come.
Eager to appease the impatient Winslow, Hoover sent
the draft to the congressman on June 12 without going
over it. Later that day he discovered to his horror
that he had forwarded a bill to establish a Department
of Air. In a chagrined note to Winslow, Hoover said,
"I regret that I sent on to you the Bill drafted by
the Committee without having first given it more
attention. I was so anxious to get it into your hands
that I sent it on as soon as it reached me through the
mail." The idea of a secretary of aeronautics Hoover
dismissed as a "political dream" saying it "has never
been discussed by the Administration and . . . I do
not think it will receive support." Hoover's
opposition apparently persuaded Winslow to abandon a
Department of Air. He made no further reference to
it, and simply suggested the secretary "endeavor to
cause a new bill to be prepared as expeditiously as
possible." Hoover dispatched a new bill on June 19
but Winslow, plainly indifferent, replied it would
create more problems than it would solve. The measure
was finally introduced on January 8, 1923, much too
late to be passed before the March adjournment.(23)

        The proponents of aviation regulation, including
Hoover, contributed a great deal to their own defeat
in the 67th Congress. Although the industry tended to
favor the Winslow bill after the Wadsworth

measure because they felt it had the best chance to
pass. A weak law, they contended, was better than no
law. Another group agreed with MacCracken that
industry should demand a stronger bill even if it
meant defeat. By cooperating with the second group,
Hoover contributed to a legislative strategy that in
effect divided the proponents of air legislation and
brought the defeat of both bills. The stalemate
continued in the 68th Congress as both bills were
re-introduced with the Wadsworth proposal again
passing the Senate, but Winslow, who had decided to
retire at the end of the session, let them languish in
his committee.(24)

While Congress debated legislation, Hoover built
a strong case for the government-sponsored development
of commercial aviation. A thriving commercial
aviation industry would help sustain in peacetime the
manufacturing capability that would be needed in case
of war and also provide a ready reserve of trained
personnel and planes. Without commercial aviation,
the government alone would have to bear the expense of
maintaining an air capability, probably through a
subsidy program that Hoover considered unwise.
Furthermore, Hoover realized that faster
transportation would bolster the national economy by
saving time, a concept that fit nicely with Hoover's
general policy of reforming industry through the
elimination of wasteful practices. In the 1920s,
commercial aviation was much more advanced in Europe
than in the United States but Hoover saw this as a
temporary condition. The United States did not have
the political barriers that Europe did, and its
greater distances put a premium on speed. Over the
long run, Hoover was convinced that America was better
suited than Europe to commercial aviaion.(25)

Despite this potential, however, Hoover agreed
with industry leaders that aviation would not progress
without federal assistance. He justified this
departure from his usual attitude by comparing
aviation with shipping. The public owned the airways
just as it owned the navigable waterways, and just as
the government provided basic services to shippers on
water, so it should provide precisely the same
services to shippers by air. This meant supplying
navigational aides such as laying out airways,
equipped with emergency landing fields and properly
lighted, marked, and mapped. Hoover considered
lighting especially important beause it opened the way
to night flying which in turn meant the faster

47.

delivery of goods and passengers and a stronger
competitive position for air transport.(26)

Hoover also believed the federal government
should uphold the safety of flying by licensing pilots
and certifying the air worthiness of aircraft. Again
this flowed from his shipping analogy because the
government performed the same services for that
industry. Only the government imprimateur, Hoover
felt, could counteract the tremendous amount of bad
publicity the industry had reeived and restore a
measure of public confidence. By reducing accidents
and building public respect, government inspection
would, therefore, help to reduce insurance rates and
attract more capital for investment.(27)

Still pursuing his comparison with shipping,
Hoover staunchly opposed federal involvement in
establishing airports. Each locality was responsible
for its own docks, so each city must provide for its
own airport although the facility had to conform to
federal standards. In this area Hoover was closer to
the more conventional workings of his philosophy on
business and government. He approved a federal
propaganda campaign to publicize the economic
advantages of airports and stressed that they should
be close to centers of population so the time gained
by flying would not be lost again, but he refused to
endorse the use of federal money in their
construction. This was a proper area for local
initiative.(28)

Hoover also had definite ideas about the
financing involved in his proposals. He was strongly
opposed to direct subsidy on the European model.
Instead he advocated using the airmail as a form of
indirect subsidy to stimulate growth through private
initiative. Hoover argued that the government should
stop flying the airmail and contract various routes to
private companies at generous rates. He envisioned a
system wherein the mail planes would carry passengers
and freight as well, with the airmail contract
ensuring the enterprise would be profitable. The
airmail contracts would provide a firm base for the
creation of a self-sufficient commercial aviation.
Hoover admitted the navigational aids, safety
inspection, and airmail contracts would be expensive
but he believed these steps would save the government
money in the long run. Although his plan would cost
roughly one to four million dollars depending on the
volume of traffic, he predicted a ten-to-one ratio of

savings in military expenditures if commercial
aviation developed. Encouraging commercial aviation,
he said, was "a most constructive drive for immediate
economy in government."(29)

If Hoover modified his usual policy in dealing
with aviation, by no means did he abandon it entirely.
Throughout his tenure as secretary of commerce he
encouraged the industry to put its own house in order
through the kind of voluntary associations that he had
suggested to Maurice Cleary in 1921. The two existing
aviation organizations, the Aero Club of America and
the Manufacturers Aircraft Association, had been
discredited by the wartime scandals, so Samuel
Bradley, the general manager of the declining MAA,
proposed an Aeronautical Chamber of Commerce which
would include manufacturers and others interested in
commercial aviation. Chartered on January 1, 1922,
with Bradley as general manager, its membership
included twenty-six manufacturing and engineering
companies, thirty-one operators, twenty-nine
manufacturers of accessories, eight trade
publications, one insurance underwriters association,
and a hundred individuals. On entering the
government, the ACC noted, "Secretary Hoover . . .
laid down the principle of co-operation with national
trade Associations as the surest means of teamwork
between the Government of this nation and the Business
of this nation." With the formation of the ACC, "The
aircraft industry thus follows the example of all
other modern industries which owe their present
greatness in no small measure to the trade
association." The first act of the new organization
was to make contact with the Department of Commerce by
submitting a review of the major events in aviation
during 1921.(30)

Almost simultaneously, Howard Coffin began to
work for the formation of another organization.
Acting "at the instance of responsible officers of the
Government," probably Hoover, Coffin wanted to disband
the faltering Aero Club and replace it with a new
National Aeronautic Association. While the ACC, as a
spin-off of the MAA, was largely the voice of the
manufacturers, the NAA would represent a broader range
of aviation interests. The group officially came into
being at a 1922 meeting in Detroit where the annual
air races were being held. Hoover indicated his
approval by attending the races, one of the few times
he accepted such invitations. The secretary left
early but did stay long enough to see General Billy

Mitchell set a new airplane speed record.(31)

In conjunction with these organizations, Hoover and the Department of Commerce acted on several fronts to encourage aviation. Most of his actions centered on expanding the market for aircraft and improving safety. One way of increasing the market was to demonstrate the usefulness and versatility of the airplane, so department spokesmen publicized its value to farmers as a crop duster, to geographers through aerial photography, and to conservationists in patrolling forests and fighting fires. To underscore its economic value, in 1923 Hoover announced with great fanfare that the department had begun sending its foreign market surveys to the West Coast by airplane. The surveys provided important leads on export possibilities, but western businessmen were usually 60 hours behind their eastern competitors in receiving the material, a gap Hoover said the speed of the airplane would substantially reduce. He frequently pointed out that the airmail would speed up the transfer of banking documents and suggested the cost of airmail would be balanced by a saving on interest. Simultaneously, the Bureau of Foreign and Domestic Commerce prepared and distributed abroad pamphlets on American planes and directed its overseas representatives to submit information on foreign aviation. Along these lines, Hoover ordered a world-wide study of commercial aviation with emphasis on what the United States might learn from the experience of others.(32)

Safety and standardization remained important concerns for Hoover. As part of his continuing concern for safety, in 1922 he convened an industry-wide conference to consider steps to reduce accidents. The discussions led to a partnership between conferees and the Bureau of Standards in a three year effort to prepare an aeronautical safety code. The analysis connected with this program drew the bureau into aviation research with many of its members attaching themselves to various aviation-related scientific and technical societies. By 1925 when the code was published, a statement of the bureau's work in aviation given to the House Select Committee on Air Services (Lampert Committee) covered fifty pages. As a consequence of this concern for safety, the bureau became deeply involved in efforts to standardize aircraft, work, the Aeronautical Chamber of Commerce described, as "extremely important."(33)

Hoover's involvement with efforts to develop
dirigible transports illustrates his willingness to
provide informal assistance for aeronautics. After
World War I, Germany turned a dirigible over to the
United States Government with the stipulation it would
not be used for military purposes. Renamed the Los
Angeles, it was made a navy training ship. In
December, 1924, Hoover told a congressional committee
that he would like to see lighter-than-air craft tried
on a commercial basis "so that we could get some real
determination of what the working costs of it are." A
few months later, a group of New York businessmen led
by John Hays Hammond and Herbert Satterlee contacted
Hoover about securing the use of the Los Angeles to
test the possibilities of a commercial airship. They
explained they had acquired the rights to certain
German-held patents considered crucial to the further
development of lighter-than-air vehicles and were
seeking more information before exercising their
option. Specifically they were anxious to have a firm
government commitment to aeronautics, assurances that
supplies of helium would be available, and any advice
the department could provide as to the feasibility of
their enterprise.(34)

Obviously Hoover could not speak for the
government nor could be made promises about helium,
but he asked P. E. D. Nagle, communication chief of
the Transportation Division for an assessment of the
commercial potential of airships. Nagle reported the
Rocky Mountains were a tremendous obstacle for a
transcontinental airship but he was more optimistic
about the use of dirigibles on trans-Atlantic flights
assuming a ship could be built that was large enough
to carry sufficient cargo. While admitting problems
existed, Nagle concluded that, "the difficulties
confronting the commercial application of
lighter-than-air craft, at present, present merely
problems for solution and not obstacles which could at
all be said to be insurmountable."(35)

Encouraged by Nagle's findings and aware of the
importance of the German patents, Hoover arranged a
meeting with President Calvin Coolidge for Hammond and
Satterlee where the two investors explained their
interest in leasing the Los Angeles for an
experimental New York-Chicago route. Coolidge was
receptive to the scheme and issued a statement
expressing the commitment of his administration to
commercial aviation and dirigible development. The

president stated his willingness to lease the
Shenandoah, as well as, the Los Angeles to private
enterprise and directed Hoover, the War Department,
and the Navy Department to cooperate with Hammond and
his friends.(36)

Hoover was also instrumental in securing private
support for aeronautical research. He believed that
neither the government nor private industry could
engage in "pure" research because they had to concern
themselves with work that had direct applicability.
To fill this gap, at a White House luncheon in 1925
Coolidge and Hoover discussed with Harry Guggenheim,
son of the wealthy New York mining family, the
possibility of his father, Daniel, providing funds for
such work. Interested in aviation since his pilot
days in World War I, Guggenheim had earlier persuaded
his father to establish a school of aeronautics at New
York University. As a result of the White House
conversation, on January 16, 1926, Daniel Guggenheim
wrote to Hoover announcing the establishment of a $2.5
million fund to encourage aviation research. The
senior Guggenheim praised the secretary saying, "Under
your general direction the United States Government
has made substantial progress in the promotion of
civil aviation," and pledged the trustees of the new
fund would cooperate with Hoover's department "in
every possible manner." Indeed the first statement
issued by the trustees closely corresponded to
Hoover's often-repeated recommendations for the
future of aviation.(37)

Also in 1925, Hoover launched his most extensive
investigation of aviation. Utilizing the kind of
administrative techniques that characterized his
tenure as secretary of commerce, he suggested to the
board of a professional organization, the American
Engineering Council, that it ask the Department of
Commerce to make a survey of commercial aviation. The
AEC responded favorably so Hoover appointed a joint
committee composed of members from the Department of
Commerce and engineers from the AEC under the
chairmanship of Assistant Secretary of Commerce J.
Walter Drake. Since the department had no funds for
such a study, Hoover and the AEC raised several
thousand dollars in private donations to finance it.
The committee was charged with answering three
questions. It was to investigate the possibility of
developing a useful air transportation service,
establish its value to national defense, and provide a
definite plan for commercial air development in the

52.

United Staes. In origin and structure the Joint
Committee on Civil Aviation is a near-classic example
of Hoover's approach to public policy. It represented
a cooperative blending of public and private resources
to bring the force of the "best minds" to bear on an
important economic problem.(38)

The Joint Committee convened in the midst of a
tumultuous period in the history of American aviation.
The recently passed Kelly Air Mail Act authorizing the
postmaster general to contract privately for air mail
delivery gave aviation a tremendous boost, just as
Hoover and others had predicted. Shortly after the
Kelly Act was passed, Henry and Edsel Ford announced
their intention to enter the field of commercial
aviation. As early as 1922, the Fords had been
backing a promoter and inventor named William B. Stout
in his work on a new aircraft that could carry
substantial loads great distances. After Stout
developed a prototype he puckishly christened the
Maiden Detroit, the Fords bought him out and in
April, 1925, Henry Ford announced the nation's first
regular commercial airline which would run between
Detroit and Chicago. Shortly afterward, he wrote
Hoover a glowing review of the enterprise and assured
the secretary, "We are planning on increasing the
service as fast as conditions will permit." Taking
advantage of the Kelly Act, Ford bid successfully for
an air mail route and in February, 1926, became the
first private operator to fly the mail.(39)

Ford's involvement greatly enhanced the public
credibility of flying. As comedian and aviation
enthusiast Will Rogers put it, "Now you know that Ford
wouldn't [sic] leave the ground and take to the air
unless things looked pretty good to him up there."
The New York Times noted that Ford's action ignited
"something like a boom" in commercial aviation. He
drew famous names such as Rockefeller and Whitney into
the field and thereby, helped to ease the chronic
capital shortage that had hobbled the industry's
advance. By the end of 1925, five new air transport
companies had been set up including the large National
Air Transport capitalized at $10.5 million.(40)

In the midst of this surge of optimism came
disquieting reminders that aviation safety still left
much to be desired. On September 3, the navy airship,
Shenandoah, broke up in a thunderstorm over Ohio
killing fourteen of the forty-three people aboard.
Coming within a few weeks of Coolidge's endorsement of

dirigible development, the accident was a devastating setback for lighter-than-air advocates. Writing to Herbert Satterlee, Hoover expressed the hope that "wrongly founded prejudice" caused by the accident would not block future progress but said for the moment, nothing further could be done. During the same week, two navy flying boats failed dismally in an effort to reach Hawaii from San Francisco. One boat went down two hundred miles from its take-off point and was ignominiously towed back. The other one also went down and was presumed lost until a patrolling submarine found it, converted into a sailboat by its ingenious crew, sailing peacefully toward its destination. These accidents sparked a spectacular blast from Billy Mitchell charging the nation's military establishment with incompetence and negligence in developing aviation for defense. Aware his outburst would probably result in his court-martial, Mitchell hoped to use his trial as a forum for his views on aviation.(41)

Partly at Hoover's suggestion, Coolidge decided to appoint a blue-ribbon panel to investigate Mitchell's charges as well as conduct a broad review of American aviation. Although a House Select Committee and Hoover's Joint Committee were already addressing these issues, they did not have the stature of a presidential commission. Hoover's claim that the President's Aircraft Board was his idea is probably not accurate because as early as March, 1925, Coolidge had suggested to Dwight Morrow of the House of Morgan the possibility of Morrow's investigating the air industry. Hoover was, however, important in persuading his reluctant fellow cabinet members, Secretary of War Dwight Davis and Secretary of the Navy Curtis Wilbur, to accept an investigation of military aviation by the independent engineers on the Aircraft Board. The nine member panel included representatives of government, industry, the military, and private citizens. Morrow was selected as chairman in spite of his protests that he knew nothing of flying.(42)

The President's Aircraft Board conducted a thorough inquiry into all facets of aviation. The shrewd Morrow summoned Mitchell as a witness but let him talk on without interruption until the officer's points were lost in the verbage. Much more effective was the blunt, concise Hoover who came "primed with facts" according to the New York Times to reiterate his views on government establishment of airways,

federal licensing of pilots and aircraft, and local
sponsorship of airports. "Without such services . .
.," Hoover stated, "aviation can only develop in a
primitive way." Looking to the Mitchell charges of
inadequate air defense, he again expressed his
conviction that a strong commercial aviation would
bolster national security while keeping the cost to
the government low. Although this policy involved
more government action than Hoover usually liked to
see, he felt these actions lay within his concept of
positive, but limited government: "With this minimum
extension of government activity, we can secure a
commercial aviation in the United States without
subsidy."(43)

Within a six-week period in late 1925, three
committees, the House Select Committee, the Joint
Committee, and the President's Aircraft Board,
reported similar findings with regard to commercial
aviation. They rejected the idea of a single
Department of Air and opted instead for delegating
commercial aviation to the Department of Commerce. In
effect, this represented the establishment of a
consensus among the executive branch, Congress, and
private industry on the proper course for civilian
flying. Under these circumstances, it was very likely
that the 69th Congress, which convened on December 7,
one week after the Morrow Board reported to the
president, would finally act on the demand for air
legislation.(44)

The leader of the regulation forces in the 69th
Congress was Senator Hiram Bingham of Connecticut.
Like many people interested in flying during this
period, his involvement went back to his days as a
pilot in World War I. More recently a member of the
President's Aircraft Board, Bingham and Congressman
James Parker of New York, another PAB member,
introduced similar measures in the Senate and House
embodying the board's recommendations. Hoover and the
Department of Commerce worked closely with Bingham in
preparing the initial draft of the bill. While the
Morrow Board was still in session, Hoover and Bingham
agreed that department solicitor Stephen B. Davis
would produce a bill for Bingham to introduce. As
Davis drafted it, the new bill was similar to the old
Wadsworth bill but with some significant differences.
Like the Wadsworth measure, it restricted federal
authority to interstate flying and contented itself
with providing a general outline of regulation rather
involving itself in many specifics. Hoover strongly

55.

endorsed the bill's vagueness noting, ". . . difficulties can be solved equally well or better when they arise than by anticipation." The major difference lay in the new administrative procedure embodied in the Bingham bill. Over the years, Hoover had moved away from the creation of a bureau of civil aeronautics and toward the idea that services to aviation could best be provided by extending the functions of existing department agencies and simply creating an assistant secretary of commerce to coordinate them. For example, the Bureau of Lighthouses could assume responsibility for lighting airways, or the Bureau of Standards could make available research facilities. In testimony before the President's Aircraft Board, Hoover argued this method would prove cheaper and more efficient than a new government bureau, and the board wrote this approach into its final report. In a letter to Senator Wesley Jones, Hoover described the new bill as a "much simplified method of setting up a civilian aviation agency."(45)

Passed on May 20, 1926, the Air Commerce Act represented an important milestone in the growth of commercial aviation in the United States. NACA hailed it as the "legislative cornerstone" of the industry, and a later historian styled it the "Bill of Rights of the aviation industry." Its impact was enormous. During the period 1922-1926, the nation added only 369 miles of regular air service operated by private enterprise and three thousand miles of air mail lines run by the Post Office that did not carry passengers or express. After the passage of the act, Hoover later recalled, "We went at it with great zest." He summarized progress by 1929 with an outpouring of his beloved statistics: 25,000 miles of government-improved airways of which 14,000 were lighted and beaconed; 1,000 airports built and 1,200 in progress; 6,400 licensed planes making 25,000,000 miles in regular flights annually; a manufacturing output of 7,500 planes a year. "I know of no satisfaction," Hoover concluded, "equal to the growth under one's own hand of a great economic and human agency."(46)

Hoover's blueprint for aviation called for private initiative that was structured by federal supervision. Industry should prepare the general plan of development while the government provided basic navigational aids and rationalized flying through a national air code. The most significant part of this

scheme was the unusually large role Hoover allotted to
the federal government. Hoover dropped his usual
opposition to direct regulation by the government
because he recognized the unique public dimension of
the transportation industry. If a private company
built the airways, it would have a monopoly over them,
something Hoover feared almost as much as the growth
of a powerful state. Private business could not
credibly license its own pilots or inspect its own
aircraft. For the airways to be open to all and for
public safety standards to have meaning, the
government must take a hand. Hoover was willing to
see direct government action in this regard, but he
believed it was temporary. Once the industry had
matured to the point of self-regulation through
voluntary association, then the government could
reduce its part.(47)

Hoover's aviation policy illustrates the
continuity of reform through the 1920s. Like many
pre-war progressives, he was trying to use government
to achieve orderly economic development, but he
adopted a new strategy born of the national response
to World War I. Rejecting the New Freedom, as well
as, the New Nationalism, Hoover instead sought to
orchestrate growth through cooperative action between
the industry and government patterned on such war-time
agencies as the War Industries Board. This new
approach, Hoover believes, would provide the optimal
blend of freedom and order to encourage maximum
creativity within a stable framework. Hoover's
involvement was by no means the only factor in the
rapid expansion of commercial aviation after Congress
passed the Air Commerce Act in 1926, but he had helped
to lay much of the foundation for that success. The
future stability and prosperity of American aviation
were in large part due to the reform-minded leadership
of Herbert Hoover.(48).

Footnotes

1. Herbert Hoover, The Memoirs of Herbert Hoover: The Cabinet and the Presidency, 1920-1933 (New York: Macmillan Company, 1952), 42.

2. Ellis Hawley, "Herbert Hoover, the Commerce Secretariat, and the Vision of an 'Associative State,' 1921-1928," Journal of American History, 61, (June, 1974): 116-140; Hawley, "Herbert Hoover and American Corporatism, 1929-1933," in Martin Fausold and George Mazuzan, eds., The Hoover Presidency: A Reappraisal (Albany: State University of New York Press, 1974), 101-119; Hawley, essay and rejoinder, in J. Joseph Huthmacher and Warren I. Susman, eds., Herbert Hoover and the Crisis of American Capitalism (Cambridge: Schenkman Publishing Company, 1973), 3-34, 115-120; Hawley, The Great War and the Search for a Modern Order, A History of the American People and Their Institutions, 1917-1933 (New York: St. Martin's Press, 1979), 9-11, 59-68; William Appleman Williams, "What This Country Needs . . .," Some Presidents, from Wilson to Nixon (New York: Review of Books, 1972), 33-49; Williams, The Contours of American History (Chicago: Quadrangle Books,1961), 425-438; James Weinstein, The Corporate Ideal in the Liberal State (Boston: Beacon Press, 1968); Herbert Hoover, American Individualism (Garden City and New York: Doubleday, Page and Company, 1922), 32-62.

3. Hawley, "Associative State," 127-128.

4. Robert Wiebe, Businessmen and Reform: A Study of the Progressive Movement (Cambridge: Harvard University Press, 1962); Wiebe, The Search for Order, 1877-1920 (New York: Hill and Wang, 1967); Samuel P. Hays, The Response to Industrialism, 1885-1914 (Chicago: University of Chicago Press, 1957).

5. President's Aircraft Board, Report of the President's Aircraft Board (Washington: GPO, 1925), 4; John B. Rae, Climb to Greatness, The American Aircraft Industry, 1920-1960 (Cambridge and London: MIT Press, 1968), 2-3; Elsbeth S. Freudenthal, The Aviation Business from Kitty

Hawk to Wall Street (New York: Vanguard Press, 1940), 63; John Hicks, Republican Ascendancy, 1921-1933 (New York: Harper Torchbook, 1963), 174; Henry Ladd Smith, Airways: The History of Commercial Aviation in the United States (New York: Russell and Russell, reissued 1965), 39-40; Lawrence F. Schmeckebier, The Aeronautics Branch, Department of Commerce: Its History, Activities, and Organization (Washington: Brookings Institute, 1930), 4.

6. Editorial, "Necessity of a Federal Bureau of Aeronautics," Chicago Commerce, March 8, 1924 in "Aviation Clippings, 1923-1926," William P. MacCracken, Jr. Papers, Herbert Hoover Presidential Library, West Branch, Iowa; Hicks, Republican Ascendancy, 176; Will H.Hays, The Memoirs of Will Hays (Garden City: Doubleday and Company, 1955), 310; Donald Whitnah, Safer Skyways: Federal Control of Aviation, 1926-1966 (Ames: Iowa State University Press, 1966), 3, 7, 14.

7. "Aircraft Production in the United States," Senate Report, No. 555, in Congressional Record, 65th Congress, 2nd Session, 9329-9334; Congresional Record, 65th Congress, 3rd Session, 883-914 Congressional Record, 68th Congress, 1st Session, 1625-1626.

8. Report of the PAB, 7; Aircraft. Hearings Before the President's Aircraft Board, Washington, GPO, 1925, 1097; Edward P. Warner, "Commercial Aviation, 1923," Journal of the Society of Automotive Engineers, 15, (August,1924), 136; Nick Komons, Bonfires to Beacons: Federal Civil Aviation Policy Under the Air Commerce Act, 1926-1938 (Washington: United States Department of Transportation, Federal Aviation Administration, 1978), 28; Whitnah, Safer Skyways, 3, 14.

9. Congressional Record, 67th Congress, 2nd Session, 1924; United States House of Representatives, 68th Congress, 2nd Session, Inquiry into Operations of the United States Air Service Hearings Before the Select Committee of Inquiry, House of Representatives, 68th Congress, Washington, GPO, 1925, 909; "Extracts from Civil Aviation Report by Joint Committee of the Commerce Department and American Engineering

Council," "Aviation, 1926," Commerce Papers,
Hoover Library; Aeronautical Chamber of Commerce,
Aircraft Yearbook of 1922 (New York: ACC, 1922)
15; Komons, Bonfires, 29.

10. Robert Burkhardt, The Federal Aviation
    Administration (New York, Washington, and London:
    Frederick A. Praeger, 1967), 5; Komons,
    Bonfires, 26; Schmeckebier, Aeronautics Branch,
    6-8; Whitnah, Safer Skyways, 7.

11. United States Senate, 67th Congress, 2nd Session,
    "Bureau of Aeronautics in Department of
    Commerce," Senate Reports, No. 460 (Washington:
    GPO, 1922), 2; New York Times, February 24,
    1924 in "Aviation Clippings, 1923-1926,"
    MacCracken Papers, Hoover Library; Herbert
    Hoover to Frederick C. Hicks, December 30, 1921,
    "Commerce Department; Aeronautics, Bureau of
    Legislation, 1921," Commerce Papers, Hoover
    Library.

12. Hoover to Maurice Cleary, June 25, 1921,
    "Aviation, 1920-1921," Commeerce Papers, Hoover
    Library.

13. Hoover to Israel Ludlow, July 21, 1921; Hoover
    to Senator Joseph Frelinghuysen, July 11, 1921;
    Richard Emmet to Julius Meirick, July 15, 1921.
    "Aviation, 1920-1921;" Clarence Stetson to W. L.
    Brackett, September 9, 1921. "Commerce
    Department; Aeronautics, Bureau of; Legislation,
    1921," Commerce Papers, Hoover Library; Thomas
    Worth Walterman, "Airpower and Private
    Enterprise: Federal-Industrial Relations in the
    Aeronautics Field, 1918-1926" (Ph. D.
    dissertation, Washington University, 1970),
    147-152.

14. Theodore Roosevelt, Jr. to Hoover, April 8, 1922,
    "Commerce Department; Aeronautics, Bureau of;
    Legislation, 1922;" Charles D. Walcott to Hoover,
    March 23, 1921. "Aviation, 1920-1921;" Charles
    T. Menoher to John Weeks, April 1, 1921.
    "National Advisory Committee on Aeronautics,
    1921-1926," Commerce Papers, Hoover Library; New
    York Times, April 20, 21, 1921; Robert Murray,
    The Harding Era: Warren G. Harding and His
    Administration (Minneapolis: University of
    Minnesota Press, 1969), 125, 164, 410-411;
    Eugene P. Trani and David L. Wilson, Presidency

of Warren G. Harding/(Lawrence: Regents Press of
Kansas, 1977), 57.

15. Lester D. Gardner to Hoover, June 18, 1921.
    "Aviation, 1920-1921," Commerce Papers, Hoover
    Library; New York Times, June 21, 1921;
    Walterman, "Air Power and Private Enterprise,"
    314-315.

16. "Notes for Meeting of Air Craft Men Monday," July
    16 1921; Clarence Stetson to Maurice G. Cleary,
    July 8, 1921; Luther K.Bell to Stetson, July 20,
    1921. "Aviation, 1920-1921;" Samuel Bradley to
    Hoover, April 11, 1922; Howard Coffin to Hoover,
    April 18, 1922. "Commerce Department;
    Aeronautics, Bureau of; Legislation, 1922,"
    Commerce Papers, Hoover Library; New York
    Times, July 5, 1921 and January 10, 1923;
    Editorial, Aviation November 20, 1922), 683;
    Aircraft Yearbook of 1922, 33; Waterman, "Air
    Power and Private Enterprise," 327-329.

17. Luther Bell to Hoover, November 12, 1921.
    "Commerce Department; Aeronautics, Bureau of;
    Legislation, 1921," Commerce Papers, Hoover
    Library; New York Times, September 20, November
    20, 1921; Hearings, House Select Committee on
    Air Services, 815.

18. United States House of Representatives, "Bureau
    of Civil Air Navigation in the Department of
    Commerce," Hearings Before the House Committee on
    Interstate and Foreign Commerce, 68th Congress,
    2nd Session, Washington, GPO, 1925, 20, 21;
    Hearings, House Select Committee on Air Services,
    815.

19. New York Times, January 10, 1923; Walterman,
    "Air Power and Private Enterprise," 328-330;
    Komons, Bonfires, 46, 50-53.

20. Hoover to Howard Coffin, April 18, 1922.
    "Commerce Department; Aeronautics, Bureau of;
    Legislation, 1922;" James W. Wadsworth, Jr. to
    Hoover, November 27, 1925, "Aviation;
    President's Aircraft Board, 1925 and undated,"
    Commerce Papers, Hoover Library; New York
    Times, December 31, 1921; Komons, Bonfires,
    46-53.

21. Richard Emmet to William Lamb, December 14, 1921.

61.

"Commerce Department; Aeronautics, Bureau of;
Legislation, 1921," Commerce Papers, Hoover
Library; Michael Osborn and Joseph Riggs, eds.,
"Mr. Mac:" William P. MacCracken, Jr. on
Aviation, Law, Optometry, (Memphis: Southern
College of Optometry, 1970), 33, 40-41.

22. Samuel Bradley to William Lamb, August 3, 1922;
Julius Klein to Richard Emmet, May 25, 1922;
William Lamb to Hoover, May 26, 1922; Hoover to
Lamb, June 2, 1922;; Lamb to Hoover, June 9,
1922. "Commerce Department; Aeronautics, Bureau
of; Legislation, 1922," Commerce Papers, Hoover
Library; Komons, Bonfires, 57.

23. Hoover to Samuel Winslow, June 12, 1922; Hoover
to Winslow, June 13, 1922; Winslow to Hoover,
June 14, 1922; Winslow to Hoover, September 15,
1922. "Commerce Department; Aeronautics, Bureau
of; Legislation, 1922," Commerce Papers, Hoover
Library; New York Times, January 9, 1923.

24. Komons, Bonfires, 55-57.

25. Herbert Hoover, "Statement on Commercial
Aviation." 'Aviation, 1925;" Hoover, "Speech
Before San Francisco Chamber of Commerce."
"Aviation, 1926," Commerce Papers, Hoover
Library.

26. Ibid.

27. Ibid.

28. Ibid.

29. Ibid.

30. "Aeronautical Chamber of Commerce Organizes,"
Aviation (January 2, 1922), 6; "Annual Report of
the Aeronautical Chamber of Commerce of America,
Inc.," Aviation (February 19, 1923), 219; New
York Times, January 1, 2, 1922; Walterman, "Air
Power and Private Enterprise," 265-269, 324;
Howard Mingos, "The Rise of the Aircraft
Industry," in Gene Roger Simonson, ed., The
History of the American Aircraft Industry, An
Anthology (Cambridge and London: MIT Press,
1968), 57-61.

31. Howard Coffin to Hoover, October 11, 1922;

Sidney Waldon to Hoover, October 20, 1922.
"Aviation, 1922-1924," Commerce Papers, Hoover
Library;   Hearings, House Select Committee on
Air Services, 1281; Komons, Bonfires, 53-55.

32. Herbert Hoover, "Speech Before San Francisco
    Chamber of Commerce." "Aviation, 1926;" Press
    release, "Hoover Plans Greatly Improved Trade
    Service for West Coast." "Aviation, 1922-1924;"
    J. Walter Drake, "Civil Aviation in the United
    States," "Aviation, Commercial, 1925," Commerce
    Papers, Hoover Library; "Annual Report of the
    Aeronautical Chamber of Commerce of America,
    Inc.," Aviation (February 19, 1923), 219-220 and
    (February 11, 1924), 150.

33. United States Department of Commerce, Tenth
    Annual Report of the Secretary of Commerce, 1922,
    Washington, GPO, 1922, 14, 157; Hearings, House
    Select Committee on Air Services, 1507-1556;
    New York Times, July 22, 1922; "Annual Report of
    the Aeronautical Chamber of Commerce, Inc.,"
    Aviation (February 19, 1923), 220; "Aeronautical
    Safety Code Completed," Aviation (June 1, 1925),
    600.

34. W. C. Mullendore to Hoover, January 13, 1925.
    "Aviation, 1925:" Jesse Jackson to Hoover, March
    19 1925. "Aviation, Commercial, 1925," Commerce
    Papers, Hoover Library; New York Times, August
    12, 1925.

35. P. E. D. Nagle to Hoover, January 30 and May 1,
    1925, "Aviation, 1925," Commerce Papers, Hoover
    Library.

36. Hoover to Dwight Davis, August 12, 1925.
    "Aviation, Los Angeles, 1925-1926;" Herbert
    Satterlee to Hoover, November 23, 1925.
    "Aviation, Commercial, 1925;" Satterlee to
    Hoover, January 21, 1926 and Hoover to Satterlee,
    January 25, 1926. "Aviation, Commercial,
    1926-1927," Commerce Papers, Hoover Library;
    Hearings, House Select Committee on Air Services,
    816-817; New York Times, August 12, 1925.

37. Harry Guggenheim to Hoover, January 11, 1926;
    Daniel Guggenheim to Hoover, January 16, 1926;
    Hoover Press Statement, January 18, 1926; Daniel
    Guggenheim Fund for the Promotion of Aeronautics,
    "Report Concerning the Aeronautical Situation in

Europe." "Aviation, Daniel Guggenheim Fund, 1926
and Undated," Commerce Papers, Hoover Library;
Harvey O'Connor, The Guggenheims: The Making of
an American Dynasty (New York: Covici, Freide,
1937), 425-426.

38. Herbert Hoover, "Statement on Commercial
Aviation," September 24, 1925. "Aviation, 1925;"
E. S. Gregg to J. Walter Drake, September 19,
1925. "Commerce Department; Aeronautics, Bureau
of; 1925-1926;" Commerce Papers, Hoover Library;
New York Times, May 8, 1925; Walterman, "Air
Power and Private Enterprise," 457-458.

39. Henry Ford to Hoover, August 14, 1925.
"Aviation, Commercial, 1925," Commerce Papers,
Hoover Library. Smith, Airways, 94; Allan
Nevins and Frank Earnest Hill, Ford: Expansion
and Challenge, 1915-1933 New York: Charles
Scribner's Sons, 1957), 238-245; Roger
Burlingame, Henry Ford, A Great Life in Brief
(New York: Alfred Knopf, 1969), 125-126.

40. New York Times, August 23, 26, 1925; Komons,
Bonfires, 67-68; Airways, 106-108.

41. Hoover to Herbert Satterlee, January 25, 1926.
"Aviation, Commercial, 1926-1927," Commerce
Papers, Hoover Library; Elizabeth Stevenson,
Babbits and Bohemians: The American 1920s (New
York: Macmillan Company,1967), 157-158; Alfred
F.Hurley, Billy Mitchell: Crusader for Air Power
(Bloomington and London: Indiana University
Press, new edition, 1975), 100-101.

42. New York Times, September 13, 1925;
Schmeckebier, Aeronautics Branch, 8-9; Hoover,
Cabinet and the Presidency, 133; Donald R.
McCoy, Calvin Coolidge: The Quiet President (New
York: Macmillan Company, 1967), 304-305; Harold
Nicolson, Dwight Morrow (New York: Harcourt,
Brace and Company, 1935), 280-281.

43. Hearings, President's Aircraft Board, 318-330;
New York Times, September 25, 1925; McCoy,
Coolidge, 305.

44. Report of the PAB; United States House of
Representatives, Report of the House Select
Committee on Operations of the United States Air
Services, Washington, GPO, 1925; Joint

Committee, "Summary of the Report of the
Committee on Civil Aviation Organized Last June
by the Department of Commerce and the American
Engineering Council." "Advisory Committee on
Civil Aviation, 1925-1926," Commerce Papers,
Hoover Library; New York Times, November 6, 1925
and January 26, 1926; Walterman, "Air Power and
Private Enterprise," 9, 450-451, 456, 458-461,.
475-478.

45. Hoover to Hiram Bingham, September 23, 1925;
     James Wadsworth, Jr. to Hoover, December 5, 1925;
     Clarence Young to Hoover, December 7, 1925;
     Hoover to Wesley L. Jones, December 9, 1925;
     Young to Hoover, December 30, 1925. "Commerce
     Department; Aeronautics, Bureau of; Legislation,
     1925-1926," Commerce Papers, Hoover Library;
     Congressional Record, 69th Congress, 1st Session,
     828-830, 7314-7317; New York Times, December 9,
     1925; Komons, Bonfires, 80-81.

46. Hoover, Cabinet and the Presidency, 134; Smith,
     Airways, 98; Freudenthal, Aviation Business, 77.

47. Hawley, "Associative State," 127-128.

48. Hawley, The Great War and the Search for a Modern
     Order, 9-10, 226-229; Hover, American
     Individualism, 32-62.

"ORGANIZING THE PRODUCTION OF LEISURE":
HERBERT HOOVER, FISHING AND OUTDOOR RECREATION IN THE
1920s

by   Carl E. Krog

The history of conservation in America in the
twentieth century is sometimes pictured as a topic
which gained national attention at the beginning of
the century and then was largely ignored by both
historians and the American public durng the 1920s
until there was renewed interest in conservation again
during the New Deal. This paper will examine the
continuing interest and progress of outdoor recreation
and conservation in the twenties, particularly Herbert
Hoover's interest and role in emphasizing the
recreational importance of National Parks for a much
larger number of Americans. It can also be argued
that Herbert Hoover, first as an influential official
in the Harding and Coolidge administrations and then
as President, worked for conservation measures during
the years of all three Republican Administrations.

The supporters of conservation could claim
progress in a number of areas by the end of the 1920s.
Although the Republican administrations opposed
Senator George Norris' plans for an expanded and
multipurpose development of Muscle Shoals, the
government did adopt a multi-use policy for flood
control and land reclamation during the decade.
Supporting a conservative philosophy which opposed
large scale development, the Army Corps of Engineers
emphasized only levee construction rather than
multi-purpose development until the Mississippi flood
of 1927. The disastrous flood and the increased
pressure of conservationists forced the engineers to
study reservoirs, reforestation, diversion channels,
and "safety valve" levees. Although the dams were
completed in the 1930s, the initial planning for both
the Boulder and Grand Coulee dams was begun during the
late twenties. These large multipurpose dams served a
number of purposes such as generating electric power,
flood control, and holding reservoirs for irrigation.

Secondly, scientific research became the commonly
accepted basis for resource planning and policy
decisions during the twenties. A number of the
federal agencies, such as the Bureau of Fisheries, and
of Mines, in the Department of Commerce, the
Geological Survey, Park Service, and Reclamation

Service in Interior, and the Biological Survey and
Forest Reclamation Service in Interior, and the
Biological Survey and Forest Service in Agriculture,
had a number of highly trained specialists who
provided the government with competent and expert
advice in a number of areas affecting conservation
policy. Further, in keeping with one of the
Progressive traditions, the agencies relied on merit
and on professional competence, in most cases, when
making promotions, usually resisting political
pressures and patronage considerations. The emphasis
of the agencies, like the Republican governments of
the twenties, was on service and specialized expertise
rather than on a strong regulatory role, following a
timid fiscally conservative course rather than
embarking on a new expansive course of action. The
Forest and Park Services with an expanding clientele,
were exceptions to this generalization.

President Hoover's record in conservation is by
far the strongest of the Republican Presidents during
the twenties. The leading scholar on conservation in
the 1920s, Donald Swain, has written, "Herbert Hoover
in contrast to his immediate predecessors was a key
conservation figure."(1) Influential in both the
Harding and Coolidge administration as Secretary of
Commerce, Hoover, even before he became president,
took an active role in conservation. He was
particularly concerned about more effective
propagation of fish, regulation of the Alaska salmon
fishing, a better control of water pollution along
American coastal waters, especially oil pollution
which contaminated offshore oyster and clam beds.
Although the Bureau of Fisheries was in his Commerce
Department, Hoover's interest was also based on his
lifelong love of fishing and the outdoors.

Herbert Hoover has been stereotyped as a
humorless, hard working, and conscientious man, but
another side of Hoover emerged whenever he discussed
his favorite hobby, fishing. To complement his love
of fishing, Hoover was concerned about effective and
beneficial use of leisure. These two interests
constitute an unexplored side of Hoover's career
during the 1920s. Hoover, in speeches on the Bureau
of Fisheries' policies and in speeches to various
nature and conservation organizations, such as the
Izaak Walton League, and in his Memoirs, has left a
sharply etched record of his love and concern for
fishing. He wrote, for example, that the Declaration
of Independence endowed men with certain inalienable

rights, such as "life, liberty, and the pursuit of happiness, which obviously includes the pursuit of fish."(2)

Like some of his contemporaries in the 1920s, Hoover believed that as Americans moved to the cities they would lose their ties to the country. Hoover wrote, "I was a boy in the days before our civilization became so perfect, before it was paved with cement and made of bricks. Boys were not so largely separated from Mother Earth and all her works." Hoover went on recalling "the most vivid and joyous recollections of my Iowa boyhood days are of patient angling in Iowa streams for the very occasional fish with a willow pole and a properly spat upon worm."(3)

Hoover felt that given the pressures of modern urban industrial life, fishing and a return to a natural setting perioidically were a necessity. He wrote, "Izaak Walton did not spend his major life answering a bell. He never got the jumps from traffic signals or the price of wheat." Hoover noted that the "blessings of fishing include discipline in the equality of men, meekness and inspiration before the works of nature, charity and patience toward tackle makers and the fish, a mockery of profits and conceits, a quieting of hate, and a hushing to ambition."(4)

Hoover particularly appreciated the new opportunities and expanded mobility that the car made possible, especially for fishermen, who could now more easily reach what had formerly been inaccessible fishing spots. The mass production of cars had both a beneficial and baneful effect on American society in the 1920s. The car paradoxically brought Americans closer to nature making it more easily possible to travel into the country and to camp in the woods. To Americans in the twenties, the small addition of cement, asphalt, and gasoline fumes were a small price to pay for the greater degree of mobility.

Observing that 10,000,000 Americans went fishing in 1926, ten times the number in 1906, Hoover was delighted over the increased number of fishermen, but also concerned over the pressure the large number of fishermen brought to the sport. Since he felt fishing was a constructive way of spending leisure time, Hoover was concerned about the low rate of return on fish caught, noting that it would be necessary to improve the number of fish caught if the government was to keep the "population from further moral turpitude." Elsewhere, Hoover had written that fishing in a quiet brook can "reduce our egotism, soothe our troubles and shame our wickedness." Humorously noting that fishermen never lie, Hoover suggested that the 191 state gamefish hatcheries, the sixty private, and forty federal gamefish hatcheries, would have to increase production.(5)

The 1920s might be regarded as a transitional decade. Although a majority of Americans during that decade lived in cities, and only a quarter of the American people lived on farms during the 1920s, the great majority of adult Americans, like Hoover, were born in nineteenth century rural America. Although people moved to cities and in the case of Hoover became a sophisticated world traveller, nonetheless, they retained many of the values of their earlier years. Hoover, like many of his contemporaries, kept some of those sentimental feelings. Speaking at his birthplace, West Branch, Iowa, in 1928 Hoover remarked, "I am often conscious of sentimental regret for the passing of those old time conditions. I have sometimes been as homesick for the ways of those self-contained farm homes of forty years ago as I have been for the kindly folk who lived in them"(6)

The conflict between a central government which intervenes in a complex urban industrial society, versus the ideal of a simpler, self-reliant, earlier America, where nature solved its own problems, in due time would force a man like Hoover, born in one age but living his adult life in another, into some interesting philosophical contortions. Noting that there were 291 hatcheries to provide fishermen with more fish, Hoover continued, "In addition to these paternal and maternal endeavors on the part of the government, I am aware that Mother Nature has herself been busy also. Private enterprise in the shape of a responsible mother fish is working upon the same problem; they are probably doing more than the paternal government for, I know, private enterprise usually does."(7)

In spite of his reservations on artificial intervention into nature, Hoover believed if fingerings were kept in the hatcheries a little longer they would have a better chance of reaching maturity. Typical of the voluntarism philosophy of the period, Hoover suggested that sportsmen's clubs take the small

69.

fry from the hatcheries and raise them to three inches
so that the fish might have a fighting chance, noting
that clubs in Minnesota, Pennsylvania and New Jersey
had already adopted such a program. In keeping with a
second characteristic of the period, a conservative
fiscal policy, Hoover pointed out that one hundred
couples in specially prepared pools could produce
200,000 offspring for a total outlay f $500, which
broken down came to four fish for a penny.(8)

Once the fish left the holding tanks, Hoover saw
another problem--"we still have another fish enemy to
deal with. That is pollution." Noting that nature
adapted fish to clean water because nature foresaw no
fishing along a sewer, Hoover saw no easy solution to
the needs of an urban industrial society versus the
need to keep as many streams in their pristine
condition for fishing as possible. Hoover's
suggestion was to divide streams into three
categories--those which of necessity would remain and
be designed as industrial streams, those streams which
were uncontaminated by industrial waste and were to
remain in their pristine condition, and the third
category of streams was made up of those where an
effort should be made to clean them up.(9)

Given his lifelong love of fishing, it should not
be surprising that Hoover, during his years as
Secretary of Commerce, and his time as President of
the Izaak Walton League, retained a strong interest in
the Bureau of Fisheries within the Commerce
Department. The bureau, however, was sometimes caught
between the conflicting wishes of sport and commercial
fishermen. Hoover, speaking to the Izaak Walton
League in Chicago a few years later, observed of
commercial fisherman, "To have restrictions thrown
about their livelihood in the interest of the future
generations has never been palatable to them."
Hoover, in asking for understanding of the commercial
fishermen's plight, reminded the more fortunate
members of the Izaak Walton League, "For them, it
means hard work, the earning of a livelihood for
themselves and their families ... Conditions under
which they must work are frequently unduly severe nd
unnecessarily hard. We can all lend in influence
toward its correction."(10)

This conflict became apparent at the Conference
of State Fish Commission Anglers and Producers in
June, 1921. Both commercial and sport fishermen were
concerned about the decreasing number of fish and the

70.

increasing amount of pollution, but sport and
commercial fishermen parted ways on what role the
government should play in enforcing stricter
regulations. The decline of Chesapeake Bay's crab
industry suggested to many delegates at the Migratory
Fish Conservation Commission that Maryland and
Virginia could not handle the problem. One
participant, an officer in the Camp Fire Club of
America, noted, "At the Washington Conference, there
was a unanimous opinion that water pollution was a
factor in the fish decrease and that there should be a
Federal control to do away with the evil." Another
participant at the meeting recalled that commercial
fishermen were mostly opposed to government
regulation. A third participant, George Shiras,
outdoor photographer for National Geographic, felt
that such conferences became bogged down between the
position of states' rights commercial fishermen versus
sportsmen who favored federal regulation. For Shiras,
at least, the issue was easy to resolve. The United
States Constitution assigned the role to the Federal
government for "the settlement of controversies
between the states."(11)

     Hoover's philosophy and position on the
relationship between state and federal government and
the limitations on federal power were closely
consistent and tended to fit reasonably with the
prevailing views in the 1920s, although the
limitations of such a philosophy became painfully
obvious after the crash of 1929. A key consideration
for Hoover was voluntary agreement rather than using
the direct coercive power of the federal government.

     At the Migratory Fish Conservation Committee
meeting, "A resolution was offered to put the
conference on record as being in favor of federal fish
control. Secretary Hoover stated that he did not care
to have it voted on, as the conference was intended to
enlighten the Department and not to instruct it."(12)
Hoover's concern over "Big Government" becoming
dominant in American life was a consistent theme
throughout his life. Shortly after the won te
Republican nomination for the Presidency, he returned
to West Branch, Iowa, his home for the first ten years
of his life. Although the rural nineteenth century
American of West Branch had changed for many Americans
to the vastly more complex interdependent, industrial
urban America of the 1920s, Hoover, nonetheless,
stated, "It is fortunate indeed that the principle
upon which our government was founded requires no

71.

alteration to meet those changes." At the same time, aware that many other Americans like himself had left the West Branches of America behind, he went on, "We have to pioneer through economic problems, through scientific development and invention. The test of our generation will be whether we can overcome these frontiers, whether we can hold mastery over he system we have created."

Although his actions were hedged by what he thought was the proper sphere of the federal government, Hoover could act decisively within those philosophical constraints. Hoover's handling of the Alaska Fisheries question is an example of his decisiveness. Accompanying President Harding on his trip to Alaska during the summer of 1923, Hoover emphasized that half of Alaska's people's livelihood and half of the Territory's revenue were derived from the salmon fishing industry and that the fishing industry was the largest in Alaska, twice the value of Alaska's mining industry. Further, there was need to restrict salmon industry fishing, in order to restore the fishery. Hoover was succinct, and to the point, "Our primary purpose is to restore this industry. Pious statements, scientific discussion, and political oratory will not spawn salmon." In a speech drafted by Hoover and delivered in Seattle shortly before his death, President Harding spoke forcefully in favor of conservation and added, "If Congress cannot agree upon a program of helpful legislation, the reservation and their regulation will be further extended by executive order."(13) Hoover seems to have had a much greater solicitude for state sovereignty than he did for a deliberative body such as Congress, which, to Hoover, was sometimes agonizingly slow and inefficient in dealing with problems which needed immediate attention.

In a little over three years, as Secretary of Commerce in charge of the fisheries, Hoover could point to a number of notable achievements, including confirmation by the Senate, of the Pacific Coast Halibut Treaty with Canada to prevent the continued depletion and destruction of the Halibut fisheries; enactment of the Alaska Fisheries Conservation Bill, by which the depletion of the fisheries, could be controlled and eventually restored to full productivity; passage of an Oil Pollution Bill to stop pollution by oil burning and oil carrying ships of fisheries and oyster beds; and enactment of Upper Mississippi Game and Fish Refuge Bill.(14)

A short time after he was appointed Secretary of Commerce, Hoover briefly explored the possibility of transferring the Bureau of Fisheries to Agriculture. Senior officials in the Bureau resisted the proposed transfer on the grounds that although the Bureau performed a number of seemingly different functions, all of the functions, nonetheless, focused on some aspect of the fishing industry, and if these functions were separated it was argued the Bureau's efficiency and administration would suffer. Hoover dropped the proposal to restructure, or to transfer the Bureau of Fisheries, but not the idea of seeking a unified administrative approach to conservation.(15)

Hoover's efforts to secure a unified approach to conservation continued during his years as Secretary of Commerce. Hoover was particularly interested in having sportsmen and conservation groups such as the Izaak Walton League support a proposed Division of Conservation within the Department of Interior. Writing to Charles Folds, President of the Izaak Walton League, Hoover pointed out: "We have ten bureaus and agencies devoted to conservation of our natural resources and our outdoor life. They are scattered through five Departments of the Government . . The major functions of the Secretaries of Agriculture, Commerce and Navy, for instance, are not conservation of our natural resources and our recreational opportunities . . . But of more importance than this, no definite, long time coordinated policies are possible under such disintegration of control and under one single direction, the force of public opinion, which is always a guardian, would be multiplied in its effectiveness."(16)

The Izaak Walton League held its meeting in Chicago in the spring of 1927 and adopted a resolution favoring the establishment of a Division of Conservation. Later, however, during the summer of 1927, President Coolidge made his famous announcement in Rapid City, South Dakota, that he did not choose to run for the presidency in 1928, and perhaps, Hoover had decided that there were more important matters than reshuffling cabinet bureaus, in order to unify the government conservation agencies. In any case, the matter was dropped, although Hoover's interest in outdoor recreation and conservation were interests which would persist from his cabinet days into the Presidency. Presidential interest in outdoor

73.

recreation was an interest shared by Hoover's two
Republican predecessors during the 1920s. This
presidential interest in the National Parks was shared
by a growing number of middle class Americans during
the 1920s. (17)

A number of factors contributed to a renewed
interest in nature, the National Parks, and outdoor
recreation. Living in the city, away from an earlier
rural environment, Americans in the twenties benefited
from modern industrial techniques and a lessening of
worktime, modern conveniences, mass produced cars with
an increase in mobility, but they, nonetheless,
retained an interest in the country and the outdoors.
In short, the desire to retreat to the country, the
leisure, and mobility for travel and extended
vacations, formerly a luxury primarily of the upper
classes, were now shared by a growing segment of the
middle class. The numbers visiting the National Parks
speak for themselves. In 1910, 200,000 visited
National Parks; that number had grown to 490,000 in
1917 and to over 1,280,000 by 1923.(18)

Capitalizing on this increased popularity of the
parks, the National Park Association, founded in 1919,
was an organization which acted as a lobby to promote
and publicize the interests of the National Parks,
while at the same time serving as a watchdog
organization to protect the parks from encroachment by
politicians and private interests. The increased
number of visitors to the National Parks in the West
created both an opportunity and a challenge. An
opportunity, because the increased number of visitors
were potential supporters of the National Parks, but
also a challenge because many of the large numbers of
visitors camped and saw the parks, not only for their
scenic natural beauty, but also as a recreational
place to enjoy the outdoors. By the early 1920s, the
received doctrine was that the National Parks were to
preserve scenic natural beauty and to be kept as
inviolate as possible. Robert Sterling Yard, an
employee of the Park Service during the early years of
the first National Park Director, Steven Mather, and
close personal friend of Mather, served as Executive
Secretary and prime mover of the National Park
Association after World War I. Yard, an effective
publicist, if a bit cantankerous at times, was opposed
to what he considered the mindless spread of
campgrounds in proposed new National Parks.
Testifying at a Congressional hearing in January,
1923, to oppose Secretary of Interior, Albert Fall's

74.

proposed Mescalero Indian Reservation bill, Yard
stated that the National Park Association was opposed
"Because a group of small isolated spots chosen
because they are good camping places, cannot make a
park in any national park sense." Yard also argued
that the Fall proposal would create an administratve
nightmare with overlapping jurisdictions among the
Indian Bureau, Forest Service, and Park Service, but
the thrust of his argument was "the public policy of
complete conservation was originated, and many times
confirmed, by Congress, and nurtured by the
government. Yellowstone, created in 1872, 'was to be
a reservation of nature, a national museum, preserving
for all time this wonderful region in its original
condition of nature.'" Yard failed to mention that
the legislation founding the park also include another
provision, namely that the government was establishng
"a park or pleasuring-ground for the benefit and
enjoyment of the people."(19)

The proposal of Secretary of Interior Fall and
the opposition of the National Park Association merely
were part of a larger philosophical battle among
conservationists which began earlier in the century.
This initial impulse for conservation was primarily
utilitarian--to save what was left from the maw of an
ever expanding industrial complex. Calvin Coolidge
summed up the utilitarian view by stating, "a tree
saved is a tree earned." A second consideration soon
entered conservation thought and that was simply
preservation of natural beauty for its own sake.
Aesthetic conservationists such as John Muir, founder
of the Sierra Club in 1892, believed that there were
other ways to measure the values of a stand of white
pine besides calculating its value in board feet. The
dispute between utilitarian conservationists under
Gifford Pinchot and aesthetic conservationists under
John Muir went back to the 1890s, when Muir and his
group opposed the damming of a beautiful chasm within
the boundaries of Yosemite National Park to provide
electricity and water for San Francisco, while
Pinchot, for a time with the Forest Service, supported
the project and castigated Muir and his followers as
unrealistic "nature lovers."(20) In spite of the
articulate opposition of Muir, the utilitarians won in
1913 and the dam was built. The philosophical debate,
however, continued down into the 1920s with the
Department of Agriculture's Forest Service continuing
the utilitarian point of view and Interior's Park
Service continuing the Muir tradition of preserving
natural beauty for its own sake.

The proposal of Fall, setting up scattered campgrounds in his home state of New Mexico, as part of an expanded National Park System, was regarded as a sharp break with what had been previous policy. Up to the time of the Fall Campground proposal, the National Park Association had distrusted Fall but had not opposed him. The Association was reassured with the continuation of Steven Mather, a professional, as Parks Director. The Association also supported Fall's opposition to Senator Thomas Walsh's bills for the damming of the Yellowstone River in Yellowstone Park, but was greatly troubled by the reasons Fall gave for his opposition; the dam was not necessary, at present, and the government should operate the dam in the park, not private Industry. The National Park Association felt that preserving the natural beauty of the park was a more appropriate and valid reason for opposing Walsh's bills.(21)

The National Park Association's resistance to Fall's proposal for a recreational National Park System was total and unremitting. The National Park Association Bulletin of February 7, 1923, carried the headline, "Fall's National Parks Policy Fully Revealed: Wants Huge Recreational System of Little Campgrounds at Sacrifice of Scenic Distinction and the Complete Conservation of America's World Famous System of Nature's Masterpieces. The Bulletin was opposed because, "The Fall policy sought to debase the National Park System to a merely recreational system and enormously expand it while, incidentally, abolishing its scenic distinction and its complete conservation." Fall, the article continued, recognized the concrete value of recreation, but "failed to comprehend the less tangible, but enormously greater values which he proposes to sacrifice."

When Fall resigned in early March, the March Bulletin went from the defensive to the offensive, stating that Fall had resigned, and Montana Senator Thomas Walsh's efforts to dam the Yellowstone River had failed. The article noted, "For three years, our allied clubs, associations, and federations have been busily nailing down our fine old national parks policy in the minds of this generation of Congressmen . . . When selfseeking legislators refuse to bring local invasion bills, not because they cannot be passed, but because they are contrary to the national policy, the war will be over."(22)

The March, 1923, Bulletin was also devoted, in part, to defining the place and role of National Parks. Taking its information from the House Committee on Public Lands, the Bulletin reiterated previously held policy, namely, the parks were to be maintained for their natural beauty, with a policy of complete conservation to be followed, and reliance on experts rather than on politicians, in defining suitable sites for parts.

Looking ahead to the future, Yard observed, "The era of travel, of outdoor living, of recreation in the open has dawned these several years, and is in the beginning of a wonderful expansion." Because of this expansion, Yard thought that additional campgrounds in the National Forests, and in state and local parks should be created, warning, "So far the National Parks have borne the brunt of this immense demand . . . it is not at all impossible that our national parks shall become so crowded very soon that they will lose much charm to the very people who crowd them."

Having successfully resisted potential encroachment on the part of Fall and Walsh, the National Park Association was able to secure a strong ally in the government when the trustees, meeting at the Smithsonian Institution, offered the presidency of the organization to Hoover in late February, 1924, and Hoover accepted. In his acceptance letter, Hoover noted that he did not have the time to raise money for the organization. Stating in his letter of acceptance that "the defense and preservation of our national parks is a most worthy effort," Hoover went on to add that "I should like to see the Association . . . expand its activities in the promotion of other forms of recreational areas. The interests of the millions of automobile campers and tourists who now annually visit our parks should be even further advanced by the reservation for them of camping grounds and other recreation opportunities from the public lands and forests."(23)

The February National Parks Association Bulletin of 1924, echoing the basic ideas in Hoover's acceptance letter, observed that "our National Park System, however, cannot remain a museum system of undisturbed nature and meet also the demands of this budding age of outdoor recreation. The automobile has begun a new era of wholesome contract with open air and nature whose benefit to the physical, mental, and spiritual welfare of the American people are

77.

inestimable." (24)

Yard wrote privately to a friend, "Mr. Hoover
wants the National Park Association to enlarge its
scope to the leadership of the strong popular movement
toward a National Recreational organization." (25)

Hoover was obviously interested in conservation
and outdoor recreation before he assumed the
presidency of the National Parks Association, but as a
member of the Coolidge cabinet in charge of the Bureau
of Fisheries, Hoover found that there could be
political advantages in being associated with the
wholesome outdoors and conservation. In a letter from
Henry Stimson to Republican Sentor George Pepper of
Pennsylvania, which was passed on to Hoover, Stimson
wrote: "The President should be thinking of a
constructive defense to all this criticism to which
the Republican Party has been subjected. In as much
as the attack on Fall is concentrated on the question
of conservation, the most natural subject matter ofr
counter attack on his part in the shape haimself and
his Administration emphatically in the forefront of
the conservation movement? He has the advantage of
having Hoover at his righthand with an essentially
constructive mind of those subjects."(26)

The March issue of the National Park Association
Bulletin in an article entitled, "About Our New
President" stated "Mr. Hoover is working in and out of
government for the sane conservative utilization of
the natural resources of the country. He believes
profoundly in irrigation and water power and has made
important contributions toward the superpower plans of
the future...He also believes profoundly in the
usefulness of conserving from all industrial
utilization one system of public reservations, our
National Parks, to serve as perpetual museums of
undistributed natural condition; and in the fullest
possible development of outdoor recreation." In a
letter to Hoover a few days later, Robert Yard, the
Executive Secretary of the National Parks Association,
wrote, "your entrance into the field of organized
recreation and nature conservation...will in spire the
conservation sentiment of the entire counrty as
nothing else could." (27)

A short time after Hoover assumed the presidency
of the National Parks Association, President Coolidge
appointed the commerce secretary and a number of other
Cabinet members to the President's Committee on

78.

Outdoor Recreation. This presidential advisory
committee was composed of the Secretaries of Interior,
Hubert Work; Agriculture, Henry C. Wallace; War, John
Weeks; Labor, James Davis; and Assistant Secetary of
Navy, Theordore Roosevelt, who, like his famous
father, was an avid outdoorsman. In making the
announcement of the appointment of his Outdoor
Recreation Committee on April 14, 1924, President
Coolidge observed, "particularly within the last
decade, the outdoor recreation spirit among our people
has increased rapidly." Believing that to expand
recreational opportunities would have a value in
"physical vigor and moral strength," Coolidge stated
that "Life in the open is a great character builder"
and a "lead should be taken by the National
Government." (28)

Ten days later, on April 24, 1924, President
Coolidge announced that a National Recreation
Conference would be held in Washington on May 22, 23
and 24, 1924, with Col. Roosevelt as Chairman of the
conference. A few days later, either to keep
administrative lines clear or else to protect his
chairmanship from the energetic Secrtary of Commerce
(who was sometimes referred to as "the Assistant
Secretary of Everything else), Theodore Roosevelt sent
a memorandum to Hoover stating that all correspondence
and other information regarding the Outdoor Recreation
Conference should pass through Roosevelt's office.
Hoover, as Secretary of Commarce in charge of the
Bureau of Fisheries, was asked to speak on
conservation and the propagation of fish. (29)

The National Outdoor Recreation Conference was
opened with an address by President Coolidge. The
President traced the need for recreation, noting that
in earlier times most people led a far more active
life. "There is still a large of manual labor, but to
a large extent this has become specialized and too
often would be designated correctly as drudgery...With
the development of our industrial an⁻ commercial life
more and more people are employed in clerical
activities...All of this, "the President continued,
"makes it more necessary than ever that we stimulate
every possible interest in out-of-door health giving
recreation."

President Collidge was hopeful that the
conference could coordinate and make an inventory of
national resources and opportunities, with the
pssibility of opening new fields, but keeping

amusements which emphasize the developmentof
character. In closing Coolidge observed, "There are
those who engaged in our industries who need an
opportunity for outdoor life and recreaton no less
than they need an opportunity of employment."(30)

The Outdoor Recreation Conference program stated,
"It represents the first recorded instance in the
history of the United States in which the moral,
spiritual and economic values of outdoor recreation
have been recognized by the head of the nation."

National Conference on Outdoor Recreation were
held during the years 1924-1928 in Washington. The
conference might be considered as quasigovernmental
because they were officially sponsored by the
president and various government agencies and, in
fact, drew on government staff, particularly the
National Park Service. A number of the delegates to
the conference representing various conservation and
outdoor organizations were also government officials.
William Greeley, Chief Forester, for example, was also
President of the Camp Fire Club of America; Ray Lyman
Wilbur, later Hoover's Secretary of Interior and one
of the founders of Save the Redwoods organization,
came as a representative of the National Education
Association; and Herbert Hoover, of course, attended
in the dual role as a cabinet officer and member of
the President's Committee on Outdoor Recreation, as
well as president of the National Parks Association.
In all, 309 delegates representing 128 organizations,
but mainly nature and conservation societies, attended
the Washington meeting. In addition to the general
delegates, a ninety-two member Advisory Committee was
chosen to further the work was active in Girl Scouts.
In all, there were seven women on the Advisory
Committee. The Advisory Committee, along with its
Executive Committee, included distinguished leaders of
American education and culture of the 1920s. The
Chairman of the Conference was Chauncey Hamilin,
President of the American Association of Museums; the
two vice-chairman were: Dr. Vernon Kellogg, head of
the Natioal Research Council. These people and ohers
on various conference committees, did more than lend
their names to stationery. As the minutes of the
conference show, the members of the committee actively
participated and were interested and involved in the
various profects of the conferences. When vacancies
occurred, Secretary of Commerce Hoover often filled
them. (31)

Although conservation and nature societies had members attending, various commercial and business organizations such as the Chamber of Commerce were also represented at the conference. In fact, the conference program stated that the conference "recognizes that many natural resources valuable for purposes of outdoor recreation are also the basis of extensive economic enterprises or sources of individual livelihood and believes that the conflicts in forms of use which now exist or which may develop, can frequently be worked out by processes of mutual arbitration and adjustment; consequently it welcomes to its membership the economic organization whose fields impinge upon that of outdoor recreation."

As a follow-up to the May confernce, two meetings of the President's Committee on Outdoor Recreation were held in late August and September. The two meetings were primarily concerned about the various Cabinet Departments cooperating in the formulation and execution of a comprehensive national policy and program on outdoor recreation. (32)

A follow-up meeting of the advisory committee of the National Conference on Outdoor Recreation was held at the Red Cross building in December, 1924. Eighty-five of the ninety-two members of the committee attended the meeting. Delivering the opening address on December 11, 1924, Hoover pledged the federal government to give the recreation movement as much support as possible, to coordnate the various agencies, and went on to suggest that the committee should make a "determination of our facilities and a clear development of the service you wish them to render." In his speech, Hoover neatly bridged the interests of commerce and leisure, noting that "one of the by-products of our increasing production and standards of living is greater leisure." This greater amount of leisure, Hoover believed was the result of the development of science and invention, the elimination of waste, and the inproved organization in commerce and industry, but the increased leisure "must be provided for by increases facilities of recreation and education. It will be of no avail to us to increase leisure without its constructive occupation. For leisure which is idleness will generate a disastrous train of degeneration." Hoover concluded by warning "We have directed ourselves to recreation." (33)

The National Conference on Outdoor Recreation of

1925 was devoted primarily to the organization of surveys and projects. Building on the general programs of the previous year, a number of specialized were undertaken. A survey of Municipal and County Park Systems, a Reactional Survey of State Lands, and a Recreational Survey of Federal Lands were begun in 1925 with the Laura Spelman Rockefeller Memorial providing $26,600., $12,500., and $15,000., for each of the surveys. as part of a fourth project, a committee was chosed to study the co-ordination of National Forests and Parks. Steven Mather, Director of the Park Service and William Greeley, Chief Forester, in addition to some outside members made up this Co-ordination Committee.

One of the most ambitious projects of the conference, a survey of the country's highway system was undertaken by the Chamber of qcommerce, with the United States Bureau of Roads, and the Highway Departments of Maryland, Pennsylvania, and Connecticut providing staff support. Drawing on reports from Connecticut and Pennsylvania, it was claimed that 60-65% of the vehicles in those states were used for recreational purposes. Inthe West, the figure was 75%. The project noted that "highway classification like city zoning, will stabilize rural property values and preserve or develop the aesthetic values of the raodside through tree planting and regulation of advertising." Both the Highway Beautification Act and the Outdoor Recreation Bureau set up in the Department of Interior during the 1960s had their origins in the mid 1920s. The material was prepared by authorities in their field, and the committee itself had representatives from the National Autombile Association, the National Conference on Street and Highway Safety, and the American Forestry Association. (34)

In all, thirty projects grew out of the 1925 conference. Some of the others included expenaded game refuges and bird sanctuaries, survey of wild lands, popular education in nature study. Project #20 called for the establishment of a National Recreation Area, and Project #21, for a National Arboretum.

Project #15 dealt with the "Recreational Needs of Industrial Workers." The Program stated rather succinctly, "One of the objectives of the Conference is the establishment of the principle that the mental and physical monotony of modern industrial employment can in large measure be offset or relieved by wholesome outdoor recreation." The report on the project was published in 1928. The Bureau of Labor Statistics compiled the study which gave an incomplete picture of the situation. Brief statistical surveys of medium sized cities such as Portland, Oregon, and Oakland, California, were taken and then a statistical comparison of 213 companies in such diverse fields as auto manufacturing, textiles, paper, food, electrical supplies, among others, employing 678,517 workers, was taken. Not all compaines in a particular industry apparently responded; the picture therefore is impressionistic at best. Although textile companies did not pay particularly well, and in many cases were open shops, of the thirty-six textile companies surveyed, employing 63,927, thirty-one, well above the surveyed averagae, had baseball teams. In contrast, only 160 of the 213 firms surveyed sponsored baseball teams and only 126 had baseball diamonds, but of the companies which responded, baseball was clearly the national pasttime. After baseball, compnay supported or sponsored recreational programs fell off sharply. Of the 213 firms surveyed, for example, only forty-two had Athletic Clubs; twenty-nine, tennis courts; nine, golf courses; thirty-six football or soccer teams; and ten had summer camps.(35)

In addition to the surveys, a number of bills supported by the member organizations of the conference were publicized and pushed toward passage, such as the Migratory Bird Reform Bill, Woodruff-McNary Bill for forest acquisition and McSeveny Bill for forest and biological research.(36)

Hoover, as a member of the Coolidge Cabinet, was involved in the National Outdoor Recreational Conference of the 1920s. In 1927, for example,Hoover gave the address at the dinner of the conference. Sounding a theme that he would use again, again, and again, Hoover reminded the delegates that "life is not comprised entirely of making a living, arguing about the future or defaming the past. It should be comprised in part of the outdoors and fishing."(37)

His involvement with the conference sometimes led to success, sometimes to failure. Hoover was interested in having the National Parks Association, the American Civic Association, the State Parks Conference, the Park Executive Institute, and the American Park Society unite into a more powerful lobby, a proposed Federation of Parks and Planning. Hoover learned that the Executive Secretary, Robert

Yard, was opposed to joining the proposed federation because he thought that the National Parks Association was distinctive and would lose both its lobbying ability with Congress and its specialized support if the National Parks Association joined the super-organization. A similar position was taken by the National Forest Association. The Trustees supported Yard's position. Of the Association's twenty trustees, seventeen were opposed to joining, two favored it, and one trustee was non-committal. Faced with this difference of opinion, Hoover resigned the presidency of the Ntional Park Association in May, 1925. In acknowledging Hoover's resignation, Yard wrote, "I am conscious that our entire viewpoint during your incumbency has very greatly enlarged...we have become a more useful organization. We shall always look back upon administration as making our great stride forward."(38)

Although unsuccessful in a policy difference with the National Parks Association Executive Secretary, Hoover was more successful in helping to choose the second Executive Director of the National Conference on Outdoor Recreation. The first director, Leon Kneipp, wished to return to the Forest Service. The man who succeeded Kneipp, Arthur Ringland, had previously worked for Hoover in the American Relief Administration. Trained at the Yale School of Forestry, Ringland spent the earlier years of the century in the Forest Service in the Southwest. During the years immediately following World War I, Ringland was involved in the food relief program in Central Europe, primarily in Czechoslovakia, and then had a similar position at Constantinople where he handled Russian relief. Ringland had orginally approached "the chief" about work in government in the spring of 1924, but it was not until December, 1924, that Ringland was chosen to be Executive Director of the National Conference on Outdoor Recreation at a salary of $7,500. a year. Described by Hoover as a man of excellent character and possessing high administrative ability, Ringlands' career during the two decades after the twenties followed the same pattern as the two decades before 1920. During the thirties, Ringland was involved with forest conservation work, and during the forties, he was again active in the World Relief program.(39)

The National Conference on Outdoor Recreation had its greatest impact during the first years the conferences were held. In 1928, it was decided to

84.

descontinue the conferences. In place of the
conference, it was suggested that a joint committee of
the Secretaries of Agriculture, Commerce, and
Interior, serve as a board in federal land planning.
This plan fell far short of Hoover's interest in a
Division of Conservatio, but Hoover's interestin
coordinated and constructive outdoor leisure persisted
into his presidency. While surveying a boundary on
the Yellowstone River during January, 1929, as part of
a study sponsored by the National Conference on
Outdoor Recreation, Ringland received a phone call
from President-elect Hoover's Assistant, Strothers,
asking for an estimate for a study on leisure.
Ringland suggested $25,000, but Hoover responded by
suggesting that the figure be increased to $250,000.

It is fitting that the story of the National
Conference on Outdoor Recreation should end in
Yellowstone Park in 1929. For it was in Yellowstone
that the National Park System was really begun, and it
was at Yellowstone during the 1920s that large numbers
of predominately middle class Americans discovered the
Great National Parks of the West for the first time,
although the attraction of the West was an old one
going back to the late nineteenth century.(40)

Americans went West in the late nineteenth
century for a variety of reasons. One attraction,
particulary of the Southwest, was a mild, warm
climate. The stationary of the Hotel del Coronado in
San Diego, for example, proudly quoted a testimonial
for "weak hearts, disabled lungs, and worn out
nerves." As late as 1925, Hot Springs National Park
had more visitors than any other national park.
Although by the 1920s, in addition to its baths and
purges the park invited visitors to try hiking and
riding.(41)

While it is true that the larger numbers of
campers coming in cars date from the 1920s, campers
began coming to National Parks in the West during the
closing decades of the nineteenth century. By the
1890s, the Southern Pacific Railroad was advertising
special campers' fare with free checking of tents,
stoves, and other camping equipment. Most of these
early railroad campers were from the cities of the
West, attracted to Yosemite and Yellowstone Parks.
The Pacific coast statles tended to have an above
average urban population--defined as an incorporated
place with a population of more than 2,500. In 1870,
for example, one third of the Pacific coast's states'

population lived in towns of 2,500 or more; the
national average was one-quarter. In California the
trend was even more marked, one quarter of the
population lived in cities in 1900, two-thirds in
1920, and three quarters in 1930.

By the beginnng of the century, western railroads
were encouraging wealthy Easterners to put their cars
on railraod cars and ship them west. Change occurred
with great rapidity during the second decade of the
century. In 1912, there were one million car licenses
in the country; eleven years later there were
15,222,658 cars and trucks on the nation's roads. In
1923 one million Americans visited the National Parks
and three million the National Forests. In fact, in
the previous year, 1,173,000 people visited the two
National Parks and the seventeen National Forests in
Colorado alone. Of the 1,173,000, only 277,000 came
to the National Parks and Forests by other means than
in cars. A writer in Sunset magazine claimed, "the
automobile and municipal camps have so cheapened
travel that the wonders of the West's National Parks
today are accessible to hundreds of thousands who ten
years ago had as much chance to see them as Hobson has
of becoming admiral of the Swiss navy." A reporter
for the Saturday Evening Post observed, "A family in a
motor car can travel one thousand miles a month with
an expense of $35.00 to $50.00 for rent, gasoline and
oil, the variation being due to the difference in gas
an oil consumption of various types of cars."(43)

The increased numbers of visitors to National
Parks and Forest attest to the increased popularity of
the National Parks and Forests during the 1920s. In
1920, 920,000 people visited National Parks and
4,833,000 visited National Forests. By 1930, that
figure had risen to 2,775,000 for Parks and 31,905,000
for Forests. As was noted earlier, the overwhelming
preponderance of visitors came in cars--92% of the
visitors in National Forests and 85% of the visitors
to National Parks.(44)

The National Conference on Outdoor Recreation on
its report on Major Fact Finding Surveys published in
1928 observed, "Swift and cheap motor transportation
has now opened up a great hinterland to city
dwellers." Millions now visit state and national
forests and parks which "afford phases of outdoor life
which admirably supplement the necessarily restricted
types of recreation use of municipal playgrounds and
parks . . . The whole aspect of the land, its value

for public social use, has undergone a radical change
in so short a period as the last decade." Repeating
what a number of articles in various magazines had
pointed out earlier in the decade, the report
continued, "Outdoor recreation did not become a
widespread popular Institution until the prosperity
following the close of the World War put the country
on a motorized basis." Noting that the federal lands
had unique opportunities for outdoor recreation and
education, the report stated that providing for such
services "is now an accepted and established function
of government." With that end in mind, the Fact
Finding Survey argued that "outdoor recreation in a
form of land economy that must find its place in the
national planning as well as in city or regional
planning if the vast Federal lands are to serve their
highest usefulness." The Fact Finding Survey also
noted that Federal Lands of recreation value are an
asset to be preserved and enjoyed and that National
Parks are the only major system which is wholly
non-utilitarian." Observing that "though National
Parks have not yet been defined in law, their purposes
and uses, and standards which govern their creation
have been established by government practice during
fifty-six years." A statement whose force both
Secretary of Interior Albert Fall, with his ill-fated
scheme of National Parks wtih scattered campgrounds
and Senator Thomas Walsh of Montana, with his project
of damming the Yellowstone River, had quickly
discovered. "Proposed parks," stated Steven Mather,
Director of the Park Service, "are measured by
standards set by the major parks of the system."(45)

Paradoxically, as the popularity of the parks
increased after World War I, agitation and concern
began to be expressed about keeping some federal lands
as wilderness areas. Aldo Leopold, of the Forest
Service, in a number of articles, warned that
Americans having cut the forests, "the next resource,
the exhaustion of which is due for discovery, is the
wilderness, already being invaded by motor cars and
tourist camps." Hoover, an outdoorsman and fisherman
himself, had read the article, and as president,
Hoover would act decisively in furthering the National
Parks and Forests, adding 3,000,000 acres to the
National Parks and Monuments, increasing the National
Parks System by forty per cent, and adding 2,000,000
acres to the National Forests and giving an order that
all leasing of forests for new lumbering operations
should cease on May 4, 1931. It is not within the
scope of this study to examine the conservation

policies of the Hoover Presidency, but some of the
conservation programs of the Roosevelt Administration
were built on the policies of the Hoover Presidency.
The idea, for example, of putting unemployed men to
work in the National Forests appeared as early as
November, 1929. By March, 1931, 5,500 men were
working in the National Forests. It can be argued
that Hoover's interest in recreation and conservation
during his years as Secretary of Commerce, helped
shape some of his decisions as president.(46)

     As Secretary of Commerce, Hoover's work,
interest, and support of standardization, efforts to
lessen waste, and increase efficiency are well known.
His efforts and interest in conservation in the Bureau
of Fisheries and his support of constructive outdoor
recreation are less well-known. His ideas on
efficient and effective use of both work and play are
cut of the same cloth. With somewhat shorter working
hours and more mobility with the greater availability
of cars for many Americans, Hoover was concerned that
a good use of leisure be found. His support of
Prohibition is another side of this same concern. In
his Memoirs, Hoover wrote, "This civilization is not
going to depend upon what we do, when we work, so much
as what we do in our time off. The moral and
spiritual forces of our country do not lose ground in
the hours we are busy on our jobs; their battle is the
leisure time. We are organizing the production of
leisure. We need better organization of its
consumption. We devote vast departments of
government, the great agencies of commerce and
industry, science and invention, to decreasing the
hours of work, but we devote comparatively little to
improving the hours of recreation."(47)

FOOTNOTES

1. Donald Swain, Federal Conservation Policy, 1921-1933, Berkeley & Los Angeles; University of California Press, 1962, The background information for the opening pages of this essay are taken from Donald Swain's excellent book. p. 161.

2. Herbert Hoover, The Memoirs of Herbert Hoover: The Cabinet and the Presidency, 1920-1933, Col. II, New York, The MacMillan Co., 1951 p. 157 Douglas Drake, "Herbert Hoover, Ecologist: The Politics of Oil Pollution Control, 1921-1926" Mid America, July, 1973. Hoover claimed in Fishing for Fun that the days spent fishing were not counted as part of one's life. Hoover lived to be ninety.

3. Herbert Hoover, Fishing For Fun And To Wash Your Soul; New York: Random House, New York, 1963, pp. 35 & 36.

4. Herbert Hoover, Memoirs, Vol. II, p. 158. The material was originally written as his Inaugural Speech as President of the Izaak Walton League, given on April 9, 1927.

5. Herbert Hoover, Memoirs, Vol. II, pp. 158 & 159.

6. Herbert Hoover, The New Day, Campaign Speeches of Herbert Hoover, "West Branch, Iowa, August 21, 1928," p. 52, Stanford University Press, 1928, p. 52.

7. Herbert Hoover, Memoirs, Vol. II, p. 160.

8. Herbert Hoover, Memoirs, Vol. II, p. 162.

9. Herbert Hoover, Memoirs, Vol. II, p. 165.

10. Speech to the Izaak Walton League, April 9, 1927 and April 12, 1924; "Conservation, 1924-1928," Commerce Papers, Herbert Hoover Presidential Library, West Branch, Iowa, (Henceforth abbreviated HHPL).

11. George Shiras to Herbert Hoover, June 13, 1921, "Report of Migratory Fish Conservation Commission," Commerce Papers, HHPL.

12. "Report of the Migratory Fish Conservation Committee" Bureau of Fisheries, Commerce Papers, HHPL.

13. Statement by Herbert Hoover, USS Henderson, Sitka, Alaska, July 23, 1923. Conservation of the Fisheries of Alaska, Commerce Papers, HHPL. Donald Swain, Federal Conservation Policy, 1921-1933, p. 160.

14. Press Release, June 30, 1924, Conservation, 1924-1928, Commerce Papers, HHPL.

15. Memorandum: H. F. Moore, Acting Commissioner, Bureau fo Fisheries to Secretary of Commerce, Febraury 27, 1922, Government Reorganization, Fisheries to Department of Agriculture, Commerce Papers, HHPL.

16. Herbert Hoover to Charles Folds, March 16, 1927, April 6, 1927, Conservation 1924-1928, Commerce Papers, HHPL.

17. Conservation, 1924-1928, Commerce Papers, HHPL. There has been a great deal of speculation over why Coolidge decided not to run in 1928. Hoover hints in Fishing for Fun that it was to spare the Secret Service from further danger whenever the President went fishing: "President Coolidge apparently had not fished before his election. Being a fundamentalist in religion, economics and fishing, he began his fish career for common trout with worms. Ten million fly fisherman at once evidenced disturbed minds. Then Mr. Coolidge took to a fly. He gave the Secret Service guards great excitement in dodging his backcast and rescuing flies from trees. There were many photographs. Soon after that he declared he did not choose to run again." Fishing for Fun, p. 70. In addition to Hoover's suggestion of a Division of Conservation and the possibility of transferring the Bureau of Fisheries to Agriculture, there were other possibilities of transfers among Departments. Albert Fall, for example, was interested in having the Forest Service moved from Agriculture to Interior. (cfr. Donald Winters, Henry Cantwell Wallace as Secretary of Agriculture, 1921-1924, Ch. VIII, and Harold Steen, U.S. Forest Services A History, 1921-1924, pp.

148-152.) This paper focuses only on Hoover's interest in establishing a Division of Conservation, not any of his interests in bureaucratic empire building.

18. National Parks, 1023-1928, Commerce Paper, HHPL.

19. National Parks Assoc. Bulletin #32, February 7, 1923, National Parks, 1923-1928, Commerce Papers, HHPL. Swain, op. cit. p. 123, Robert Shankland, Steve Mather of the National Parks, New York: Alfred Knopf, 1970, Third Edition. Yard served as best man at Mather's wedding. Mather was a descendant of the famous Massachuetts ministerial family of Increase and Cotton Mather.

20. Swain, Conservation Policy, p. 16 and p. 124.

21. National Parks Association Bulletin #32, February 7, 1923, National Parks, 1923-1928, Commerce Paper, HHPL. Fall, knowing that Mather was cool to his proposal of a National Park in New Mexico, did not demand that his subordinate testify on its behalf. Donald Swain, Wilderness Defender, Horace M. Albright, and Conservation, Chicago: University of Chicago Press, 1970, p. 146.

22. National Parks Association Bulletin #33, March 8, 1923, National Parks 1923-1928, Commerce Papers, HHPL.

23. By the mid-twenties, the National Parks Association was able to raise a little over $10,000, with John D. Rockefeller giving $2,500, and Miss Laughlin $2,000. Robert Yard to Herbert Hoover, April 3, 1924, National Parks Association, Commerce Papers; Herbert Hoover to Charles D. Wolcott, Febraury 26, 1924, Yale to Town-Yarr, Commerce Papers, HHPL.

24. National Parks Association Bulletin #37, Febraury 28, 1924, National Parks Association, Commerce Papers, HHPL.

25. Robert Yard to H. W. de Forest, March 18, 1924, National Parks, 1923-1928, Commerce Papers, HHPL.

26. Henry Stimson to George Pepper, March 31, 1924, Conservation, Commerce Papers, HHPL.

27. National Parks Association Bulletin #38, March

21, 1924, Robert Yard to Herbert Hoover, April 3, 1924, National Parks, Commerce Papers, HHPL.

28. *National Parks Association Bulletin #39*, April 30, 1924, National Parks, Commerce Papers, HHPL.

29. Theodore Roosevelt to Herbert Hoover, April 4, 1924, May 5, 1924, National Conference on Outdoor Recreation, Commerce Papers, HHPL.

30. National Conference on Outdoor Recreation, Commerce Papers, HHPL.

31. National Conference on Outdoor Recreation, Commerce Papers, HHPL. Interview with Arthur Ringland, "National Conference on Outdoor Recreation" Regional Oral History Office, 486 Bancroft Library, University of California, Berkeley, 94720.

32. President's Committee on Outdoor Recreation, August 27, 1924, September 11 & 20, 1924, National Conference on Outdoor Recreation, Commerce Papersm HHPL.

33. National Conference on Outdoor Recreation, 1924, Commerce Papers, HHPL.

34. National Conference on Outdoor Recreation, 1924, Commerce Papers, HHPL.

35. *NAtional Conference on Outdoor Recreation: Report on Major Fact Finding Surveys*, 70th Congress, Senate Document #158, Washington: U.S. Government Printing Office, 1928.

36. Interview with Arthur Ringland.

37. National Conference on Outdoor Recreation,1927, Commerce Papers, HHPL.

38. Memorandum, January 21, 1925, Robert Yard to Herbert Hoover, May 22, 1925. Yard also wrote: "In spite of the small amount of attention you have been able to give to the affairs of the National Park Association...your service to it has been very great indeed...the hill-top vision has lifted us." National Park Association , 1925, Commerce Papers, HHPL.

39. Leon Kneipp later served as Assistant Forester.

Interview with Arthur Ringland. Christian Herter
to George Barr Baker, February 2, 1924; Arthur
Ringland to Frank Page, April 15, 1924; Paul
Clapp, Assistant to Hoover, To Ringland, April
18, 1924; Christian Herter to Harold Chauncy
Hamlin, December 10, 1924; Arthur Ringland,
Commerce Papers, HHPL. Perhaps because of
divided loyalties, Ringland tends to play down
the rivalry between the Interior's Park Service
and Agriculture's Forest Service. Ringland is of
the opinion that the Park Service's Steven Mather
and Forest Service's William Greenley were both
professionals who avoided any rivalries between
their two Services. Donald Swain in Federal
Conservation Policy, 1921-1933, p. 134-137, and
Harold Steen's The U.S. Forest Service: A
History, p. 157, have suggested that beneath the
surface cordiality, some rivalry persisted in the
twenties. Because Ringland was trained in the
Yale School of Forestry and worked during the
years before World War I in the Forest Service,
and relied on Park Services personnel for staff
work for the National Conference on Outdoor
Recreation, Ringland tended to play down any
rivalry between the two Services, although he did
recall that on a boundary rectification between
Yosemite National Park and a National Forest
where the two Yale School of Forestry trained
members of the Coordinating Committee, William
Greenley and Barrington Moore voted against the
Yosemite addition, losing by a vote of three to
two. Ringland, also a Yale University School of
Forestry graduate and Chairman of the
Coordinating Commission, did not vote, (Ringland
interview.)

40. Interview with Arthur Ringland.

41. Earl Pomeroy, In Search of the Golden West: The
     Tourists in Western America, New York: Alfred
     Knopf, 1957, p. 119.

42. Pomeroy, In Search of the Golden West, p. 121
     dd.

43. Pomeroy, In Search of the Golden West, p.130;
     Saturday Evening Post, August 9, 1924; Sunset,
     September, 1924.

44. Recent Social Trends in the United States:
     Report of the President's Research Committee on

Social Trends, Vol. II, "Recreation and Leisure
Time Activities," J. F. Steiner, New York:
McGraw-Hill Book Company, 1933, (Henceforth
Recent Social Trends) pp. 921 and 922.

45. National Conference on Outdoor Recreation:
     Report on Major Fact Finding Surveys, 70th
     Congress, Senate Document #158, Washington: U.S.
     Government Printing Office, 1928, "Recreation
     Resources of Federal Lands: Report of the Joint
     Committee on the Recreational Survey of Federal
     Lands of the American Forestry Association and
     National Park Association," pp. 54-60 passim.

46. Aldo Leopold, "The Last Stand of the Wilderness,"
     American Forests and Forest Life, October, 1925.
     A. Martin Hyde & Raqy L. Wilbur, The Hoover
     Policies, New Uork: Charles Scribner & Sons,
     1937, p. 234. Donald Swain, Federal Conservation
     Policy, 1921-1933, p. 25.

47. Herbert Hoover, Memoirs, Vol. II, pp. 165-166.
     There was a phenomenal increase in American car
     ownership during the 1920s. In 1920 one
     passenger car was registered for every 13
     Americans, in 1930 there was one for every 5!
     Americans. During the twenties the American
     automobile population grew more than seven times
     as fast as the human population. Emma
     Rothschild, Paradise List: The Decline of the
     Auto Industrial Age, New York, Random House,
     1973, p. 26.

HERBERT HOOVER'S
INDIAN REFORMERS UNDER ATTACK:
THE FAILURES OF ADMINISTRATIVE REFORM

by William G. Robbins

The formulation and administration of federal
Indian policy in the United States has alternated
between the aggressive pursuit of assimilating Indian
people as quickly as possible into the dominant
society, and programs which give some attention to
preserving the Indian cultural heritage along with a
less aggressive assimilationist ideology. The
identifying characteristics of this policy were
paternal - denying traditional native political
structures and making indigenous people dependent on
non-native governing bodies and non-native
resources.(1) This dichotomy characterizes Indian
policy in the United States in the first half of the
twentieth century.(2)

Three assumptions define federal reforms in the
twentieth century: [1] that Indian people desire and
should be integrated into the dominant society, [2]
that the immediate social and economic conditions of
Indian people should be ameliorated, and [3] that the
federal government is the appropriate agency to carry
out such programs. For the first twenty years of the
new century, reformers showed little interest in
Indian affairs; indeed it was not until the 1920s that
one hears the first rumblings about federal
administration of Indian policy. For many years after
the passage of the General Allotment Act of 1887, it
was widely assumed that Indians were being
successfully integrated into American society. But by
the 1920s it was apparent to many that not all was
well in the field, that somehow the government's
assimilation program had failed to achieve its
goals.(3) Finally, in 1929 the administration of
Herbert Hoover made a commitment to extend the
benefits of its New Era reforms to the American
Indian.(4)

The General Allotment or Dawes Act was predicated
on the assumption that individualizing the Indian
pattern of collective landholding would speed the
erosion of tribalism, promote assimilation, and lead
to the full integration of Indian people into American
life.(5) As the years passed it was obvious that the
allotment policy was perpetuating Indian poverty,

95.

contributing to ever-worsening health conditions, and accelerating the alienation of Indian people from their land base.(6)   These matters were made public in a notorious series of incidents centered around the Pueblo land controversy in the early 1920s and the subsequent efforts of reformers to bring an end to the allotment policy.(7)

The struggle to determine the direction of Indian policy during this period produced knights in shining armor, crusading reform organizations, and a sprinkling of first-rate villains.   Two hold-over officials, Charles H. Burke and Edgar Meritt, appointed by former Secretary of Interior Albert B. Fall, held the offices of Commissioner and Assistant Commissioner of Indian Affairs until Herbert Hoover replaced them shortly after his inauguration in the Spring of 1929.   Burke, a former Congressman from South Dakota, had continued to allot reservation land and was contemptuous of reformers like John Collier and his American Indian Defense Association.(8)   And, these critics were not passive.   Early in 1929 Harold Ickes, then an ambitious Chicago attorney, castigated the Fall appointees for perpetuating a "shameful record" in their treatment of American Indians.(9)   It remained to be seen, however, if a new administration would bring a new direction to Indian affairs.

As part of an effort to engage the expertise of social scientists to help solve the government's persisting Indian problems, Secretary of the Interior Hubert Work commissioned the Institute for Government Research and an investigative team headed by Lewis Meriam of the University of Chicago to make a survey of economic conditions on Indian reservations. Popularly known as the Meriam Report, the study was a scathing indictment of health and economic conditions, and educational policy (especially the off-reservation boarding schools).   And the allotment policy was singled out as a special case for failure.(10)

Although the Meriam Report was published in the midst of an election year (1928), all indicators suggest that Indian affairs was not a major election issue.   But there is evidence that Republican Party campaign strategists may have withheld distribution of the report until the adjournment of Congress to avoid the onus of having failed to act on its recommendations.(11)   And, the leading Republican candidate was the energetic Secretary of Commerce, Herbert Hoover, a man widely identified as a humanitarian and reformer.(12)

David Burner, a recent Hoover biographer, has
claimed that Herbert Hoover "had strong reasons for
addressing himself to the problems of American
Indians" because of his long and intimate association
with Indian people through childhood experiences,
relatives in the employ of the Indian service, and the
"Quaker tradition of fair treatment for Indians."(13)
The claim is misleading. An examination of the Hoover
presidency shows that the chief executive had little
interest in Indian affairs. Even the significant
Meriam Report, for instance, seems to have escaped
Hoover's attention for some time.(14) And when he did
respond to an inquiry from the American Defense
Association, Hoover was ambivalent and vague in his
references to the report.(15)

From the outset, therefore, it seems unlikely
that Herbert Hoover would be an activist reformer on
behalf of Indian people; his reluctance to intervene
on controversial Indian issues during his presidency
bears out this assumption.(16) Thus, his
administration's reputation for Indian policy reform
rests with the successes and failures of cabinet and
Indian service appointees and not with the chief
executive.

Beause of the paternal and colonial relationship
between Indian people and the United States
government, white activist organizations had
traditionally lobbied with the federal government to
influence the direction of Indian policy. The Indian
Rights Association, long identified with missionary
groups, followed an assimilationist and integrationist
program best expressed in the philosophy of the Dawes
General Allotment Act. That temper still prevailed
among its membership in the late 1920s as evidenced in
its monthly publication, Indian Truth. (17)

The more recent American Indian Defense
Association originated in the Pueblo land controversy
of 1922-1924. The social engineer and moral reformer,
John Collier, was its inspirational leader and most
influential spokesman, but the association also
attracted others who believed in the use of social
science tools and research techniques to solve social
problems. Although there was some friction between
these two reform organizations, both regularly
attacked Commissioner Charles Burke's Indian policy
during the late 1920s. And the cooperation between

these two groups carried over to the first year of the administration of Herbert Hoover.(18)

Moreover, the appointment of Hoover's longtime friend, Ray Lyman Wilbur, as Secretary of the Interior heartened most Indian reformers. As an educator, president of Stanford University, and with an active interest in Indian affairs, Wilbur brought impressive credentials to the Interior office. Indian Truth praised the new administration for offering "a new and better day. . . for the American Indian."(19) In quick succession the addministration fired Charles Burke and Edgar Meritt and appointed two Quakers--Charles J. Rhoads, a wealthy Philadelphia banker, as commissioner, and J. Henry Scattergood, an equally successful businessman, as assistant commissioner. Both men were active members of the Indian Rights Association, and at the time of his appointment to the Indian bureau Rhoads, was president of the association.(20)

Wilbur, Rhoads, and Scattergood represented the assimilationist approach of the Indian Rights Association, and they also worked in close harmony with the quasi-private, missionary-oriented Board of Indian Commissioners. Perhaps the most aggressive tone to the administration's Indian program was Wilbur's zeal in pressing for an early version of the infamous "termination" policy of the early 1950s. In an earlier letter to his predecessor, Hubert Work, Wilbur had listed six steps to an equitable Indian policy: [1] the use of intelligence tests to determine which children should advance beyond the sixth grade, [2] a requirement that all Indian children attend public school, [3] that the federal government should get out of Indian affairs "as soon as possible" and that allotment should be speeded up, [4] that health and education for Indian youth should be improved, but on the basis of Indian responsibility, [5] that school integration should be accelerated, and [6] that tribal assets should be liquidated and each enrolled Indian granted prorated shares.(21)

After his appointment as Interior Secretary, Wilbur proposed (in a memo to the President) "to make of the Indian a self-supporting, self-respecting American citizen just as rapidly as this can be brought about." He recommended that education and health programs be placed under the respective jurisdictions of the Bureau of Education and the

Public Health Service, or, where feasible, made the responsibility of the various states. He proposd that the activities of the Indian bureau be decentralized, that Indian agents gradually be phased out, that children should attend public schools where they were accessible, and that, except for large reservations, there "should be a continued allotment of land." Finally, the Interior Secretary urged improved facilities for Indian people "with the general plan in mind of eliminating the Indian bureau within a period of say 25 years." Hoover accepted the proposals but suggested that Wilbur consult with the commissioners on Indian affairs "which I think is called the Board of Indian Commissioners. . . . They are all sane people."(22) The President displayed a lack of familiarity with the workings of the Indian office, but, more importantly, Hoover and Wilbur indicated from the beginning that, like previous administrations, they were inclined to favor the missionary-oriented board.(23)

One of the most influential congressional figures the Hoover administration would have to confront to obtain funding for its Indian programs was the Republican chairman of the House Appropriations Committee, Representative Louis Crampton of Michigan. And Crampton had forewarned the administration to be on guard. In a letter to the President on April 17, 1929, he expressed alarm about dropping Indians as "wards of the Nation" (Wilbur's language), and opposed the transfer of Indian health and education policies to the states or to other executive departments. Crampton directed his major criticism at Wilbur's support for the allotment policy. Allotment, he argued, "has been more permanently disastrous to the welfare of the Indians" than any other policies advocated "by idealistic, but ill-informed Indian administrators. "Indian people, he said, were "suffering from a too rapid application of the policy of allotment of land." The Interior Secretary, therefore, should "avail himself of the views of men in Congress" who have had years of experience on the subject. The President's response to the Michigan congressman was blunt and undiplomatic: "I suggest that you reserve judgment in the matter until you have had an opportunity to take matters up with him.(24)

During Hoover's first year in office, the administration became embroiled in a controversy over appropriations to provide food and clothing for children attending Indian boarding schools. The issue

centered on Congressman Louis Crampton's efforts to
cut appropriations designated to increase allocations
for food and clothing (referred to as the Deficiency
Bill). The intervention of the American Indian
Defense Association and the restoration of funds in
the Senate effected a compromise and partial victory
for the administration. But Senate progressives and
the arguments of the American Indian Defense
Association forced the issue. The Nation charged
Commissioners Rhoads and Scattergood for defending
Crampton's recommendations and criticized the
President for his unwillingness to discipline members
of his own party and for his failure to support Indian
legislation.(25)

The controversy over the Deficiency Bill marked
progressive alienation between the American Indian
Defense Association and Hoover's Indian policy makers.
But, what other reformers characterized as failure,
the Indian Rights Association described as "the dawn
of a new era in Federal administration of Indian
affairs." The Indian, it announced, "is getting a new
deal," and Rhoads and Scattergood "have disarmed
believers in the old order, harmonized discordant
elements, and gained adequate financial support." The
Board of Indian Commissioners in its annual report for
1930 also applauded Rhoads and Scattergood for their
cautious approach and for avoiding "sensational
upheavals" and "dramatized reforms." The "captious
critics" who berated the hard-working commissioners,
the board noted, was an unpleasantness inseparable
from the office; beter they be praised for making
progress "step by step" and not by "sensational leaps
and bounds."(26)

Others disagreed. The American Indian Defense
Association accused Wilbur, Rhoads, and Scattergood of
promising the millenium, raising the "highest hopes,"
and accomplishing "practically nothing." Haven
Emerson, the association's president, chastized Wilbur
and his subordinates for their failure to "fight to a
finish for such elementary things as the prevention of
starvation of the Indian children." The Indian
Bureau, Emerson charged, "is, if anything, in worse
plight now than under their predecessors, Burke and
Meritt."(27) The Interior Department soon became
obsessed with attacks such as this.

Because of his excessive sensitivity to
criticism, Wilbur must share responsibility for the
increasing alienation of his department from the

Indian reformers. And this "sensitivity" turned to outright rancor as the months passed and the charges mounted. In May 1930, Wilbur complained that the attacks of the American Indian Defense Association "have required a great deal of the time of the Commissioners." It was easy for the association to criticize, Wilbur contended, because it "has no responsibility" and its charges were not based on reality. Moreover, such "outrageous and unworthy" criticism hurt "the opportunities of the government officials to obtain and retain the confidence of the Indian population." The association should discontinue its "widespread, intemperate and illy digested emotional attacks."(28) And in his memoirs Wilbur refers to "confusion . . . created by the constant agitations of certain zealots" who "consumed a good deal of the time of government officials which might have been better used for th benefit of the Indians."(29)

There was more to this story than Wilbur was willing to reveal, because the Department of Interior and the Indian office had become involved in matters of great controversy. One of the most troublesome for the Interior Secretary was the disposition of the Flathead Indian power issue, a dispute that had been simmering for some time. The turmoil centered around the application of the Rocky Mountain Power Company, a subsidiary of the Montana Power Company (and with close ties to Anaconda Copper), to develop a hydroelectric site on the Flathead reservation in Montana.(30) Secretary Wilbur, as titular head of Indian affairs and chairman of the three member Federal Power Commission, was deeply involved in the Flathead case.

When the Federal Power Commission rendered its decision to lease the site to the Rocky Mountain Power Company in May 1930, the administration's Indian policy already was under attack. Assistant Commissioner J. Henry Scattergood, who negotiated the terms of the lease, involved the Flathead Indians only peripherally in the discussions, a process that was not unusual because the government seldom consulted Indian people in such matters. And the lease arrangement was singled out for criticism because the case was the first of its kind.(31)

The Flathead decision set Wilbur and the Indian office against progressive forces who made the Flathead power issue their cause celebre. These included public power advocates, the National Popular Government League, and a coalition of Senate progressives who were critics of the administration of Indian policy.(32) Then, to add fuel to these charges, the President failed to intervene in the dispute despite numerous requests to do so. The disposition of the Flathead case, therefore, worsened Hoover's problems with Congress and tended to discredit his Indian administrators. The nation's rapidly contracting economy made matters even more difficult.

Moreover, there are indications that the Flathead decision embarrassed the Hoover administration. In a news release hailing the Indian Bureau's achievements during his first year in office, the President made no mention of the Flathead power issue. Yet, in the original memorandum to the President, Commissioner Rhoads included a full-page discussion of the Flathead decision (in a six-page memo). The President released the commissioner's memorandum to the press with the exception of the information under "Flathead Power Site."(33)

But the administration was not without supports. Joseph W. Latimer, a New York attorney, defended the administration although he "utterly opposed. . .many policies which are apparently those of the present Commissioners." Latimer commended them for asking Congress to assist in "abolishing the Bureau," and praised the new commissioners for being "open-minded" and "honest men, free. . .from any political entanglements." He attacked John Collier and the Senate Committee Investigating Indian Affairs. The committee, he argued, allowed too much of its testimony from one source--its "star and perpetual witness" who dramatized his opinions "so that they appear in the record as facts." He referred disparagingly to Collier as the "Professional Benevolent," and defended Charles Rhoads, "the mild-mannered, patient Commissioner," who testified before the "inquisitorial Committee."(34)

The mounting congressional attacks and criticism from the American Indian Defense Association jeopardized the administration's Indian legislative program. In a candid letter to the President,(35) Secretary Wilbur dismissed the possibility of getting legislation through Congress and proposed a typically Hooverian solution--a commission with legislative authority "to study the tangled treaties, laws, rights

and other pressing problems, and to make
recommendations for a fresh start." The growing
crisis of the depression killed this effort to deal
with Indian affairs through an elitist commission.
When the Bureau of the Budget informed Wilbur that the
expenditure was not in accord with the President's
financial program, the Interior Secretary appealed to
the President. Hoover replied that he would support
"a moderate appropriation only if no expenditures were
to be undertaken until after the fiscal year 1933.(36)
Wilbur's unsuccessful attempt to circumvent a
recalcitrant Congress suggests that the federal Indian
program depended on legislative approval.

And to confound matters some of the
administration's early supporters turned up among its
most strident critics. One of these was John
Collier.(37) Because he wa intimately associated with
reform activities, it is easy to exaggerate the
ideological differences between Collier and Rhoads.
Although both men previously had worked with
white-dominated Indian reform organizations, -- the
Indian Rights Association and the American Indian
Defense Association -- there was considerable
collaboration between the two groups and both had
cooperated to push specific Indian legislation in
Congress. John Collier and the American Indian
Defense Association assisted Rhoads in drafting much
of his legislative program and subsequently lobbied
for its passage through Congress.(38) Rhoads,
moreover, was not an unrepentant assimilationist,(39)
and some of his views anticipate the rhetoric and
policy of Collier's tour in the Indian office. In his
annual report for 1930 Rhoads argued that the federal
government should preserve what is best in Indian
"traditions, arts, crafts, and associations" and
"encourage their development and survival."(40) If
anything, Rhoads offered a less forceful and less
arbitrary administration of Indian policy than his
successor.

Most of the resistance to the more progressive
proposals of the Indian office was undoubtedly
Secretary Wilbur. Although he had formulated his own
program and had endorsed the initial legislative
schemes of Commissioner Rhoads, he was unable to get
the measures through Congress. And Wilbur's support
for the allotment policy made it unlikely that he
would pursue vigorously Rhoads' recommendation that
Congress reverse the direction of the Dawes General
Allotment Act. Indeed Wilbur reiterated his

long-standing opinion in his annual report for 1930:
"The Government must be divorced more and more from
supervision over the Indian's person, through the
gradual breakup of the old reservation system.(41)

Moreover, Wilbur and Hoover offered little
support to Rhoads and Scattergood when they testified
in front of congressional committees. Then, there is
the note of pessimism in Wilbur's November 17, 1930,
letter to the President that Congress likely would
oppose any Administration-sponsored Indian legislative
program.(42)   And Charles Rhoads and Henry Scattergood
were not forceful personalities. John Collier
recalled in later years that the administration had a
promising beginning, but "No amount of persuasion
could...bring the Secretary and the Commissionner to
press in Congress for enactment of the necessary
legislation. They furnished, in other words, what
could have become an 'ad interim' change of spirit
within the Indian Service."(43)

The Hoover Administration also was developing a
sense of paranoia. Even when its Indian policies were
praised, the administration kept a wary eye on its
chief critic, the American Indian Defense Association.
When Hoover signed a bill authorizing payment of over
$1,000,000 to the Ute Indians for land taken from them
through an executive order of President Theodore
Roosevelt, he did so "with certain reluctance,"
because the "bill provides that fees and expenses
shall be taken from the Indians and allowed to the
lobby promoting the bill." Although this was common
practice in most Indian claims appropriation bills, in
this case the "lobby" was the American Indian Defense
Association. Hoover fumed that the "whole background
of lobbies in Washington, pushing and profiting, on
behalf of helpless people is most repugnant." He
contended that the "Government ought to be able to do
justice by it's wards without feeding these
professional lobbies." Hoover vetoed other claims
appropriations, because the government should not
"undertake the revision of the efforts of our citizens
in building this nation."(44)   And with the worsening
of the depression, such legislaion usually fell victim
to the administration's economy drive.

Herbert Hoover clearly had a fetish for
administrative reform, and this is illustrated in his
handling of the Indian bureau.(45)   He selected
Charles Rhoads as commissioner because he "has some
understanding of the problems and at the same time has

the large business experience necessary to thoroughly
reorganize this Bureau." In his first two years as
commissioner, Rhoads completed a thoroughgoing
reorganization of the Office of Indian Affairs. He
divided the bureau into five field divisions --Health,
Education, Agricultural Extension and Industry,
Forestry, and Irrigation--with a director at the head
of each division. The new system replaced a
fifty-year-old organizational structure and was
designed to simplify management and to make he Indian
office more responsive to "the needs of the
field."(46)

The Indian bureau which historically has resisted
change, administrative or otherwise, opposed Charles
Rhoads' reorganization scheme,(47) and employees in
the field led the opposition to the plan. Shortly
after the commission implemented his revamped
administrative formula, complaints filtered into the
Indian office regarding the new requirements for
appointment to the Indian service. The
tradition-bound Board of Indian Commissioners
complained "that a considerable number of the older
employees are at a disadvantage when promotions are
under consideration." The board also contended that
graduates of Indian schools were being discriminated
against because they lacked academic requirements:(48)

 The board submits that strict adherence to
 these academic standards will often work an
 injustice toward faithful and competent
 Indian employees and will discourage young
 and promising Indians from preparing
 themselves for government service.

 The board belives that in closing the door
 of opportunity to graduates of Indian
 schools, the Indian Office is departing from
 its declared policy of developing Indian
 leadership... The board further suggests
 the inconsistency of opening placement
 offices to secure employment for Indians
 while, at the same time, denying the
 opportunity of employment in the Indian
 service itself.

The missionary-oriented board feared that bureau
personnel with missionary backgrounds might be
replaced in the administrative reshuffling. Its
complaints went unanswered and reports of discharges,
promotions, transfers, and demotions continued to

cause unrest among field personnel.(49)

Hugh Scott, a respected member of the Board of Indian Commissioners who conducted a survey of conditions in the field service during the summer of 1931, delivered the most damaging critique. He praised the increases in medical and educational facilities and the improvements in dietary provisions for Indian children, but he was less enthusiastic about "the general administration of the Service." The "Washington Office," he noted, "has always...lacked consideration for its field force but I have never seen such a lack since the establishment of the civil service in the Bureau of Indian Affairs." Although the reorganized Indian bureau was "hostile to the field employees," Scott directed his most devastating criticism at the administration's claim that it had decentralized lines of authority. Because the organization plan had delegated authority to division heads, he charged, "this decentralization has never gone further than the Washington Office," and it has not reached the superintendents who were in closest contact with Indian people. Scott's report was a damning indictment of one of the administration's chief claims to achievement in the field of Indian affairs.(50)

As the depression deepened, reports of starvation and demoralized conditions in Indian country became more frequent. These problems and a hint of corruption made irreversible any reapprochement between the Hoover administration and its Indian policy critics. The latter concerned the mounting attacks of the Senate Indian Investigating Committee and the American Indian Defense Association against Herbert Hagerman, an Albert J. Fall appointee as the Indian bureau's Special Commissioner to the Navajos. Hagerman's association with land speculators, railroad interests, cattle companies, and his questionable decisions as an Indian bureau official, made him an ideal target for Senate progressives and Indian reformers.(51) John Collier, who led the investigation, underscored Hagerman's significance as the "make-or-break component of Rhoads' administration." The affair, Collier argued, remained in the spotlight because Wilbur and Rhoads defended Hagerman "with a zeal approaching fanaticism."(52)

With Collier doing most of the leg work, the Senate Indian Investigating Committee compiled documents and evidence which, at the very least,

106.

embarrassed the administration and made Hagerman's
continuation as Special Commissioner a real liability.
When the Senate committee and Collier's associates
released information about Hagerman's activities,
Indian Truth lashed out against the "vicious and
unwarranted attack on Herbert J. Hagerman." The
Indian Rights Association Journal accused Senator Lynn
J. Frazier, chairman of the Senate committee, of using
Hagerman in a political attack on the Hoover
administration. When the Senate Indian Investigating
Committee issued its report in February 1932, it
condemned Hagerman's conduct (primarily for failing to
gain fair market value for Pueblo lands when he served
on the Pueblo Lands Board) and recommended his removal
from office. The House and Senate subsequently
removed Hagerman from the government's payroll.(53)

     Through all this furor, Secretary of the Interior
Wilbur staunchly defended Hagerman, insisting that the
Senate Committee's activities in the Spring of 1932
were election year politicking. In his memoirs,
however, he recalled that "the attacks on
Commissioners Rhoads and Scattergood were so unfair,
and at the time so outrageous, that I reached the
limit of my patience." Indeed, Wilbur was so incensed
at John Collier's testimony to the Senate committee
that he wrote Stella Atwood, a member of the American
Indian Defense Association, urging the organization
"to get some other leader than Mr. Collier if they
want to be of service to the American Indians."
Collier, according to Wilbur, had become "a definite
handicap to the welfare of the Indians," because he
was neither fair nor factual, caused dissension,
obstructed legislation, and through personal attacks
pursued "his projected victim with the spirit of the
Inquisition."(54)

     John Collier reflected at the time that the
Hoover-Wilbur years were tragic because the
administration "did imagine the alternatives; did
challenge the organic essentials of the inherited
system; did make detailed and public announcements of
an intention to take the lead in changing them." And,
he argued, Hoover enjoyed a Senate favorably disposed
toward Indian reform and a Republican controlled House
for two years. But the Administration failed to
provide leadership. Collier claimed, "beyond the
initial stage of verbal undertakings." Moreover, the
Indian office attempted to secure the needed
legislation without the support of "the Executive or
against his passive or active opposition;" the

administration's policy, therefore, lapsed into "those
identical features of the Indian system which the
Executive had condemned in 1929." With the Congress
juxtaposed against an inert and "Executive
reactionary," Collier saw little likelihood for
change.(55)

The heightened tone of the charges and
countercharges in 1932 indicates the degree to which
relations between Hoover's Indian administrators and
their critics had deteriorated. The political
maneuvering of an election year obviously explains
part of the furor. But not all. The Hoover
administration simply proved itself inept in its
handling of Indian policy issues and the worsening
depression crisis exacerbated these difficulties. The
Herbert- Hagerman affair, for instance, should be
placed in the context of already strained relations
between the administration and its critics. Hagerman
could have been dismissed, perhaps with some partisan
grumbling, instead the administration tenaciously
defended him, and as a consequence, Hagerman became
another of the administation's increasing number of
liabilities.

Strong and active support from the executive
branch is a prerequisite for conventional reform
programs directed at minority groups. This is
especially true for subject people like American
Indians who are relatively powerless and lack the
influence to push ameliorative legislation through
Congress. In the instances discussed here, President
Hoover never intervened to push the Indian legislative
program through Congress. And, after a series of
legislative setbacks in 1930, (and amidst the mounting
criticsm of the American Indian Defense Association),
Secretary Wilbur became increasingly pessimistic about
the prospects of getting any legislation through
Congress. These congressional problems probably date
from the Spring of 1929 when the President scolded
Louis Crampton, the chairman of the House
Appropriations Committe, for his criticism of Wilbur's
Indian policy. After Crampton's defeat in 1930,
economic conditions were worsening and a new and more
formidable opposition emerged--the Senate
progressives. Senators Lynn Frazier, Burton K.
Wheeler, and Elmer Thomas supported public power
development, the McNary-Haugen farm bills, and public
relief programs. And they effectively used their
positions on the Senate Indian Affairs Committee to
further embarrass Hoover.(56)

David Burner and other writers who praise
Hoover's Indian policy, cite increases in
appropriations for Indian programs as one of the
administrations's accomplishments in the field of
Indian affairs. Burner praises the administration for
increasing Indian service appropriations from $16
million to $25 million between 1929 and 1932. His
commendation is misleading. Of the $25,612,046
appropriated in 1932, $1,243,000 was designated for
Alaskan natives (in March, 1931, responsibility for
the health and education of Alaskan natives was
transferred to the Bureau of Indian Affairs). In
addition, the Indian service had hired nearly 1,000
new personnel, and salary raises for staff amounted to
more than $1 million. There were obvious increases in
appropriations, but Hoover's Indian administrators and
some biographers have exaggerated the amount.
Moreover, a good case can be made that the Senate
progressives were responsible for the increment.(57)
And, from all indications, much of the money simply
went to inflate the federal bureaucracy.

If we define reform in terms of changing the
system to give those at the bottom a better break, the
Hoover adminstration's Indian policy did not work
well. Wilbur, Rhoads, and Scattergood were more
concerned with visible change at the top --
organizational restructuring, shifting school policy,
and administrative efficiency -- with the idea that
this would ameliorate conditions at the grass roots
level. These alterations represented little more than
administrative manipulation. The respected Hugh Scott
of the Board of Indian Commissioners said the
organization caused "apprehension," a "demoralization
of morale," and a "feeling of distrust of the Bureau."
Some of his remarks might represent concern for old
sinecurists in the field; however, the mere volume of
such complaints would indicate otherwise. At the
onset of Franklin D. Roosevelt's administration, the
respected anthropologist Franz Boas, observed that
Rhoads and Scattergood made the error of assuming that
mere administrative change would better the lot of
Indian people.(58)

Added to the Wilbur-Rhoads propensity for
administrative restructuring, were very real
limitations in their ideology and vision. The
missionary-assimilationist view of the Indian Rights
Association dominated their thinking, and neither man
felt comfortable in the presence of John Collier and

others who advocated more radical approaches to social problems. These ideological strictures limited their field of action to measures directed in one way or another to speedy assimilation. As criticism of their policies mounted, they became increasingly combative toward social scientists like Collier who were anxious to carry the goverment's programs much further. (59) When the administration's legislative program for Indian afffairs became lodged in a recalcitrant Congress, neither Wilbur nor Rhoads was able to rescue it. And the man at the top was preoccupied with the awesome problems of the economic crisis.

FOOTNOTES

1. J. E. Chamberlin, The Harrowing of Eden: White
    Attitudes Toward Native Americans (New York
    Seabury Press. 1975), 93. For a provocative
    insight into the relationship between colonial
    governments and indigenous people see Franz
    Fanon, The Wretched of the Earth (New York: Grove
    Press, 1968. First published, 1961).

2. For variations on the reform theme see Kenneth
    Phillip, "Herbert Hoover's New Era: A False Dawn
    for the American Indian, 1929-1932," Rocky
    Mountain Social Science Journal 9 (April 1972),
    53-60; Michael T. Smith, "The Wheeler-Howard Act
    of 1934: The Indian New Deal," Journal of the
    West 10 (1971), 521-524; Charles J. Weeks, "The
    Eastern Cherokee and the New Deal," North
    Carolina Historical Review 53 (July 1976),
    316-317; B. T. Quinten, "Oklahoma Tribes, the
    Great Depression and the Indian Bureau,"
    Mid-America 49 (January 1967), 29-43; Randolph C.
    Downes, "A Crusade for Indian Reform, 1922-1934,"
    Mississippi Valley Historical Review 32 (December
    1945), 331-345. Articles contemporary to the
    period include Ray Lyman Wilbur, "The Dawn of a
    New Era for the American Indian," The Sunday
    Star, May 24, 1931 (copy in "Indian Affairs," Ray
    Lyman Wilbur Papers, Herbert Hoover Presidential
    Library); John Collier, "The Indian Bureau's
    Record," The Nation 135 (October 5, 1932),
    303-305; "Editorial," The Nation 136 (April 26,
    1933), 459; Oliver La Farge, "The American
    Indian's Revenge," Current History 40 (May 1934),
    163-168. The only book-length treatment of
    Indian reform for the period is Kenneth R.
    Phillip, John Collier's Crusade for Indian
    Reform, 1920-1954 (Tucson: University of Arizona
    Press, 1977). Also see Hazel Hertzberg, The
    Search for an American Indian Identity: Modern
    Pan-Indian Movements (Syracuse: Syracuse
    University Press, 1971); John Collier. From Every
    Zenith: A Memoir and Some Essays on Life and
    Thought (Denver: Sage Books, 1963); Arthur M.
    Schlesinger, Jr., The Coming of the New Deal, Vol
    2 of The Age of Roosevelt (Boston: Houghton,
    Mifflin Company, 1958).

3. D'Arcy McNickle, Native American Tribalism:
    Indian Survivals and Renewels (New York: Oxford

University Press, 1973), 85-88; Harold E. Fay and D'Arcy McNickle, Indians and Other Americans: Two Ways of Life Meet (New York: Harper and Row, 1959), 91-103.

4. David Burner, Herbert Hoover: A Public Life (New York: Alfred A. Knopf, 1979). See especially the chapter, "The Reform Presidency," 212-244.

5. An odd assortment of special interest groups had combined to force congressional passage of the measure: railroad and cattle spokesmen who wanted to break up the reservation system in the American West, reclamationists who wanted access to reservation water, and a strong assimilationist-minded group of Christian reformers centered in the Indian Rights Association. The background to the Dawes Act is treated in Francis Paul Prucha. American Indian Policy in Crisis: Christian Reformers and the Indian, 1865-1900 (Norman: University of Oklahoma Press, 1976), 227-257; Robert W. Mardock, The Reformers and the American Indian (Columbia: University of Missouri Press, 1971). 192-228; Henry Fritz, The Movement for Indian Assimilation, 1860-1900 (Philadelphia: University of Pennsylvania Press, 1963), 198-222, Loring Benson Priest, Uncle Sam's Stepchildren: The Reformation of United States Indian Policy, 1865-1887 (New Brunswick: Rutgers University Press, 1942), 167-252.

6. For the consequences of the Dawes Act see Prucha, American Indian Policy in Crisis, 257-264; Wilcomb E. Washburn, The Assault on Indian Tribalism: The General Allotment Law (Dawes Act) of 1887 (Philadelphia; J.B. Lippincott Co., 1975), 28-31; D.S. Otis, The Dawes Act and the Allotment of Indian Lands, edited by Francis Paul Prucha (Norman: University of Oklahoma Press, 1973), 124-155.

7. The turmoil of the 1920s is discussed in Downes, "Crusade for Indian Reform," 334-340; Collier, From Every Zenith, 124-155.

8. Downes, "Crusade for Indian Reform," 343-344.

9. Congressional Record, 71 Cong., 2 Sess., 2498. Undoubtedly, the association of Burke and Meritt with Fall and their seeming reluctance to

consider even the mildest of policy changes
sharpened the differences between them and the
Indian reformers.

10. According to the report the policy was mistaken,
because it had failed to "Individualize" Indian
people and to make them into self-supporting
members of the communities in which they lived.
Actually the report proposed a very limited
reform program. Lewis Meriam, et al., The
Problem of Indian Administration: A Summary of
Findings and Recommendations (Washington: U.S.
Government Printing Office, 1928) 460-488.

11. Stella M. Atwood to Herbert Hoover, Sept. 18,
1928, "Pres-Presidential, 1928-1929, General
Correspondence, American Indian Defense
Association," Campaign and Transition Papers,
Hoover Papers, Hoover Library (hereafter CTHP).
Haven Emerson, a Columbia University professor
and president of the American Indian Defense
Association made the original charge according to
Atwood's letter.

12. Secretary of the Interior Hubert Work, the person
chiefly responsible for the handling of Indian
affairs, resigned his cabinet post to become
Hoover's campaign manager. See Burner, Herbert
Hoover, 199.

13. Ibid., 224-227. Burner's brief account of
Hoover's concern and interest in Indian affairs
is exaggerated and poorly documented.

14. P. Narcha to Hoover, July 26, 1928, and Akerson
to Narcha, Aug. 13, 1928. "Pre-Presidential,
1928-1929, General Correspondense, Na-Nas," CTHP.

15. "Our Citizens: Their Crisis," Letter Addressed
to the Presidential Candidates by the American
Indian Defense Association, Oct. 6, 1928; Jay B.
Nash to Hoover, Oct. 15, 1928; Harry E. Thomas to
Alvin Hart, Oct. 18, 1928 and Hoover to American
Indian Defense Association, Oct. 20, 1928,
"Pre-Presidential, 1928-1929, General
Correspondence, American Indian Defense
Association," CTHP.

16. The administration's unwillingness to press
forcefully for measures before Congress
exasperated contemporary critics like John

Collier. See Collier, "The Indian Bureau's Record, "303-305; Collier, From Every Zenith, 152.

17. The Indian Rights Association, founded lr, 1882, was the oldest of the Indian reform organizations. See Prucha, American Indian Policy in Crisis, 138-143. Indian Truth first was published in February 1924. See Downes, "Crusade for Indian Reform," 337.

18. John Collier, "No Trespassing," Sunset 50 (May 1933), 60 Collier, From Every Zenith, 134-135; Philip, John Collier's Crusade for Indian Reform, 26-54; Philip, "Herbert Hoover's New Era," 55.

19. Downes, "Crusade for Indian Reform," 344; Philip, "Herbert Hoover's New Era," 53; Indian Truth 6 (April 1929), 1.

20. Burner, Herbert Hoover, 224; Downes, "Crusade for Indian Reform," 345; Philip, "Herbert Hoover's New Era," 53. In his memoirs Wilbur says Hoover knew Rhoads and Scattergood through their work with the American Red Cross and the Y.M.C.A. In France at the end of the First World War. See Edgar Eugene Robinson and Paul Carroll Edwards, eds., The Memoirs of Ray Lyman Wilbur (Stanford: Stanford University Press, 1960), 482n. Elsewhere Wilbur claims Rhoads recommended Scattergood for the position of Assistant Commissioner. See Wilbur to Hoover, Mar. 16, 1929, "Interior-Indian Office," Presidential Papers, Hoover Papers (hereafter PPHP).

21. The Board of Indian Commissioners dates from the administration of Ulysses S. Grant and the inauguration of what was termed "Grant's Peace Policy." See Prucha, American Indian Policy in Crisis, 33-46; Henry Fritz, "The Making of Grant's Peace Policy," Chronicles of Oklahoma 37 (Winter 1959-1960), 411-432. A critical discussion of termination policy is in Vine Deloria, Jr., Custer Died For Your Sins: An Indian Manifesto (New York: Macmillan, 1969), 54-77 Wilbur to Hubert Work, Dec. 15, 1924, "Box 15," Wilbur Papers, Hoover Library.

22. Wilbur to Hoover, Mar. 23, 1929, and Hoover to Wilbur, Mar. 25, 1929, "Cabinet--Interior--Indian Office," PPHP.

23. Hoover's ignorance of his Quaker heritage is surprising, especially since Quakers were chiefly responsible for the creation of the original Board of Indian Commissioners in 1869. See Prucha, American Indian Policy in Crisis, 47-49.

24. Philip, "Herbert Hoover's New Era," 54; Crampton to Hoover, April 17, 1929, and Hoover to Crampton, April 18, 1929, "Interior--Indian Office," PPHP.

25. Ruby A. Black, "A New Deal for the Red Man," The Nation 130(April 2, 1930), 388-390.

26. Indian Truth 7 (Feb. 1930), 4; U.S. Department of Interior, Annual Report of the Board of Indian Commissioners (1930), 1-3.

27. Emerson to Wilbur, May 6, 1930, "Indian Affairs," Wilbur Papers.

28. Wilbur to Emerson, May 7, 1930, Ibid. Copies of the letter were mailed to twelve members of the Indian Defense Association's Board of Directors who had signed the May 6 letter to Wilbur.

29. Robinson and Edwards, eds., Memoirs of Ray Lyman Wilbur, 485.

30. The Federal Power Commission was charged with licensing federal power sites. This is only a brief outline of the Flathead controversy as it involved the Interior Secretary. (A subsequent paper will explore in detail the many ramifications of the issue.

31. A summary discussion of the Flathead case is in Philip, John Collier's Crusade for Indian Reform, 85-87, 167-169. Also see Burner, Herbert Hoover, 227. It should be noted that the pro-administration monthly publication of the Indian Rights Association, Indian Truth, makes no mention of the Flathead controversy. See Indian Truth 7 (May and June 1930).

32. Philip, John Collier's Crusade for Indian Reform, 167-169.

33. Rhoads to Hoover, Aug. 6, 1930, "Indian Office," Wilbur Papers.

34. Joseph W. Latimer, Let My People Go, No. 5 (Aug. 1930), copy in "Presidential Subject File--Indians, 1929-1930," PPHP. Latimer had served as secretary, confidant, and propagandist for Carlos Montezuma, a leading pan-Indian writer and vitrolic critic of the Bureau of Indian Affairs until his death in 1923. After Montezuma's passing, Latimer continued to spread his message through his newsletter. The American Indian: Captive or Citizen. See Laurence M. Hauptman, "Alice Jemison: Senaca Activist, 1901-1964," The Indian Historian 12 (Summer 1979), 19.

35. Wilbur to Hoover, Nov. 17, 1930. "Interior -- Indian Office," PPHP.

36. Wilbur to Hoover, Jan. 13, 1931, and Hoover to Wilbur, Jan. 15, 1931, "Interior--Indian Office," PPHP.

37. The pro-New Deal historiography exaggerates the influence and successes of John Collier as Commissioner of Indian Affairs under Franklin D. Roosevelt. Collier served as commission from 1933-1945. See William E. Leuchtenburg, Franklin D. Roosevelt and the New Deal, 1932-1940 (New York, Harper and Row, 1963), 86, 329, Hauptman, "Alice Jamison: Seneca Political Activist," 15.

38. Philip, "Herbert Hoover's New Era," 54; Burner, Herbert Hoover, 227.

39. U.S. Department of Interior, Annual Report (1929), 14. Wilbur's entry in his first report shows the breadth of his assimilationist views: "The white man, wanting wholesome food, a comfortable place to live in, opportunities for education and advancement, has a single way of getting them. He works for them. The Indian has often failed to satisfy these same needs because he has not learned the way to competence and happiness through work."

40. Ibid., Annual Report of the Commissioner of Indian Affairs (1930), 1-2.

41. Philip, "Herbert Hoover's New Era," 54; Black, "A New Deal for the Red Man," 389; U.S. Department of Interior, Annual Report (1930),25.

42. Wilbur to Hoover, Nov. 17, 1930, "Interior--Indian Office," PPHP.

43. This assumption is based on remarks made by both critics and supporters of the two men. See Collier, From Every Zenith, 152.

44. Hoover to Wilbur, Feb. 13, 1931, and Wilbur to Hoover, Feb. 13, 1931, "Interior--Indian Office," PPHP, Hoover to the Senate, Feb. 18, 1931, "Subject File, Indians," PPHP.

45. The emphasis on administrative efficiency and administrative reorganiztion emerged early in Hoover's career. See Burner, Herbert Hoover, 159-189; Ellis Hawley, "Herbert Hoover, the Commerce Secretariat, and the Vision of an 'Associative State,' 1921-1928," Journal of American History 61 (1974), 116-140.

46. Hoover to Senator David A. Reed, n.d., "Interior--Indian Office," PPHP; Memorandum for the Press, Mar. 30, 1931. "Interior--Indian Office," PPHP.

47. See the highly amusing chapter on Bureau of Indian Affairs lethargy in Deloria, Custer Died For Your Sins, 125-145.

48. Annual Report of the Board of Indian Commissioners (1931), 14.

49. Ibid., 17. Indian Bureau teachers employed at the elementary level now were required to have three years of education beyond high school. See Annual Report of the Commissioner of Indian Affairs (1931),9.

50. Hugh L. Scott to Samuel A. Eliot, Chairman of the Board of Indian Commissioners, Oct. 1, 1931, "Interior--Indian Office," PPHP.

51. Philip. "Herbert Hoover's New Era," 56-57. Philip correctly sees the Hagerman affair as the final breaking point between Hoover and his critics on Indian policy.

52. Collier, From Every Zenith, 153-154.

53. Philip, "Herbert Hoover's New Era," 57; Indian

Truth 8 (Feb. 1931), 1; Subcommittee of the
Senate Committee on Indian Affairs, Report on the
Charges of Misconduct of Mr. Herbert J. Hagerman,
Special Commissioner to Negotiate with Indians
and a Former Member of the Pueblo Lands Board,
Feb. 16, 1932, copy in "Interior--Indian Office,"
PPHP.

54.   Robinson and Edwards, eds., Memoirs of Ray Lyman
       Wilbur, 490-491; Wilbur to Stella M. Atwood, Mar.
       19, 1932. "Indian Affairs, 1932," Wilbur Papers.

55.   John Collier, The Indian Affairs Tragedy Since
       1929 and a Suggestion of Political Realism (April
       28, 1932), copy in "Indian Affairs, 1932," Wilbur
       Papers.

56.   Hoover to Crampton, April 18, 1929,
       "Interior--Indian Office," PPHP, Phil, "Herbert
       Hoover's New Era," 57.

57.   Burner, Herbert Hoover, 226; U.S. Department of
       Interior, Annual Report (1931), 85; Annual Report
       of the Commissioner of Indian Affairs (1931), 26;
       Ibid. (1932), 21; Charles Rhoads to Senator
       William H. King, Jan. 18, 1933, "Interior--Indian
       Office," PPHP.

58.   Hugh Scott to Samuel A. Eliot, Oct. 1, 1931,
       "Interior--Indian Office," PPHP, For the many
       letters of complaint to the Indian office see
       "Interior--Indian Office," PPHP, Boas to Louis M.
       Howe, Secretary to President Roosevelt, Mar. 18,
       1933, Official File, 6c (Department of Interior,
       Office of Indian Affairs), Franklin D. Roosevelt
       Library, Boas, incidentially, did not support
       John Collier for Commissioner of Indian Affairs.
       His choice was Lewis Meriam.

59.   This point is illustrated in a letter from George
       W. Hinman to Wilbur, April 23, 1933, "Indian
       Affairs, 1933," Wilbur Papers. Hinman was
       Secretary to the Service Committee on Indians of
       the Home Missions Council:

       "What we shall be able to do in contacts
              with the Indian Bureau hereafter will
              depend very much on the character and
              policy of the new Commissioner. There
              could have been no finer cooperation

than we have had with Commissioners
Rhoads and Scattergood. If John
Collier should be the appointee of the
Roosevelt administration, I would be
doubtful about the future."

HERBERT HOOVER AND BLACK AMERICANS

by Larry Grothaus

The recent literature on Herbert Hoover reveals him as a forgotten progressive who continued to pursue reform in the 1920s and 1930s. (1) Hoover's relationship to black Americans has received less attention and has been viewed as part of an era of Republican neglect and overt animosity. Hoover, critics charge, support the so-called lily-white movement, an effort to reduce black power in the southern GOP, and stress his ignorance and lack of sympathy with the problems and needs of blacks.(2)

While the criticisms are appropriate, they do not acknowledge recent scholarship on Hoover. The Iowa-born Quaker was a reformer who occoasionally gave race relations and the place of blacks in American life some thought, and he formulated plans, radical for the times, to alleviate their plight. Yet, Hoover's thinking on racial issues was limited by his personal views on race, his views on the methods of social progress, black powerlessness, the depression, a failure to recognize social and political change among blacks, and by his own and his staff's political ineptitude. The results were, therefore, more disappointing because the man who had achieved so much and who had been a great humanitarian chose those goals and policies which reduced the significance and recognition of blacks.

When Hoover appeared on the national political scene in 1920, he knew little about American blacks but had some general views on race. His education and experience as an engineer caused his thinking to be naturalistic, and, while he was no Social Darwinist, he accepted natural law and the concept of inherent racial characteristics. He readily accepted Anglo-Saxon superiority and decided that white workers were far superior to non-whites. His experiences in the Orient led him to conclude that the United States should exclude Oriental immigrants and avoid a mixture of races. On the other hand, Hoover believed that the evolutionary development of inferior groups could be enhanced through science and education. Furthermore, he had traveled the world and had had the opportunity to broaden his views. His most recent experiences in feeding Belgians and others, during and after World War I, suggested a humane man and a

successful organizer of extensive programs. These
successes gave evidence that Hoover's Quaker beliefs
and youthful exposures to Quaker missionary activity
would be benevolent factors in determining his racial
policies.(3)

To these experiences Hoover also brought certain
ideas to his government service which were often
determining factors in his thinking and in his
behavior. In 1922 in a short book, American
Individualism, he strongly emphasized that a just
social and political system depend on equality of
opportunity. Society, he wrote, must be kept "free
from the frozen strata of classes" and must recognize
"that social injustice is the destruction of justice
itself." Those on the bottom should rise through
education, moral leadership and cooperative economic
efforts. Government should secure equality before the
law, voting rights and equality in holding public
office. The best method for achieving these goals, he
felt, was through voluntary cooperation of all the
principals in society and through implementation of
programs on the local level. World War I had taught
Hoover that decentralization was the best and most
effective approach to solving problems. It was not
the power of centralized government passing new
legislation but community organization that truly
solved problems. Hoover found problems in the nation,
but he was more impressed with the great strides that
had been made.(4)

Tensions obviously existed within Hoover's
concepts. Could his methods really achieve the goals?
Could his distaste for legislative solutions be
squared with the need for protecting basic political
rights, such as the right to vote? Could his elitism
lead to a democratic society? Did decentralization
and local committees always produce the best
solutions? Blacks certainly doubted the value of
states rights and decentralization. Hoover's ideas
were faulty and ineffective, and his understanding of
blacks was increasingly outmoded. Consequently, the
extent to which he was willing to intervene on their
behalf was limited. Occasionally his concepts and
sympathies led to radical proposals, but he was unable
or unwilling to act upon them. Ultimately the
powerlessness and invisibility of blacks meant the
they were of little importance to him.

The racial politics of Presidents Warren Harding
and Calvin Coolidge were educational experiences for

Hoover as their Secrestary of Commerce.(5)   President
Harding briefly repoliticized the race issue in the
1920 campaign when he urged the South to grant blacks
economic opportunities and allow qualified blacks to
vote.   As President, he appointed blacks to manage and
staff the veterans hospital at Tuskegee, Alabama, over
the opposition of local whites and the Ku Klux Klan.
Leonidas C. Dyer, a Republican, in the House of
Representatives with a large black constituency in St.
Louis, introduced an anti-lynching bill that passed
the House in 1922 but failed in the Senate after a
brief filibuster.(6).

Northern black militants, W. E. B. Du Bois, James
Weldon Johnson and Walter White of the National
Association for the Advancement of Colored People,
rejoiced in Harding's early initiatives but soon
concluded that he and his party were insincere.   The
GOP's failure to pass the Dyer bill disappointed them,
and they later learned that the Party had only played
politics with the bill.(7)   Blacks also took issue
with the President's rejection of social equality and
racial intermixture in a Birmingham speech, and they
interpreted some of his remarks as an invitation to
leave the Republican Party.   Such an invitation seemed
consistent with the renewed lily-white movement in the
southern wing of the GOP.   The continuation of
segregation in government buildings in Washington and
at the dedication of the Lincoln Memorial in 1922
further disappointed blacks.   As promises remained
unfulfilled and grievances not redressed, northern
blacks grew restive within the Republican Party. (8)

But what to do?   One NAACP answer was to reward
friends and punish enemies, and in 1922 the
organization claimed several victories over
Republicans who had voted against the Dyer bill.
Since an anti-lynching bill had never progressed so
far previously, many felt success would soon come and
urged continued pressure for the bill in four states
where blacks held the balance of power and in four
others where the black vote was significant.   However,
the NAACP probably overstated its case, and the claim
went unregcognized.   Southern black leaders such as
Robert R. Morton of Tuskegee Institute and southern
black politicians, exemplified by Perry Howard, the
Republican National Committeeman from Mississippi,
were in no position to confront the GOP.   Morton's
political style, as with his mentor, Booker T.
Washington, was to practice politics quietly.
Considering the realities of black life and

circumstances in the South, black activism seemed impossible. The lynching record revealed fifty-three victims in 1922, and the effort to staff the hospital at Tuskegee with blacks brought the Ku Klux Klan and the threat of violence to the campus. Black politicians, threatened by lily-white tendencies in the southern GOP and dependent on national Party developments for their position in the Party, were in no position to rebel. Du bois' suggestion of a third party or a switch to the Democrats were not viable alternatives.(9)

Blacks had little power and few friends to influence Republicans in the 1920s. The census showed that most still lived in the South where they were disfranchised. The extent of the wartime migration and its continuation in the 1920s and easy victory in 1924 made blacks unimportant. Nor did potential friends and allies appear. The labor movement had shown more animosity than friendship toward blacks, and various reform and minority organizations were united. Politicians reflected popular opinions in their low regard for blacks. All of this was very galling to a people who were coming of age in terms of their self-respect, identity and sense of worth. The Harlem Renaissance and the New Negro were significant developments but known only to a few whites. Marcus Garvey's ideas and programs of black nationalism furthered self-sonsciousness, but his failures and the psychological studies of black intelligence from World War I data seemed to be proof of inferiority with which the general population supported their prejudices.(10) Thus, Hoover learned that blacks were a powerless and unwanted group. Still, if he came face-to-face with a problem that plagued blacks, he might be expected to seek a solution by following his principles, his Quaker sympathies and the historic ties of his Party.

The Mississippi River flood of 1927 provided Hoover the opportunity to learn directly of the plight of southern blacks trapped in the peonage of the sharecropper system and to apply his ideas and methods to both tragedies. When the levees broke and the river inundated large areas of Arkansas, Mississippi and Louisiana, President Coolidge appointed a cabinet committee with Hoover as chairman to organize help for the stricken area and the victims. In typical Hoover fashion, he organized headquarters at Memphis, from which rescue, relief and rehabilitation programs were coordinated. Hoover strongly believed that the function of the national government should be to determine needs and organize programs for action that local governments or agencies would implement. In this crisis, the Secretary used the American Red Cross, a semi-private organization chartered by Congress and a recipient of national appropriations and supplies. The Red Cross fit well into his concept of an efficient organization that efficiently coordinated and locally executed the efforts, to combat the great flood.(11)

While the operation received much well-deserved praise, reports reached Hoover that blacks were being held prisoner in the segregated relief camps. They were freed only in the custody of planters, forced to work on levees, mistreated and required to pay for an unequal share of the relief. By tradition, blacks felt that a flood freed them from their debts and believed they could leave the area. This hope was dashed, however, when local Red Cross officials distributed relief through the planters, who in turn, sold it to their tenants. The sales violated Red Cross rules but provided planters the opportunity to keep tenants in debt slavery peonage. To obtain justice, Claude Barnett, head of the Associated Negro Press, suggested that the Red Cross appoint a black official who would sympathetically look after the needs of his people. This appointment must come from the national Red Cross, Barnett counseled, because a local appointment would have insufficient authority to be effective.(12) In short, Hoover learned that southern blacks had to look outside the local organization to the national unit because local elited opporessed them

While Hoover was very sensitive about his reputation, he was willing to act on some complaints. When alarmed blacks wrote Senator Arthur Capper of Kansas, he defended the Red Cross but ordered the agency to make an investigation. He also appointed a Colored Advisory Commission under the leadership of Dr. Robert Moton of Tuskegee Institute. Although the NAACP had resolved to investigate contions in the flooded area Hoover selected mostly southern blacks and none from the Association.(13) The Colored Advisory Commission toured the devastated region and recommended more recreational activities in camps, table utensils and cots, removal of armed white guardsmen at the camps, fairer distribution of clothing and the appointment of two black men in each state with adequate authority to visit camps and

124.

provide informaton ad answer questions on
rehabilitation programs. The Commission's suggestions
aimed at establishing an effective communications
system and a trustworthy advisory system with power to
operate beyond the conrtol of local elites. Hoover
responded favorably to most of these reasonable
requests. He hired more recreational leaders,
improved the worst of the living conditions, reported
that the National Guard was being demobilized and
recommended that state Red Cross Rehabilitation
Committees add black assistants. Hoover claimed he
followed each suggestion but did nothing to relieve
tensions caused by the presence of the Guard except to
await the end of the flood and the disbanding of the
camps. His suggestion that advisors be added to state
committees ran into difficulties. Still, he was
sympathetic and responsive to the Moton
Commission.(14)

    Hoover's sensitivity to criticism by Walter White
of the NAACP was in direct contrast to his responses
to the Moton group. When White charged the militia
with inflicting forced labor, physical abuse and
peonage, Hoover testily denied that the Red Cross
would permit such activities. He admitted the
possibility of errors in the immensity of the disaster
but claimed that the accomplishments of the Red Cross
outweighed the mistakes. Maintaining that his task
was to save lives and not to interfere in local and
state customs and economics, the Secretary did not
discuss the real issue of local Red Cross units which
discriminated in the implementation of relief. Hoover
offered to consult with White on any constructive
criticism" but was clearly annoyed when White
published them in the Nation. To counteract the bad
publicity, he arranged a public relations campaign
that placed his activities and those of the Red Cross
in a more favorable light.(15)

    As the rehabilitation phase replaced relief
operations, blacks pressed for representation on the
state rehabilitation committees. They knew that such
representation was necessary or their needs would be
forgotten by local committees who controlled the
applications for loans. Blacks who sought supplies,
needed their applications endorsed by a white person.
Furthermore, tenants had no idea of what was
rightfully theirs and under what conditions they could
participate in Red Cross programs. Hoover now pushed
for adding a black person to the Red Cross machinery,
but opposition quickly formed. Governor Dennis

Murphree objected to the presence of S. D. Redmond, an activist black politician, on the Mississippi committee. The head of Mississippi's rehabilitation program, L. O. Crosby, feared an interracial clash if blacks were fed by the Red Cross and thus freed from white domination. Crosby contended that whites could get the necessary data for relief purposes and defended Hoover's record with blacks.(16)

Hoover, however, insisted on black representation, and the Red Cross leaders fell into line. Whether Hoover's motives were directly affected by his belief in equality of opportunity, his sense of fair play or his concern for his personal reputation, and that of the Red Cross, is difficult to discern. Probably all three factors were involved. Certainly pressure from the NAACP and the northern press was a factor, and the correspondence shows Hoover's keen sensitivity to any criticism. In any event, local leaders and Hoover discovered that black representatives were very helpful both in disseminating understandable information to the masses and in inspiring confidence. Even Crosby saw the wisdom of appointing blacks who organized Red Cross chapters and obtained resolutions praising Hoover's leadership. Since Walter White had continued his complaints, Crosby wrote Hoover, "Such resolution would forever set at rest any question that might arise in the northern newspapers as to whether or not the negros in the flooded area has received the right treatment from the Red Cross, and whether or not your leadership had given them what they were justly entitled to receive." Hoover's reputation aside, black representation was very helpful in obtaining accurate data necessary to provide fair treatment. Representation was also valuable in making the administrative process more effective and efficient, goals that ranked high in Hoover's thinking. The Moton Commission performed an important function for Hoover, the Red Cross and blacks.(17)

Although the methodology of dealing with the problems of relief and rehabilitation was improved, problems remained. Both Hoover and national Red Cross leaders were reluctant to intervene with elites who controlled local voluntary associations. Concerning local elite control of socio-economic matters, one Red Cross leader reported, "It has been our position that we should not devote undue effort to discovering and rectifying things of this kind." Not surprisingly, then, the Moton Commissioners again found serious

126.

problems when they toured the area in November.
Blacks lived in very congested and unhealthy
conditions in homes hardly worthy of the name. All
were very poor. The national Red Cross was just and
fair, Moton reported, but planters nullified its good
intentions by the continued use of the whip and the
threat of death to keep tenants on the plantations.
Conditions of peonage were so bad that blacks were
afraid to talk to anyone and refused to confront the
system by complaints and testimony. Moton urged that
the responsibility for revealing these conditions
should not be placed on his people, as Hoover had
required, but that the government should send
confidential agents from Washington to expose the
corruption. Moton again suggested that black
representatives of the Red Cross be authorized to
inspect local Red Cross records to enable them to
gather sufficient data about conditions of their
people. Black representatives had become involved in
Louisiana, and conditions improved significantly.(18)

     Hoover promised Moton a vigorous investigation,
but the black community was divided in its assessment
of Hoover's latest efforts. After a personal
inspection trip, the Secretary reported that black
inspectors told him that, for the most part, they had
received cooperation. As to special investigators
from Washington, James Fieser of the Red Cross urged
Hoover to delay and cautioned against any precipitous
action. These leaders agreed to add more black
assistants with authority to obtain data but denied
intervention by federal inspectors. Moton and his
commission praised the appointments and soothed Hoover
with disclaimers that their December report had not
been meant as a criticism of him or of the Red Cross.
They publicly reported that many problems had been
overcome through the use of black advisors and praised
"Secretary Hoover as an outstanding leader who brought
them through the crisis that was trying to their
mental, moral and physical being." The NAACP,
however, feared that the Moton group had white-washed
the true conditions, and in the Association's journal,
The Crisis, charged that the Red Cross supported the
sharecropper system at the expense of poor blacks.(19)

     Notwithstanding, the improvements that had been
made, the charge rang true. Considering the
conditions of the late 1920s in the South, however, it
is doubtful that the system could not be changed by
individual complaints to authorities. In addition,
Congress, Coolidge and public opinion were not ready

for a second reconstruction. Furthermore, while confrontation of the sharecropper system by the government was not Hoover's way, it did not prevent him from considering another kind of action.

Hoover recognized the basic problem in his travels in the South, and he soon proposed a plan to solve tenancy and peonage. He suggested that the abandoned and foreclosed plantations of the South be subdivided into small farms of twenty acres which tenants might purchase. To finance the project he advocated a private land resettlement corporation which could issue loans to buy land, animals and to make improvements. Profits would extend the program to more families so that ultimately the southern tenant would be free and independent. The corporation, he advised, should include blacks on the Board of Directors. To provide these small farmers with organizational advantages, Hoover believed that all-black cooperative communities such as Mound Bayou, Mississippi, were the best hope for blacks in the South. He shared his ideas confidentially with several southern whites and members of the Colored Commission and expressed the hope that money from rehabilitation funds might be used for the project.(20) The financial plan for the idyllic small farm was typical for Hoover. No government spending or programs were contemplated. When Red Cross monies proved unavailable and the organization unwilling to participate, he turned to philanthropic groups. Although responses from these organizations were also negative, the innovative Secretary of Commerce promised to investigate further.(21)

Hoover, eager to obtain the presidential nomination, insisted on secrecy instead of a public relations promotion of the plan. He discontinued his leadership of the project for political reasons and suggested that the matter be taken up privately with those inclined to help. Moton recognized his desire to gain southern votes and urged him to attend a small, private gathering, but the lack of philanthropic support and Hoover's reluctance stymied the idea.(22) While he forsook the plan, he had projected a radical change in southern agriculture. To be sure, the plan was romantic, economically questionable and evolutionary, but Hoover had sincerely addressed himself to the problem. To have such a sympathetic and activistic man in the White House held great promise for blacks. Albon Holsey of the National Negro Business League took this view claiming, "Secretary Hoover constructed a perfect machine for handling the flood situation and it worked with precision except at the point of conflict between exact justice to the Negro and the perpetuation of the plantation system - and at that point Mr. Hoover discovered the South which was the greatest blessing of the flood."(23)

Regardless of his knowledge of the inadequacies of decentralization and local volunteerism in the South, Hoover did not seek new methods for dealing with the sharecropping system when he became President. The drought of 1930-31, like the flood of 1927, presented the problem of bringing relief to blacks in the affected areas of the South. Hoover once more turned to the Red Cross, and the result was a repeat of landowner exploitation of tenants. Planters permitted no relief until the fall crops were harvested because they feared that blacks would not work for fifty cents a day if relief were available. When relief became available, local leaders again required tenants to work for it in violation of Red Cross rules. Hoover, aware of the problem, urged that blacks receive their fair share, but they did not enjoy that kind of treatment. When Red Cross officials denied all charges of discrimination, Hoover accepted these reports, apparently assuming that the Red Cross avoided the abuses by dealing directly with the tenants.(24)

During the depression, Hoover remained sympathetic to the basic economic problems of black tenants and farmers and to the cooperative settlement idea at Mound Bayou. He did not appoint a black to the Federal Farm Board, but the President convinced the Rosenwald Fund to sponsor a study of the economic status of blacks. In his report Dr. T. J. Woofter advocated more black ownership of land, stronger cooperative communities, cooperative marketing facilities and appealed for fair treatment to blacks in agricultural programs. Wofter's basic recommendations, however, stressed only better vocational education and more agricultural extension agents as means to achieve these goals. The Woofter report, Du Bois charged, was inadequate because it did not strike at the root causes for black ignorance, lack of leadership and poor economic conditions. Meanwhile, the Administration aided black landowners and helped the Mound Bayou community secure loans, but the aid was inadequate. While such sympathy was commendable, the Administration had no program that helped black tenants and farmers.(25)

Hoover's connection to blacks and their problems
in the Mississippi River Valley came full circle in
1932-33. The NAACP charged that black laborers were
abused and held in peonage in filthy camps as they
worked on flood control projects on the river.
Initial inquiries indicated that these workers earned
only ten cents per hour, were often not paid and were
overcharged in the contractor's commissary. The War
Department denied the substance of the NAACP's
charges, but Hoover ordered an investigation by
another Motown Commission. The Commission, however,
was slow to organize and lacked funds to act. A later
report by the Army Engineers denied the extreme
conditions, and it took Senator Robert Wagner's Senate
investigation to bring improvement in conditions.(26)

If decentralization and voluntary associations
were unsuccessful ways of dealing with relief and
rehabilitation problems of blacks, the decentralized
nature of the American political party structure could
be beneficial to blacks. The strength of the party
system was on the local and state level, and, since
blacks controlled the Republican Party in many
southern states, Presidential hopefuls had to consider
their interests. However, southern white Republicans
had renewed their plan in developing a lily-white
party and had been successful in several states in the
1920s. President Harding had shown some support to
this development while Coolidge appointed the Virginia
lily-white leader, C. Bascom Slemp, as his secretary.
Lily-whites varied in their goals. Some sought to
exclude blacks altogether while others demanded white
leadership and predominace in party conventions and
offices. In either event they challenged black
leadership and power in the GOP, threatened black
politicians in the South and, symbolically, blacks
everywhere.(27)

In his campaign for the nomination, Hoover proved
to be politcally adept and interested in black
involvement in politics. Whlie Secretary of Commerce,
he made several political gestures to win black
support and eagerly sought black delegates for the
1928 convention in Kansas City. His first gesturew as
to appoint James Jackson as promoter of black business
in the Commerce Department. Hoover had rejected this
appointment earlier but now found it politically
advantageous. He eliminated segregation in the Census
Bureau when a black delegate to the national

convention and a local officer of the NAACP, called
his attention to the situation. Blacks cheered these
moves as acts of kindness, true Americanism and good
politics. Hoover called upon southern blacks such as
Moton and Holsey from Tuskegee to convince black
delegates to support his candidacy.(28)

Like most Republican candidates, Hoover's
strategy was to capture convention delegates, not to
get involved in local factional disputes. The 167
southern delegates were important because they
represented nearly one-third of those needed to win
the nomination. To assure himself of delegates,
Hoover hoped to not only gain the support of the
regular political organizations, be they
black-and-tan, or lily-white, but he also tried to
obtain delegates in the competing factions, as well.
In Mississippi, for example, he received the somewhat
reluctant support of National Committeeman Perry
Howard through the efforts of Eugene Booze, Mayor of
Mound Bayou, and other non-federal government office
holders.(29) In addiion, Hoover's friend, L. O.
Crosby, kept a wary eye on the lily-white faction in
the state, where a competing delegation was organized
to challenge Perry Howard and to support Frank
Lowden's presidential ambitions. Although it was
widely known and reported to Hoover that Howard had
been selling Post Office positions, the Hoover forces
did not wish to antagonize the national committeeman
as long as his delegation might be seated at the
convention. Meanwhile, Crosby urged Hoover's
candidacy to the lily-white faction. When Howard was
indicted for selling patronage, Hoover urged that he
be replaced with someone of unquestioned integrity,
but his campaign manager warned him to go slow. The
Howard group triumphed and voted for Hoover at he
convention.(30)

Elsewhere, the lily-white movement was stronger,
and the Hoover forces cooperated with them. In
Louisiana, Hoover's aide, George Akerson, worked with
Emile Kuntz, the national committeeman who had split
with Walter L. Cohen, the black leader. In Texas,
when National Committeeman, R. B. Creager forced out
blacks under Bill McDonald, Akerson assured Holsey
that something would be done, but he was unable to
prevent the exclusion of blacks. In Georgia, Benjamin
J. Davis, the black National Committeeman, was ousted
from his position. By the time of the convention,
Hoover had successfully worked for support in all
groups and had cautiously maneuvered through the maze

of factional southern politics.(31)

Having won the nomination, Hoover changed his strategy and ignored blacks in the campaign. This decision was based upon the rejection of Al Smith's candidacy in much of the South and Hoover's desire to prevent the race issue to be used against him as he sought to divide that section. Ignoring advice to speak out to blacks, Hoover said nothing specifically and made only a reference to equality of opportunity. At Elizabethton, Tennessee, he promised, in the tradition of William Howard Taft, not to appoint officials who were unacceptable to the community, a statement the South interpreted as meaning blacks would not receive appointments there.(32)

The race issue, however, became a major part of the campaign in the South. To attract and organize anti-Smith voters, Colonel Horace Mann, a Tennessee politician, established a Constitutional Democratic Committee and mounted a campaign outside the regular Republican organizations. Because he worked in secrecy, Mann's connection to Hoover is not clear, but he often reported to him ,as well as, to Claudius Huston, a Hoover supporter from the South and the next Chairman of the Republican National Committee. Democrats attacked Hoover and the GOP on the race issue by claiming that they favored social equality, corrupted southern politics in the sale of Post Office patronage, and threatened enforcement of the 14th and 15th amendments. Mann responded by pointing out that his group was lily-white and counter-attacked with pictures of Ferdinand Morton, a black Tammany Hall leader, dictating to a white secretary. Blacks, unimpressed with either side of this racist demagoguery, called upon both candidates to reject this use of race propaganda in the campaign.(33)

In the North, the Republican effort to win the black vote was limited and ineffective. Hoover wanted an active campaign for the black vote here, but despite his prodding, the Colored Division received little money. The nominee carefully observed campaign developments and on one occasion inquired into the speeches of President Mordecai Johnson of Howard University. Hoover's interest was inadequate, however, and Robert Church, the powerful black politician from Memphis, and his ally, J. Finley Wilson of the National Colored Voters League, were critical of the GOP. Church supported Hoover but refused to participate in the Party's campaign.(34)

        Dissatisfied with the Republicans and attracted
to Al Smith, many blacks turned away from the
Republican Party in 1928. In Texas, Bill McDonald
supported Smith, and speakers at the convention of the
National Negro Voters League threatened the GOP
because of its poor treatment of blacks in the South
and segregation in the government. Smith was
attractive because he was wet, and many blacks looked
for the end of prohibition to restore jobs. Smith
made no public appeal to black voters, but they found
Democratic political organizations such as Tammany
Hall to be responsive. Since the Klan opposed Smith
and Tammany, blacks had something in common with
northern Democrats. The post-election research of the
Republican National Committee showed that black
support declined in many areas. Texas reported that
Smith won 60 per cent of the black vote; Oregon
admitted a 40 per cent loss; Maryland, Missouri and
Ohio indicated a 20 per cent decline. The report
noted that Democrats did much better in the Northeast
and in cities while Hoover had more than doubled the
Republican vote in the South.(35)

        Despite the research findings, the disruption of
the Solid South offered an irresistable opportunity to
develop a two-party system in the region. To do so,
Hoover believed that the Party had to be made
respectable, and on March 26, 1929, he announced that
his policy was, to promote an organization in the
South that would be honest and efficient. He cited
improvements in a number of state organizations but
noted that recent exposures in the selling of Post
Office patronage in Mississippi, Georgia and South
Carolina made Republican organizations in those states
unacceptable Such corruption, he said, was
intolerable to his concept of public service and to
the principles of the GOP, and was unjust to the
South. While he expected reform to evolve from the
people in the states, Hoover indicated that his
administration would not entrust patronage to corrupt
politicians but would cooperate only with special
committees.(36)

        Had Hoover announced a lily-white policy for the
South? Hoover denied that race had anything to do
with it and claimed that honest and good service were
his goals. To correct an editorial in the Chicago
Tribune he wrote Colonel Robert McCormick that he
sought only to eliminate the abuses in patronage and
not to attack blacks. He claimed the support of black

leaders but admitted that Perry Howard was a current target. He argued that the urbanization and industrialization of the South meant that the national interest required a two-party system, and not until a healthy two-party system emerged in the South could the black person regain his franchise and his freedom.(37)

On the surface, that program made some sense. Ralph Bunche, in his studies of southern politics, agreed that if a lily-white policy could develop a true two-party system, blacks ought to support it. The black masses, he believed, would gain more from the end of the Solid South than from the patronage system of the black-and-tans. Dr. Moton supported the establishment of special committees in southern states to handle patronage, but he urged that blacks be included on these committees. From Chicago, Arthur W. Mitchell, later the first black Democrat elected to Congress, agreed that fraudulent leaders should be replaced, but he too, insisted that Hoover recognize worthy and deserving blacks.(38)

Subsequent events showed that Hoover had announced a lily-white policy that favored white leadership, but that efficient government remained an important goal. The President did not believe in the total exclusion of blacks, but he did agree to their elimination from positions of leadership and prominence. The two indictments of Perry Howard revealed both the President's concern for clean government and his lily-white policy. The latter policy was more evident in his efforts to dump Walter L. Cohen, a black officeholder in New Orleans. In cooperation with Louisiana Committeeman Emile Kunz, Hoover sought to remove Cohen by appointing him Minister to Liberia. Cohen was reluctant because of his age, the low salary of the position and the possible difficulty of confirmation by the Senate. Moton advised Hoover to allow him to remain at his position. When Cohen died in 1930, Hoover appointed a white to the position.(39)

Events elsewhere demonstrated the difficulties of imposing lily-whiteism and clean government in the South. In Florida, Hoover first cooperated with National Committeeman Glenn Skipper, who had ousted the black-and-tans. However, when Skipper proved to be primarily interested in patronage and old-style politics, the Administration rejected him. Various groups attempted to gain control of the party

machinery, but, when many appointments went to
Democrats, Florida Republicans lost interest. In the
1928 campaign Hoover forces had cooperated with
Georgia's black leader, Benjamin Davis, but turned
against him and chose Josiah T. Rose to head the party
after the election. Efforts to obtain cooperation
between Davis and Rose failed, and with Adminstration
approval, the latter's group followed a lily-white
policy of minimal black involvement in the party.(40)
In 1929 the durable Perry Howard remained as national
committeeman, but patronage went to the lily-white
faction. The Democrats, however, saved Howard from
successful prosecution for patronage sales by the
Justice Department, preferring him to a revitalized
GOP in the state. The failure of the lily-white
movement and the political ineptitude of the
Administration were more evident by 1932. Due to the
pressure of Chicago's black Congressman, Oscar
DePriest, Howard retained his power and was promised
control of patronage in return for DePriest's silence
on the political situation in South Carolina. The
lily-white leader of Mississippi resigned in
embarrassment. At the same time, Walter Newton,
Hoover's secretary, warned Florida lily-whites that
the Adminstration had to be concerned about black
voters in critical states and urged the South to
recognize the problem. The Administration simply
could not maintain black support in the North and seek
respectability through lily-white policies in the
South at the same time.(41)

     Blacks thought that such political behavior from
the President was sheer hypocrisy and poor politics.
In his drive for the nomination, Hoover had not
hesitated to associate with the likes of Perry Howard
and Ben Davis, and he had given them thousands of
dollars to work for him. Having successfully gained
the nomination, Hoover now attacked his friends and
historic allies and turned to their enemies. Not only
was political ingratitude unforgiveable, but Hoover's
strategy was also faulty. Robert Church prepared a
collection of black newspaper articles which opposed
the southern strategy and sent them to each
Congressman. In a long letter to the President, the
Memphis politician denounced lily-whiteism. He warned
Hoover that "the Negro having stood the scorn of time,
can stand the indifference and neglect of even so good
a man as you are, but I, with millions of men, many
white men of sober judgement, doubt that our country
can afford to issue so open an invitation to the
designs of oppression." Even Dr. Moton complained

that his suggestions seemed to be unwelcomed in
Washington. As to political efficiency, honesty and
respectability, Du Bois claimed that the southern
strategy would not work because the rotten borough
system, not blacks, was the real evil. Du Bois had
accepted Congressman De Priest despite the latter's
unsavory connections in Chicago because he would vote
right on issues involving blacks. By the same logic,
black leadership and recognition was necessary in the
southern GOP, and the removal of his people from party
leadership was detrimental to their interests. Du
Bois correctly perceived that Democrats would fight to
prevent any change toward a two-party system. The
Crisis editor did not believe that a two-party South
would result in the enfranchisement of blacks and
doubted whether Hoover had any place for his people in
his plans.(42)

Hoover's political perception and analysis were
also faulty in the nomination of Judge John J. Parker
to the United States Supreme Court. The NAACP feared
that the nominee would not grant justice to blacks
because as a Republican nominee for governor of North
Carolina in 1920, he had spoken against black
involvement in politics. This lily-white view
disqualified him for service on the high court, the
Association charged, because he would not enforce the
entire Constitution, particularly the 14th and 15th
amendments. Parker never answered the NAACP's query
concerning the validity of his statement and whether
he still agreed with it, but he could not deny that he
had made the statement. To others, he maintained that
he was trying to take the race issue out of politics,
not to interject it, and he promised that he would
uphold the Constitution in all its provisions.(43)

The NAACP was unwilling to take a chance that
Parker would be better than his history revealed. He
was only forty-four years old, and the prospect of an
unfriedly judge making significant decisions for a
potentially long time was not acceptable. The black
press and even the usually compliant Moton opposed the
nomination. When Hoover refused to withdraw the
nomination, the NAACP pressured U. S. Senators by an
organized write-in campaign. The opposition of blacks
was significant, and, when added to that of labor, the
result was the rejection of Parker by a vote of
41-39.(44)

The victory came over the determined effort of
Hoover to force the nomination regardless of the views

of blacks. Certainly neither Hoover nor anyone else
foresaw their opposition to Parker, but the President
believed that the race issue was extraneous to the
basic question of Parker's ability and character. To
blacks, however, a person's view on race was a very
important element in his character. When efforts to
influence the NAACP Board of Directors failed, the
Administration investigated the leadership and motives
of the organization. J. Edgar Hoover sent a summary
of the FBI's file on the NAACP, and Hoover's
secretary, Walter Newton, suggested to Representative
Hamilton Fish and he include the Association among
those being investigated for Communist activities.(45)

Hoover had ended segregation in the Census Bureau
as a candidate for the nomination, but he made no
further moves toward racial integration. He followed
the separate, but equal, doctrine of constitutional
law and allowed current practices to continue
unchallenged. When the time arrived for Mrs. Hoover's
tea for Congressional wives, plans were carefully made
to deal properly with Mrs. Oscar DePriest. Wives who
did not object to her presence were invited in the
same group, and officials tried to avoid publicity.
When the press learned of the event, the President and
his staff were careful to point out that the affair
was an official, not a social occasion and provided
research which showed that black diplomats and their
wives had been previously invited to the White House
for official receptions under both Democrat and
Republican presidents. But the incident gave southern
Democrats opportunity to renew the old charge that the
Republicans insisted on social equality and were a
threat to white supremacy. Clearly, any challenge to
racial mores was politically dangerous and especially
difficult in the midst of a southern strategy.(46)

After the DePriest affair and with the coming of
the depression, the Administration strictly followed
the segregation of races. After Congress voted to
send gold star mothers and widows to Europe to visit
the graves of their loved ones, the War Department
arranged that blacks be sent on separate ships. To
black protests the Department answered that the policy
was to avoid giving offense, a position that pleased
whites but angered blacks. When the latter complained
that they were sent on smaller ships with less
adequate facilities, the Department claimed that this
was due to the small number of blacks going, and the
ships were equal to those used when small numbers of
whites went. Many blacks cancelled the trip rather

than to submit to humiliation. The insensitivity of
the government was scored in the Nation's comment,
"Surely there was no time in the history of our
country when segregation was less necessary and more
cruel."(47)

In Washington, the Adminstration continued
segregation. In 1928 the NAACP investigated
government buildings, and Walter White discovered
segregation in all but three of the federal
departments. Even the Civil Service Commission
practiced segregation. White was critical of the
Commission's use of photgraphs on application forms
and the rule of three which allowed department heads a
choice among the top three candidates as devices which
provided the possibility for discrimination to subtly
occur. The NAACP did not push too strongly at the
time, but a later study labeled the period from 1913
to 1933 as the "critical period" for blacks in Civil
Service. This study accused the Hoover Administration
of systematically excluding blacks by order of
Postaster Walter Brown.(48) In the use of parks and
other recreational places, Ulysses S. Grant, III,
Director of Public Buildings and Public Parks in the
District of Columbia, rigidly maintained segregation.
When a white woman complained of attempted social
fraternization in the Recorder of Deeds office, the
President's secretary reprimanded the Recorder and
arranged to have reports of the situation sent from a
white employee. Blacks, he demanded, must lean over
backwards to avoid giving offense.(49)

In some instances, Hoover might have made
symbolic gestures but failed to do so. In 1928, the
Republican Congress had supported a black
organization, the National Memorial Association, in
its promotion of a major building in Washington that
would be a tribute to the contributions of American
blacks. The legislation provided minimal monetary
support from Congress, the bulk of the project to be
financed through voluntary subscription. Hoover could
hardly have disagreed with the method, but, when he
became President, he delayed naming a Commission that
would be empowered to act and allowed it a very small
appropriation. The idea was ultimately destroyed by
the depression.(50) As the depression required
government retrenchment, the NAACP learned that the
War Department had ordered limits placed on
reenlistments and required replacements to come from
existing units that would be disbanded. The order led
to the dissolution of the 25th Infantry and 10th

Cavalry, the most famous of black combat troops and symbols of black achievement, glory and manhood. Furthermore, the NAACP discovered that these reductions were made to allow increases in the Army Air Force which did not admit blacks. Considering the fact that black troops accounted for only a small per cent of he nation's armed forces, the NAACP found the action discriminatory. On another occasion, the President promised the appointment of a black Assistant Attorney General but specified that he had to come from Indiana or Illinois. Black leaders selected a man whom Hoover interviewed, but the appointment was never made. Blacks concluded that the incident was further evidence that Hoover was cold nd impassive toward them. The President received many requests to aid the Scotsboro boys being tried in Alabama, but felt he had no authority to act.(51)

Even in an area that elicited Hoover's sympathy and shocked his conscience, he decided not to act. A dramatic increase in the number of lynchings in 1930, accompanied by the constant protests of William Monroe Trotter of the National Equal Rights League and the NAACP, prompted Hoover to act on the Republican pledge to end that terrible blot on American civilization. Newton wrote Walter White that the President had recently declared that "Every decent citizen must condemn the lynching evil as an undermining of the very essence of both justice and democracy," but White insisted on stronger action. To give moral support to the anti-lynching movement, the NAACP Executive Secretary wanted Hoover to call a conference of southern governors to discuss the lynching problem. Possibly because of White's involvement in the Judge Parker fight and his dubbing Hoover as the "man in the Lily-White House," the President would not see him, and his memorandum on the conference was not acknowleged. Hoover did meet with Maurice Spencer and Trotter of the National Equal Rights League on November 15, 1930, and promised he would consider federal legislation by Lincoln's birthday. Trotter continued to prod Hoover who missed the deadline and most of 1931 before he acted, sending only an anti-lynching message to the NAACP conventon.(52)

When Hoover finally determined to act, he was stymied by constitutional and political problems. As late as December 1, 1931, Hoover told Spencer and Trotter that he was not inclined to ask Congress for an anti-lynching law, but by the end of the month he planned to add to his message on law enforcement a

139.

proposal to attack lynching through federal action.
"These actions," he proposed to add, "are the negation
of the Republican [sic] form of government guaranteed
to our citizens by the Constitution. With the modern
expedition, through aerial and motor forces of Federal
troops located at all important centers throughout the
country, it is possible to bring them almost instantly
to the assistance of local authorities if a system
were authorized by Congress that would make such
action swift and possible."(53)

In reply to Hoover's request for advice Attorney
General William Mitchell opined that the Constitution
and practical politics would prevent this proposal.
The 14th amendment could not be stretched to permit
the use of troops, and Mitchell noted, further
constitutional problems arose if the legislature or
governor of a state refused to ask for assistance.
Furthermore, he added, the measure was impractical.
If the President were to wait to see if the state
would act or not, he would be too late to prevent the
lynching. Mitchell argued that neither this proposal,
nor the old Dyer bill, had a chance to pass Congress.
It would be better, he advised, to educate public
opinion and encourage state officials to do their
duty. Hoover's idea was a radical approach to law
enforcement that was surprisingly statist for him and
reminiscent of the enforcement acts of the
Reconstruction era. Although previous Presidents had
found ways to intervene in state affairs, Hoover
dropped the idea and rejected further conferences on
the subject because of his involvement in other
meetings of "outstanding importance." Blacks never
learned of the radical proposal and remained
discontented.(54)

Many Americans were unhappy with the Hoover
Adminstration by 1932, and blacks were among them.
Loyalists such as Dr. Moton and Claude Barnett
complained of neglect, and even black politicians
criticized the President. Robert Church refused to
support him but did support the GOP. The NAACP had a
list of accumulated grievances and demanded redress.
Of course, one might expect the NAACP to be critical,
wrote J. M. Marquess, a black politician from
Pennsylvania, but, when the conservative Board of
Bishops of the A. M. E. Church spoke out for rewarding
friends and punishing enemies, it was time for
Republicans to take note. Hoover's failure to appoint
a black to the commission to investigate conditions in
Haiti disappointed many, and they resented Hoover's

reluctance to be photographed with them. For a time,
the Administration planned to drop the Colored
Division in the national party's headquarters and
changed its plans only late in the campaign. When
Hoover finally met with black political leaders, the
reiterated te historic tradition between the GOP and
blacks, which the black press ridiculed as "the same
old hooey."(55)

The Administration worried a bit about black
loyalty in 1932 but did little about it. A spy was
employed to attend meetings of the NAACP and faternal
groups to ascertain their political thinking. The
Reconstruction Finance Corporation hired a few blacks
to work in the agricultural programs. Hoover
responded to the charges of discrimination in public
works programs by ordering Treasury Department
officials who supervised the construction of public
buildings to do whatever possible to prevent
discrimination by contractors. Secretary of the
Treasury Ogden Mills made a public announcement to
that effect, and sent the word to government engineers
and contractors. Unfortunately, those moral suasions
were ineffective. The need, wrote Francis Rivers, a
black politician, was a permanent fair employment
practices commission which could immediately check
into charges of discrimination rather than appointing
a new investigative group for each reported incident.
Too often, the project was completed before anything
was done.(56)

Most blacks voted Republican in 1932, but the
election results showed some slippage in their party
loyalty and in their personal loyalty to Hoover. For
some, the Republican tradition was too strong to break
despite Hoover's apparent indifference. "Somehow,"
wrote A. M. E. Bishop W. J. Walls, "I feel it my duty
to make frinds for the Republican administration in
spite of some acts which seem to indicate the apparent
attitude of aloofness of my race group upon the part
of the present administration at Washington." Since
party loyalty and the benefits of political activity
were primarily local matters, blacks continued in
their party loyalty. Adam Clayton Powell, Sr.,
advised blacks that no matter how they felt about
Hoover, they should support local Republicans who
would be fair in providing jobs. In Chicago,
Philadelphia and Cleveland, they again voted
overwhelmingly Republican, but, where local Democratic
organizations responded to their needs, as in Kansas
City, New York and Detroit, they switched from their

historic ties in large numbers.(57)

Regardless of the election results in 1932, the
Hoover Administration had done little to maintain
black loyalty to the national party. The President
and his advisers followed old ideas, ineffective
techniques and inept politics and failed to note the
changes ocurring among blacks. While he was not a
malevolent racist, Hoover, like most Americans in the
1930s, retained the Booker T. Washington approach to
race relations by his acceptance of black
responsibility for their condition. When Hoover
appeared ready to help blacks gain land or prevent
lynchings, political ambition and political
difficulties stopped him. American racism in the
1920s and 1930s made positive innovations in race
relations difficult to achieve, but Hoover's political
ambition and political analyses led him to follow
those possibilities that promised greater electoral
rewards. Ignoring Republican slippage among blacks
and northern city voters, Hoover promoted the
lily-white movement in the South. As Hoover saw it,
blacks prevented the development of a respectable
southern GOP, and powerless blacks could be sacrificed
in the short run to develop a clean and efficient
two-party system. The policy failed, however, and led
to political dis-affection in the North.

Hoover's experience might have led him to move in
other directions. If a legislative solution to
lynching was impossible, Hoover failed to place the
onus of failure on the Democrats or to exert executive
action. To be sure, he spent much time dealing with
the depression, but his experience had suggested some
possibilities. He had learned the merits of black
representation from the Mississippi flood, but as
President, he applied the lesson only on occasion and
not as a policy. Had he made black representation a
policy, perhaps a black subcabinet might have evolved
as it did under Franklin Roosevelt. Though Hoover
recognized that decentralized authority in the Red
Cross aided the perpetuation of peonage, he did not
change the process or his ideas. Hoover never felt
the affront experienced by the gold star mothers and
did not understand the nationalism of the Harlem
Renaissance and the New Negro. Disliking the
confrontation tactics and racial militancy of the
NAACP, the President offered only pious testimonials
for the Tuskegee idea of education and the mild
approach of the Commission on Interracial
Cooperation.(58)

142.

While blacks welcomed any positive efforts, they
had advanced beyond Hoover's simple statements of good
will. The NAACP was a well-organized pressure group
which presented a decidedly militant mood for the
times. The Parker fight was very significant in
bringing cohesion to black dissatisfaction with GOP
indifference. Hoover thought the rejection of Parker
by "demagogues and Negro politicians" to be
outrageous, but the NAACP felt that Hoover had to be
confronted because an unfriendly man on the Supreme
Court was too dangerous. "In this fight," claimed an
editorial in the Kansas City Call, "to prevent John J.
Parker of North Carolina from becoming associate judge
of the Supreme Court, we have found ourselves."(59)

Not only were northern blacks restive, but the
mood also changed in the South. Black politicians
fought against the lily-white movement and opposed
Hoover by inactivity or support of Democrats. Even
Dr. Moton revealed a new viewpoint. In his book, What
the Negro Thinks, a copy of which he sent the
President, Moton complained that those who controlled
Negroes and claimed to know them, actuaully did not
understand them at all. Blacks concealed their views
and resentments from whites who recognized only
stereotypes and caricatures. But now, Moton asserted,
blacks knew and appreciated themselves. He not only
opposed segregation, but he also advocated the return
of the franchise to protect blacks' lives, property
and business. Without the vote and representation, he
wrote, "government is simply white society organized
to keep the Negro down." This was far from the old
Tuskegee view, and to a reviewer in the Crisis it was
unthinkable ten years ago. Whether Hoover read the
book is impossible to say, but Claudius Huston did and
told the President that Moton was in advance of his
times. Another Tuskegee loyalist, Albon Holsey, could
not forget the sympathy Hoover had for the Mississippi
River flood victims, and, while expressing loyalty in
the face of events he did not understand, he now asked
for assurance that the party was still sympathetic to
blacks. To many, Hoover was difficult to understand
and his policy towards blacks vague.(60)

In 1929, a scholarly observer of black culture
concluded, "The submissive acquiescence of the Booker
T. Washington attitude and era have now become
contemptuously anachronistic," but few whites,
including Hoover and his staff, realized it.(61) In
the context of the times, Hoover was a moderate in

143.

race matters and was genuinely sympathetic in the face
of disaster and tragedy. In those instances, he
responded with radical ideas, but contemporary racism
and political conditions, led him to rely more on time
than on programs to solve the "Negro problem." His
American individualism featured equality of
opportunity, the prevention of capital as an
oppressor, equality before the law, voting rights and
government by the majority, but he did not apply these
to black life. His principle of decentralization
strengthened political, economic and social oppression
in the South, and he was unwilling to abandon the
principle and unable to change conditions. Hoover
neither sought nor wielded a sword to achieve social
justice for blacks, even though he himself had
written, "social injustice is the destruction of
justice itself."

FOOTNOTES

1. Joan Hoff Wilson, Herbert Hoover: Forgotten
   Progressive, (Boston 1975); Martin L. Fausold and
   George T. Masusan, eds., The Hoover Presidency:
   A Reappraisal, (Albany, 1974); David Burner,
   Herbert Hoover A Public Life, (New York, 1978);
   Ellis W. Hawley, The Great War and the Search for
   a Modern Order, (New York, 1979).

2. Richard B. Sherman, The Republican Party and
   Black America: From McKinley to Hoover
   1896-1933, (Charlottesville, 1973); Harvard
   Sitkoff, A New Deal For Blacks: The Emergence of
   Civil Rights as a National Issue, Vol. 1, The
   Depression Decade, (New York, 1978); Pete
   Daniel, The Shadow of Slavery: Peonage in the
   South 1901-1969, (Urbana, 1972); A recent
   article by George F. Garcia, "Herbert Hoover and
   the Race Issue:" The Anals of Iowa, 44 (Winter,
   1979), 507-515 does place Hoover's views on race
   within his larger philosophical framework.

3. Herbert C. Hoover, Principles of Mining, (New
   York, 1909), 161-165; Garcia, "Hoover and the
   Race Issue," 507-515.

4. Herbert Hoover, American Individualism, (Reprint,
   Washington, n.d., first published, New York,
   1922), 4, 5, 7, 9, 17, 19, 20, 23; Wilson,
   Hoover, 61, 62.

5. The best study is Sherman, Republican Party and
   Black America.

6. Robert K. Murray, The Harding Era: Warren G.
   Harding and His Administration, (Minneapolis,
   1969), 54, 397-401; Crisis, 23 (Dec., 1921), 53;
   Pete Daniel, "Black Power in the 1920s: The Case
   of Tuskegee Veterans Hospital," The Journal of
   Southern History, 36 (Aug., 1970), 368-388;
   Donald McCoy, Calvin Coolidge: The Quiet
   President, (New York, 1967), 200, 328, 329;
   Crisis, 26 (July, 1923), 106, 107; (Sept.,
   1923), 216-218.

7. Crisis, 24 (May, 1922), 25; (June, 1922), 69-72;
   (July, 1922), 123; (Aug., 1922), 165; (Sept.,
   1922), 215, 216; (Oct., 1922), 261-264; 25
   (Nov. 922), 24; (Jan., 1923), 103, 105, 119;

Murray, <u>Harding</u>, 402; William Borah, "Negro
Suffrage," Crisis, 33 (Jan., 1927), 132, 133;
William Borah to W. E. B. Du Bois, July 17, 1926,
in Herbert Aptheker, ed., <u>The Correspondence of</u>
<u>W. E. B. Du Bois</u>, I (Amherst, 1973), 341, 342.

8. <u>Crisis</u>, 20 (Sept., 1920), 213; 21 (Mar., 1921),
   197; 22 (May, 1921), 20; (July, 1921), 101, 102;
   23 (Dec., 1921), 53; 24 (May, 1922), 11; (July,
   1922), 122; 25 (Nov., 1922), 30.

9. <u>Ibid</u>., 24 (May, 1922), 11; (Oct., 1922), 264,
   265; 25 (Jan., 1923), 103, 104, 106, 117, 118;
   (Feb., 1923), 169, 170; Daniel, "Tuskegee
   Veterans Hospital," 371-380.

10. Jarvis Anderson, <u>A. Phillip Randolph: A</u>
    <u>Biographical Portrait</u>, (New York, 1972), parts
    III and IV; Donald Johnson, <u>The Challenge to</u>
    <u>American Freedoms</u>, (Lexington, 1963), 196;
    Florette Henri, <u>Black Migration: Movement</u>
    <u>North</u>,. 1900-1920, (Garden City, 1976), 333-343;
    Sitkoff, <u>New Deal For Blacks</u>, 22, 23.

11. Bruce A. Lohof, "Herbert Hoover, Spokesman of
    Humane Efficiency: The Mississippi Flood of
    1927," <u>American Quarterly</u>, 22 (Fall, 1970),
    690-700; Bruce A. Lohof, "Hoover and the
    Mississippi Valley Flood of 1927: A Case Study
    of the Political Thought of Herbert Hoover,"
    (Unpublished PhD dissertation, Syracuse
    University, 1968).

12. Claude Barnett to Herbert Hoover, May 4, 1927.
    "Mississippi Valley Relief Work - Telegrams,"
    Commerce Papers, Herbert Hoover Presidential
    Library (Herafter cited as HHPL). Rules may be
    found in Herbert Hoover and James Fieser, "The
    Principles of Organizationa and Procedure for
    Relief and Reconstruction in the Mississippi
    Valley Flood Disaster," "Mississippi Valley
    Relief Work - Misc.," Commerce Papers, HHPL.

13. Arthur Capper to Hoover, May 10, 1927; Hoover to
    Capper, May 15, 1927; Hoover to Henry M. Baker,
    May 13, 1927; Hoover to Dr. Moulton, [sic,
    Moton] May 24, 1927; Robert R. Moton to Hoover,
    May 26, 1927. "Mississippi Valley Flood Relief
    Work - Negroes;" Baker to Fieser, May 14, 1927;
    Margaret Butler to Fieser, May 14, 1927; J.W.
    Richardson to Fieser, May 18, 1927. Mississippi

Valley Flood Relief - Telegrams," Commerce
Papers, HHPL.

14. Moton to Hoover, June 13, 1927; Hoover to Moton,
    June 17, 1927. "Mississippi Valley Flood Relief
    Work - Negroes," Commerce Papers, HHPL.

15. Lawrence Richey to George Akerson, June 9, 1927;
    Hoover to Will Irwin, June 10, 1927.
    "Mississippi Valley Flood Relief Work -
    Telegrams;" Hoover to Ida Wells-Barnett, June 17,
    1927; JJD (James D. Davis) to Hoover, June 10,
    1927; Claude Barnett to Hoover, June 10, 1927;
    Hoover to Barnett, June 14, 1927; Walter White
    to Hoover, June 14, 1927; Hoover to White, June
    21, 1927; Barnett to Hoover, June 14, 1927;
    Press release of Associated Negro Press, June 14,
    1927. "Mississippi Valley Flood Relief Work -
    Negroes," Commerce Papers, HHPL; Walter White,
    "The Negro and the Flood," The Nation, 124 (June
    22, 1927), 688, 689.

16. Memorandum of Conference Between Officials of the
    American Red Cross and Members of the Colored
    Commission on Flood Rehabilitation at National
    Red Cross Headquarters on July 8, 1927; L. O.
    Crosby to Hoover, July 15, 1927; Crosby to
    Hoover, July 15, 1927. "Mississippi Valley Flood
    Relief Work - Negroes;" R. R. Taylor and Albon
    Holsey to Hoover, June 9, 1927. "Mississippi
    Valley Flood - Rehabilitation, Arkansas;" Dennis
    Murphree to Hoover, July 15, 1927. "Mississippi
    Valley Flood - Personnel," Commerce Papers, HHPL.

17. Hoover to Crosby, July 8, 1927; T. J. McCarty to
    Hoover, July 9, 1927; Crosby Schafer to Fieser,
    N.d.; McCarty to Hoover, July 14, 1927; White to
    Fieser, July 12, 1927; Holsey to Robert E.
    Bondy, June 22, 1927. "Mississippi Valley Flood
    - Negroes;" Crosby to Hoover, July 29, 1927;
    Crosby to Hoover, Oct. 22, 1927. "Mississippi
    Valley Flood - Rehabilitation, Mississippi;"
    Fieser to Hoover, July 28, 1927; Fieser, "The
    Courage and Optimism of 'The Great Valley,' " The
    Red Cross Courier, 7 (Jan., 16, 1928), 8.
    "Mississippi Valley Flood - Reports," Commerce
    Papers, HHPL.

18. Walter Wesselius to Bondy, June 29, 1927; Moton
    to Hoover, with memorandum, Oct. 1, 1927; Moton
    to Hoover, Sept., 6, 1927; Moton to Hoover,

Dec., 12, 1927; Hoover to Moton, Oct. 17, 1927.
"Mississippi Valley Flood - Negroes;" F. E. Wood
to T. J. McCarty, Aug. 3, 1927. "Mississippi
Valley Flood - Rehabilitation, Louisiana;"
Crosby to Will Percy, June 15, 1927.
"Mississippi Valley Flood - Rehabilitation,
Mississippi;" A. L. Schafer to Bondy, July 29,
1927. "Mississippi Valley Flood - Material,"
Commerce Papers, HHPL.

19. Fieser to Hoover, Dec. 14, 1927; Fieser to
Hoover, Dec. 16, 1927; Hoover to Moton, Dec. 16,
1927; Hoover to Moton, Dec. 22, 1927; Hoover to
Fieser, Dec. 22, 1927; Bondy to Wesselius,
Buchanan, McCarty, Dec. 22, 1927; Moton to
Hoover, Dec. 31, 1927; J. S. Clark to Fieser,
Jan. 11, 1928; Moton to Hoover, Jan. 12, 1928;
Moton to Judge John Barton Payne, May 14, 1928.
"Mississippi Valley Flood - Negroes;" Moton to
Hoover, Jan. 4, 1928. "Mississippi Valley Flood
- Negroes - Land Sitation;" Joseph S. Clark,
"Survey of the Colored Advisory Commission's
Work," Robert H. Moton, "Wisdom and Helpfulness
of Interracial Cooperation," The Red Cross
Courier, 7 (June 15, 1928), 10, 11, 14, 15, 24;
"Mississippi Valley Flood - Reports;" Crisis, 34
(Nov., 1927), 311; "The Flood, the Red Cross and
the National Guard," Crisis, 35 (Jan. - March,
1928), 5-7, 26, 28, 41-43, 64, 80, 81, 100, 102.
See also T. C. Reagan, Sr. to Hoover, Feb. 20,
1928. "Mississippi Valley Flood -
Rehabilitation, Louisiana," Commerce Papers,
HHPL.

20. Memorandum, July 12, 1927. "Mississippi Valley
Flood: Resettlement;" Bruce A. Lohof, "Herbert
Hoover's Mississippi Land Reform Memorandum: A
Document," The Arkansas Historical Quarterly, 29
(Summer, 1970), 112-118; Hoover to H. C. Couch,
July 12, 1927. "Mississippi Valley Flood -
Rehabilitation, Arkansas;" Hoover to Crosby,
July 12, 1927. "Mississippi Valley Flood -
Rehabilitation, Mississippi;" Moton to Hoover,
Jan. 4, 1928. "Mississippi Valley Flood -
Negroes, Land Survey;" Hoover to Eugene Booze,
July 5, 1927. "Mississippi Valley Flood -
Congratulations;" Booze to Hoover, July 9, 1927.
"Mississippi Valley Flood - Negroes." Commerce
Papers, HHPL.

21. Moton to Hoover, Jan. 4, 1928. "Mississippi

Valley Flood - Negroes, Survey;" Edwin Embree to
Vern Kellogg, March 1, 1928; Embree to Hoover,
March 1, 1928; Hoover to Embree, March 6, 1928;
Hoover to Moton, March 11, 1928. "Mississippi
Valley Flood - Negroes, Plan;" Fieser to Hoover,
Aug. 27, 1927. "Mississippi Valley Flood -
Negroes," Commerce Papers, HHPL.

22. William Jay Schieffelin to Hoover, Jan. 9, 1928;
Hoover to Schieffelin, Jan. 12, 1928; Moton to
Hoover, Jan. 18, 1928; Moton to Hoover, Feb. 27,
1928. "Mississippi Valley Flood - Negroes,"
Commerce Papers, HHPL. At the close of Hoover's
Presidency Moton reminded him of the idea and
suggested that they take it up again. Hoover
appeared interested but nothing followed. Moton
to Hoover, Jan. 12, 1933; Hoover to Moton, Jan.
17, 1933. "Moton," Presidential Papers, HHPL.

23. Clipping, The Pittsburgh Courier, Jan. 21, 1928.
"Mississippi Valley Flood - Negroes," Commerce
Papers, HHPL.

24. Albon Holsey to Arthur Hyde, Sept. 2, 1930;
Walter Newton to E. French Strother, Sept. 9,
1930. "Better Homes," Presidential Paper, HHPL;
Nan Elizabeth Woodruff, "The Great Southern
Drought of 1930-31: A Study in Rural Relief,"
(Unpublished PhD dissertation: The University of
Tennessee, 1977. See untitled statement directed
at Senator Borah, Feb. 6, 1931, #1474, Public
Statements, HHPL.

25. E. E. Hunt to E. French Strother, Aug. 23, 1930
attached with "The Economic Status of the Negro,"
"Hunt," E. French Strother Papers, HHPL; Eugene
Booze to Richey, Feb. 6, 1931; J. A. Evans to
Mr. Warburton, Jan. 27, 1931; Richey to Booze,
Feb. 4, 1931; Booze to Hoover, Jan. 30, 1931.
"Negroes;" Booze to Richey, Jan. 15, 1930;
Booze to Richey, Nov. 30, 1929. "Booz-Booze;"
Booze to Newton, Feb. 9, 1933. "Reconstruction
Finance Corporation;" Leon R. Harris to Newton,
April 11, 1932; C. W. Warburton to Hyde, April
25, 1932. "Colored Question," Presidential
Papers, HHPL; Crisis, 38 (March, 1931), 81.

26. "Investigation of Labor Camps in Federal Flood
Control Operations," Aug. 1932; Clipping,
Washington Tribune, Oct. 28, 1932; Press
release, Oct. 26, 1932. "Colored Question," F.

H. Payne to Newton, Oct. 1, 1932; Moton to
Newton, Oct. 18, 1932; U. S. Grant, III, to
Newton, Nov. 1, 1932; Grant to Newton, Nov. 8,
1932; Major General Lytle Brown to Secretary of
War, Feb. 13, 1933. "Flood Control,"
Presidential Papers, HHPL. Sherman, Republican
Party and Black America, 250, 251.

27. Crisis, 27 (Jan., 1922), 105, 106; David James
Ginzl, "Herbert Hoover and Republican Patronage
Politics in the South, 1928-1932," (Unpublished
PhD dissertation, Syracuse University, 1977),
14-20.

28. C. C. Spaulding to Hoover, Nov. 25, 1927.
"Foreign and Domestic Commerce - Colored;"
Holsey to Hoover, March 13, 1928. "National
Negro;" Barnett to Hoover, March 24, 1926.
"Newspapers - Associated Negro;" R. R. Wright,
Jr., to Hoover, March 24, 1921; Christian Herter
to Wright, April 1, 1921. "Colored - Colton;"
Hoover to Neval Thomas, March 16, 1928; Hoover to
Dr. Hill, March 18, 1928; Thomas to Hoover,
April 6, 1928; Clippings, Washington Post, March
31, 1928; Washington Sentinel, April 21, 1928;
Washington Eagle, April 6, 1928 Commerce Papers,
HHPL. Harvey Couch to George Akerson, Feb. 25,
1928; C. C. Neal to Richie [sic] Feb. 22, 1928;
Akerson to Couch, March 22, 1928; Akerson to
Couch, April 5, 1928; Couch to Akerson, April 23,
1928; Couch to Akerson, May 21, 1928. "Couch;"
Akerson to Holsey, March 27, 1928; Moton to
Akerson, March 29, 1928; Holsey to Akerson,
March 29, 1928; Akerson to Holsey, April 25,
1928. "Colored People," George Akerson Papers,
HHPL.

29. Ginzl, "Hoover and Patronage," 14; Akerson to
Booze, Jan. 19, 1928; Booze to Work, Jan. 16,
1928; Booze to Akerson, Jan. 24, 1928; Booze to
Akerson, Feb. 3, 1928; Akerson to Booze, Feb. 9,
1928. "Hixs-Hopw," George Akerson Papers, HHPL.

30. Crosby to Akerson, Feb. 1, 1928; Akerson to
Crosby, Feb. 4, 1928; Crosby to Akerson, Feb. 6,
1928; Crosby to Akerson, Feb. 9, 1928; Akerson
to Crosby, Feb. 13, 1928; Crosby to E. E.
Hindman, Feb. 14, 1928; Crosby to Akerson, Feb.
21, 1928; Crosby to Akerson, March 14, 1928;
Crosby to Akerson, April 10, 1928; Akerson to
Crosby, April 16, 1928. "Crosby," George Akerson

Papers, HHPL; Hoover to Work, July 18, 1928;
Work to Hoover, July 21, 1928. "Work," Campaign
and Transition Papers, HHPL; New York Times, June
7, 1928.

31. Emile Kunta to Akerson, May 4, 1928; Kuntz to
Akerson, Feb. 2, 1928. "Kuntz;" Holsey to
Akerson, May 4, 1928; C. F. Richardson to
Holsey, May 12, 1928. "Colored People," George
Akerson Papers, HHPL; Paul Lewinson, Race,
Class, and Party, (New York, 1963), 172.

32. Emmett J. Scott to Hoover, July 13, 1928; Hoover
to Scott, July 21, 1928; "Scott," Campaign and
Transition Papers, HHPL; New York Times, October
7, 1928; William F. Nowlin, The Negro in
American National Politics, (Boston, 1931), 120,
121; Sherman, Republican Party and Black
America, 230 231.

33. Ginzel, "Hoover and Patronage," 70-106; "An
Appeal to America," Crisis, 35 (Dec., 1928), 416.
Mann was apparently involved with the Ku Klux
Klan. See Walter F. Brown to Hoover, March 29,
1933, Box 2, fol. 1, Walter F. Brown Papers, The
Ohio Historical Society.

34. Hoover to Work, July 14, 1928. "Work;" J.
Finley Wilson to Hoover, Sept. 15, 1928. "Nat -
Nd;" Scott to Akerson, Sept. 17, 1928; Hoover
to Scott, Sept. 21, 1928; Clipping, Washington
Eagle, Sept. 14, 1928. "Scott," Campaign and
Transition Papers, HHPL.

35. Lewinson, Race, Class, and Party, 173; Kansas
City Call, Nov. 9, 1928; Materials in "Electional
result,' Campaign and Transition Papers, HHPL.
36. Press Statement, March 26, 1929. "Appointments:
Southern," Presidential Papers, HHPL.

37. Ibid.; Hoover to McCormick, March 30, 1929;
Clipping, Chicago Tribune, March 28, 1929.
"Republican National Committee (Hereafter cited
RNC): Colored Voters," Presidential Papers,
HHPL.

38. Moton to Hoover, April 19, 1929. "Moton;"
Arthur W. Mitchell to Hoover, March 30, 1929.
"Colored Question," Presidential Papers, HHPL;
Ralph Bunche, The Political Status of the Negro
in the Age of FDR, (Chicago, 1973), 82, 83.

39. Kuntz to Akerson, March 17, 1929; Sidney Martin
and John Diaz to Hoover, July 25, 1931; Joseph
B. Mayes to Hoover, April 6, 1932. "RNC:
Louisiana;" Kuntz to Akerson, May 31, 1929;
Kuntz to Akerson, June 6, 1929; Cohen to
Akerson, June 8, 1929; Moton to Newton, Aug. 21,
1929; "Countries: Liberia," Presidential
Papers, HHPL.

40. Hoover to Fred E. Britten, Sept. 26, 1929. "RNC
- Patronage;" Resolution of Florida State
Committee, May 11, 1929; E. E. Callaway to
Newton, April 16, 1930; Callaway to Newton,
April 19, 1930; A. H. Lindilie to Newton, Jan.
8, 1932. "RNC - Florida;" Benjamin Davis to
Republican National Committee, Nov. 19, 1928;
Rose to Newton, Jan. 29, 1930; Rose to Newton,
April 14, 1930; Kittrell to Newton, April 21,
1930; Rose to Newton, July 21, 1920; Newton to
John Tilson, Sept. 27, 1930; W. H. Harris to
Brown, Aug. 20, 1931; Davis to Newton, Aug. 4,
1930; Rose to Newton, April 2, 1932; Newton to
Rose, April 6, 1932; Mrs. George S. Williams to
Newton, March 12, 1932. "RNC - Georgia;"
Colored Question," Presidential Papers, HHPL.

41. Walter Shelby to Newton, April 15, 1932; Newton
to Harry Hewitt, April 15, 1932. "RNC -
Florida;" L. G. Reese to Claudius Huston, Feb.
15, 1930; Lamont Rowland to Newton, March 21,
1930; Reese to Newton, Jan. 11, 1932; Hawkins
to Newton, June 20, 1932; Redmond to Newton,
Sept. 15, 1932; Redmond to Newton, July 5, 1932;
Rowland to Hoover, June 14, 1932; W. N. Ethridge
to Hoover, Nov. 18, 1932. "RNC - Mississippi;"
Hoover to Rowland, July 8, 1932. "Rowland;"
Hambright to Newton, Aug. 15, 1931. "RNC - South
Carolina," Presidential Papers, HHPL.

42. Robert R. Church to Hoover, Nov. 6, 1929; John
R. Hawkins to Hoover, Feb. 26, 1929; James P.
Davis to Richey, March 22, 1929; Harry H. Pace
to Hoover, April 27, 1929; Clipping, The World,
April 22, 1929. "Colored Question;" Clipping,
The Memphis Triangle, n.d., "Barnett;" Moton to
Newton, Dec. 17, 1929. "Moton;" Clippings,
Chicago Defender, March 30, 1929; New York Times,
March 27, 1929. "RNC - Georgia;" Presidential
Papers; Ernest Attwell to Eugene Rickard, Nov.
18, 1928. "Attwell," Campaign and Transition

Papers, HHPL; _Crisis,_ 36 (April - May, 1929),
131, 132, 167.

43. Walter White, "The Negro and the Supreme Court,
     "_Harper's Magazine_, 162 (Jan., 1931), 238-246;
     New York Times, March 22, 1930; Reproduced
     clipping, _Greensboro Daily News_, April 19, 1920;
     Parker to Henry D. Hatfield, April 19, 1930;
     Parker to Hamilton F. Kean, May 2, 1930; Parker
     to David H. Blair, April 9, 1930. "Judiciary -
     Supreme Court," Presidential Papers, HHPL.

44. W. M. Blount to Henry J. Allen, April 18, 1930;
     Nathan William MacChesney to Newton, April 24,
     1930; M. T. Whittico to H. D. Hatfield, April 7,
     1930; Moton to Newton, April 18, 1930;
     Clipping, _New York Times_, April 12, 1930.
     "Judiciary - Supreme Court," Presidential
     Papers, HHPL; Walter White, _A Man Called White:_
     The Autobiography of Walter White, (New York,
     1948), 104-110; Oswald Garrison Villard, "My
     Dear Senator," _The Nation_, 130 (April 30, 1930),
     512; _New York Times_, April 13, 17, 1930; May 8,
     1930.

45. J. Edgar Hoover to Assistant Attorney General
     Sisson, April 19, 1930; Carl Bachman to Newton,
     Aug. 28, 1931. "Colored Question;" J. Edgar
     Hoover to Newton, April 25, 1930; Memo on Judge
     Parker, n.d.; Memo on Spingarn, n.d.; File
     memo, n.d.; R. Barrows to Newton, April 17,
     1930. "Judiciary - Supreme Court," Presdential
     Papers, HHPL; _New York Times_, April 14, 20; May
     5, 1930.

46. Newton to Henry W. Anderson, June 12, 1929; WHN
     (Newton) to Miss Randolph, July 5, 1929; see
     generally the correspondence in "Colored Question
     - DePriest Incident," Presidential Papers, HHPL.

47. M. W. Spencer and William Monroe Trotter to
     Hoover, Feb. 19, 1930; Tom Canty to Akerson, May
     30, 1930; F. H. Payne to Richey, Oct. 25, 1932;
     Clipping, _Cleveland Call and Post_, July 19, 1930.
     "Gold Star," Presidential Papers, HHPL; _New York_
     Times, May 30; July 11-13, 1930; "Black and Gold
     Stars," _The Nation_, 131 (July 23, 1930), 86.

48. Herbert Aptheker, "Segregation in Federal
     Government Departments: 1928," _Science and_
     Society, 28 (Winter, 1964), 86-91; _Crisis_, 35

(Nov., Dec., 1928), 369, 387-390, 418; Lawrence J. W. Hayes, The Negro Federal Government Worker: A Study of His Classification Status in the District of Columbia, 1883-1938, III, The Howard University Studies in the Social Sciences, (Washington, 1941), 37, 46, 51, 66-70.

49. Newton, File Memo, April 16, 1931; William N. Fisher to Newton, August 27, 1931; Newton, Memo on telephone call from Mrs. Yost, April 10, 1931; Newton, File Memo, April 29, 1931. "District Commissioners - Recorder of Deeds;" U. S. Grant, III, to Newton, Sept. 3, 1932. "Colored Question," Presidential Papers, HHPL.

50. Committee of Library, Report, 70 Cong., 1 Sess., May 3, 1928; M. H. Thatcher to Hoover, April 19, 1929; Richey to Forster, April 20, 1929; Ferdinand Lee to Newton, July 3, 1929; Lee to Newton, June 16, 1930. "National Memorial Association," Presidential Papers, HHPL.

51. Copy of War Department order on Negro Regiment, July 2, 1931; Press release of NAACP, Aug. 8, 1931; White to F. H. Payne, Sept. 1, 1931; White to General Douglas MacArthur, Sept. 10, 1931; White to MacArthur, Sept. 15, 1931; Major General George Van Horn Moseley to White, Sept. 21, 1931; Anna E. Oliver to Hoover, Aug. 10, 1932; Simon P. W. Drew to Joslin, May 13, 1931; Mrs. E. R. Matthews to Hoover, June 22, 1931; John I. A. Byrd to Hoover, Oct. 30, 1932; Moton to Hoover, Jan. 15, 1930; Moton to Hoover, Feb. 5, 1930. "Colored Question," Presidential Papers; Barnett to Hoover, Oct. 12, 1949. "Colored Question," Post Presidential Papers, HHPL.

52. White to Hoover, Aug. 15, 1930; Newton to White, Aug. 20, 1920; Memo, telephone call from Lewis Strauss, Oct. 14, 1930; LLS (Strauss) to Richey, Oct. 14, 1930; (Akerson) to Strauss, Oct. 22, 1930; White to Hoover, Nov. 13, 1930; James Marshall to Alan Fox, March 7, 1931; Hoover to Spingarn, June 23, 1931. "NAACP;" Trotter to Hoover, Nov. 4, 1930; Trotter and Spencer to Hoover, Feb. 7, 1931; Trotter to Hoover, Feb. 9, 1931. "Colored Question - Lynching," Presidential Papers, HHPL.

53. Trotter to Hoover, Dec. 7, 1931; Trotter to

Hoover, Jan. 6, 1932. "Colored Question -
Lynching;" Hoover to Attorney General, Dec. 31,
1931. "Prohibition Enforcement," Presidential
Papers, HHPL.

54. William D. Mitchell to Hoover, Jan. 6, 1932.
"Prohibition Enforcement;" Theodore Joslin to
Charles Curtis, March 21, 1932. "Colored
Question - Lynching;" Presidential Papers, HHPL.

55. Moton to Hoover, Jan. 15, 1930; Moton to Hoover,
Feb. 5, 1930; Moton to Newton, Feb. 22, 1930;
Barnett to Akerson, Nov. 19, 1930; Mordecai
Johnson to Ray Lyman Wilbur, Dec. 8, 1931; J. M.
Marquess to James M. Beck, May 26, 1932; W. C.
Hueston to Walter F. Brown, Oct. 10, 1931;
Clipping; The Afro-American, July 2, 1932;
Francis E. Rivers to Hoover, Nov. 11, 1932; Cobb
to Newton, July 9, 1932; Hawkins to Everett
Sanders, Aug. 4, 1932; Holsey to Rivers, Oct. 12,
1932. "Colored Question," White to Hoover,
March 5, 1932. "Interior: Howard;" Charles E.
Mitchell to Joseph McCuen, March 8, 1932.
"Diplomats: Mitchell;" Presidential Papers,
HHPL; Crisis, 38 (June, 1931), 207; Kansas City
Call, June 17, July 1, 1932; Charles H. Martin,
"Negro Leaders, The Republican Party, and the
Election of 1932," Phylon, 32 (Spring, 1971),
85-88.

56. E. L. Priest to Theodroe Joslin, n.d.; Newton,
File Memo, n.d. "Nat'l - Org;" Scott to Newton,
Feb. 12, 1932. "Reconstruction Finance
Corporation;" George W. Lawrence to Hoover, Sept.
21, 1932; Confidential Memo, n.d.; Requa to
Newton, April 28, 1932; Robert F. Leftridge to
Edgar Rickard, July 7, 1931; Leftridge to
Richard, Sept. 24, 1931; Francis E. Rivers to
Hoover, Nov. 10, 1932. "Colored Question;"
Ogden Mills to T. Arnold Hill, Sept., 1932;
White to Hoover, Sept. 10, 1932; Hoover to Ferry
K. Heath, Sept. 12, 1932; Heath to Hoover, Sept.
13, 1932; Heath to District Engineers,
Inspection and Construction Engineers, Oct. 4,
1932. "Government Contracts;" Presidential
Papers, HHPL; Crisis, 37 (Feb., 1930), 65;
Kansas City Call, Sept. 2, 1932.

57. Walls to Hoover, Sept. 17, 1932. "Colored
Question;" Clipping, New York Amsterdam News,
Oct. 12, 1932. "Powell;" Presidential Papers,

HHPL: Kansas City Call, Nov. 11, 18, 25, 1932;
William Griffin, "Black Insurgency in the
Republican Party of Ohio, 1920-1932," Ohio
History, 82 (Winter/Spring, 1973), 42, 43; David
Burner, The Politics of Provincialism: The
Democratic Party in Transition, 1918-1932, (New
York, 1970), 237-241; Samuel Lubell, White and
Black: Test of a Nation, (2nd ed., New York,
1964), 56, 57.

58. Radio Address of Herbert Hoover from White House
on 50th Anniversary of Tuskegee, April 14, 1931,
"Moton;" Hoover to Moton, Dec. 3, 1929.
"Commission Interracial," Presidential Papers,
HHPL; Wayne Cooper, "Claude McKay and the New
Negro of the 1920s," Phylon, 25 (Fall, 1964),
297-306; John B. Kirby, Black Americans in the
Roosevelt Era, (Knoxville, 1980), chapter 6.

59. St. Louis Argus, April 25, 1930; Kansas City
Call, April 18, 25, July 18, 1930; Richard L.
Watson, Jr., "The Defeat of Judge Parker; A Study
in Pressure Groups and Politics," Mississippi
Valley Historical Review, 50 (Sept., 1963),
213-234.

60. Holsey to Brown, July 8, 1932; Holsey to Rivers,
Oct. 12, 1932; C. H. Hueston to Hoover, April 25,
1929. "Colored Question;" Moton to Hoover,
April 15, 1929. "Moton;" Presidential Papers,
HHPL; James Weldon Johnson, "The Militant N. A.
A. C. P.," The Southern Workman, 57 (July, 1928),
241-248; Robert R. Moton, What The Negro Thinks,
(Garden City, 1929), 6-8, 13, 25-34, 69-94,
140-155; Crisis, 36 (June, 1929), 196.

61. V. F. Calverton, "The Negro's New Belligerent
Attitude," Current History, 30 (Sept., 1929),
1086.

FOOD FROM THE PUBLIC CRIB:
Agricultural Surpluses and Food Relief
under Herbert Hoover

by C. Roger Lambert

Herbert Clark Hoover, the first modern
technocrat-managerial president, entered office in
1929 with the prediction that, given the proper
policies, poverty would be banished from America. He
pledged that the farmer, who had not shared in the
prosperity of the 1920s, would be brought into the
mainstream of society through the modern efficiency of
the business world. Four years later, Hoover left the
presidency as one of the most thoroughly rejected of
all presidents. Although the high expectations and
excessive promises contributed to the repudiation, the
Hoover failure to achieve reform of the agricultural
industry and to deal with needs of the victims of the
Great Depression proved of greatest importance. In
the controversy over relief to agriculture and to
hungry Americans the positions and tone of three years
of debate over depression relief took form.(1)

In the Depression a large part of the American
people visibly confronted hunger as a prolonged
reality rather than a transitory sensation. In the
past the excess productivity of American farmers
provided far more of a problem than the possible
starvation of any significant number of people.
Agricultural productivity and relief for hungry
Americans became inextricably intertwined in the first
year of the Depression. As the hungry searched
through garbage for food, farmers, who could not
afford to sell their bounty, left crops to rot in the
fields. President Hoover was confronted with that
great "paradox of want in the midst of plenty."(2)
The way he met the challenge became perhaps the most
important political and personal issue of the
Depression. As one of the most emotional of issues,
food for hungry Americans involved the humanitarian
character of Herbert Hoover and his continuing concern
about the well being of individual Americans; it
involved the role of government in society in the most
fundamental of ways; and, above everything else, it
involved the character and political quality of
Herbert Hoover.

Hoover expressed a concept of a "New Era"
voluntary, cooperative, managerial, elitist society.

He placed his emphasis upon individualism but it was to be a special kind of individualism in which interest groups banded together for common purposes and the common good. Economic equality of opportunity for the individual would be retained but in the new complex society association was essential. Initiative would come from the bottom but guidance would come from the elite-managerial top. Government served as the advisor, inspirer, educator, and, at times, assistant, but almost never the regulator or controller. This would maintain the "American System" as a wondrous blend of the new technical-managerial era and the traditional values that had made America unique. Hoover envisioned the necessity for this cooperation in every element of society and was particularly concerned about bringing agriculture into the "new Era."(3)

Hoover and farm spokesmen, such as Henry C. Wallace, Secretary of Agriculture, and the backers of such measures as the McNary-Haugen proposal, differed over the nature of the farm problem and its solution. Farm spokesmen looked back to prosperous times and placed the blame for farm problems on wartime dislocations and the favored political position of industry. Hoover considered agriculture as perhaps "the most disorganized and chaotic" of all the "sick" industries. While the war caused some of the surplus, price and credit problems of the farmer, the basic problems were more fundamental. Farmers, Hoover believed, refused to develop efficient, businesslike control over their industry. Without such control the farmer could not give proper management to either marketing his product or to production. The farmer, Hoover insisted, had lost and would not regain the major part of the export market. "The farmer," he wrote in 1923, "is undoubtedly over producing for the present world consumption . . . and there is no remedy for the over producer except to reduce production." He projected that this reduction would be short because in "five or ten years from now we are going to be a food importing country."(4)

Hoover insisted that others did not understand the nature of the problem and would destroy the "American System" as they involved the federal government directly in the agricultural industry. He suggested that "being naturally socialistic in mind they turn to Socialism as a solution." The Hoover solution emphasized the development of cooperative marketing associations to give the farmer the same

kind of control over marketing and then production as
business men had over their product. As farmers
gained control over their market they would find a
method to resolve the surplus production problem.(5)
At the same time Hoover urged farmers to become more
businesslike, he preached the necessity of preserving
the traditional small independent-family farm:

> an individualistic business of small units
> and independent ownership. The farmer is
> the outstanding example of the economically
> free individual. He is one of our solid
> materials of national character. No
> solution that makes for consolidation into
> large farms and mechanical production can
> fit our national hopes and ideals.(6)

As with his broader vision for the entire society, the
Hoover farm program was based on the ideal of
preserving individual initiative as the base for
society, at the same time, erecting a cooperative
structure which would build in a primary concern for
the common good. He projected not only a long term
reform instead of immediate relief for farmers but
more fundamentally a basic change of human values.

Although Hoover admitted that the "excessive
individualism" of farmers made their integration into
his "New Era" difficult, the Agricultural Marketing
Act of 1929 seemed to give him the opportunity he
sought. The Federal Farm Board, created by the act,
received a $500,000,000 revolving fund with which to
sponsor cooperatives and make agriculture efficient.
Hoover insisted that aid for the farmer must be a
"long-term reform project," and he emphasized that the
board was "to build up farmer-owned and
farmer-controlled institutions for marketing the
farmer's crops." He believed that with better control
over his marketing the farmer could be guided to
better control his production. The AMA, not
completely a Hoover measure, expressed the aim of
putting agriculture "on a basis of economic equality
with other industries," a Hoover desire but not his
immediate objective. There was also a provision for
stabilization activities, which derived from the last
McNary-Haugen concept and constituted for many farm
spokesmen the most important element in the act. Some
clearly expected the Board to immediately use the
power to bring price relief for farmers. The AMA also
expressed the intent that the Board control excessive
production but did not spell out the method and Hoover

was unwilling to use anything beyond education.(7)

The Federal Farm Board confronted an unfortunate situation as production in some export crops such as wheat was high and the Great Depression forced prices down to a disastrous level. In its first months the Board sponsored cooperatives and marketing institutions such as the Farmers National Grain Corporation. This conformed to the Hoover vision of integrating the farmer into the "New Era," but the cautious Hoover reform program put the Board in the middle between the complaints of wheat farmers who demanded immediate price-raising and the grain dealers who considered the restrained action of the Board dangerous experimentation in socialism. The Farm Board never escaped this position as the Depression caused a price collapse and endangered the cooperative movement. The Board in an attempt to save the Hoover program launched a massive price-fixing effort. Although Alexander Legge, chairman of the board, insisted that the Board was not "Santa Claus," the Board controlled some 257 million bushels of wheat when it finally ceased buying wheat in June, 1931.(8)

Hoover, who had claimed that he knew more about price-fixing than anyone and would never do it again except in a world war, defended the Board action, but he was not happy with it. With the farmer receiving less than 30 cents per bushel on the farm, farmers were convinced the effort was a total failure. Some felt the purchases had been designed more to protect bankers than farmers. The buying of wheat protected the carefully nurtured cooperatives for a time and possibly held prices up somewhat but the effect was disaster for the Board. The vast store of wheat held by the Board and the price collapse destroyed the Hoover farm program.

The wheat represented a major challenge to the Hoover Administration. Even if the desire existed, with so much money already invested, price fixing could not be continued. Too, the wheat remained as a threat to the wheat market and to prices. Another element by the fall of 1930 was a developing demand that the wheat be used for food relief. Hoover had insisted, Joan Hoff Wilson has said, that "he did not want the country to be forced in the future to use food relief as a means of price support" thus that idea had little appeal for him.(9) If the provision of surpluses to needy Americans was an unacceptable course, the Board was left with control of excessive production.

From the colonial problems with surplus tobacco
to the 1920s, American farmers suffered occasional
over-production problems. Many unsuccessful efforts,
both legislative and voluntary, had been made to
limnit production, particularly in the first and third
decades of the twentieth century. The
McNary-Haugenites hoped to dump surpluses abroad.
Hoover, certain that would not succeed, preferred
planning through farmer-owned and farmer-directed
cooperatives to reduce production. Although the board
had used a degree of coercion to get participation
with the cooperative movement, it limited its
curtailment efforts to persuasion. From its inception
the Board advocated the policy of reducing acreage.
In July 1930, Alexander Legge and Arthur M. Hyde,
Secretary of Agriculture, launched an impressive
campaign of education throughout the major winter
wheat region from Nebraska to Texas and urged a 10 to
25 percent reduction in acreage. Legge warned:(10)

> the government is not to solve the farmer's
> troubles but the farmer must solve them. It
> is his job. I'm telling you what you ought
> to do. Do as you please. I am in a position
> to tell any man to go to hell and I don't
> care what you do.

Legge concentrated on Kansas, where he met strong
opposition and told the editors of a Wichita newspaper
"to go to hell."(11) The campaign was vigorous; the
message was, in good part, correct; and it was
rejected.

The Legge message countered the basic instinct of
the farmer and the economic realities as farmers
understood them. It also conflicted with the
educational emphasis of the Department of Agriculture
since its beginning on increasing output. Farmers who
responded to the campaign through the Kansas City Star
questioned the morality of cutting production, raised
the point of underconsumption, and doubted the
economic value:(12)

> I consider the plan hot air. If his [Legge
> plan] would work with 10 per cent reduction,
> why is wheat selling so cheap now in face of
> the federal farm board after such a poor
> harvest which will equal much more than the
> 10 per cent . . .

Others raised the issue of hunger:

> Let's not let anyone go hungry if it can be
> helped. We may not get rich, but there is a
> chance to get fat. Now boys get busy raise
> all you can, don't pay any attention to this
> bunc [sic] of the farm board.

Control of farm output was widely debated during
the twenties with Henry A. Wallace leading a voluntary
reduction campaign as early as 1921. Before the end
of the decade many farm leaders advocated various
approaches to curtail output. Most of them recognized
that voluntary restriction was not adequate but were
reluctant to take the next step. Other approaches
such as greater efficiency, movements to large-scale
mechanization, development of factory farms,
price-fixing, or even the elimination of the less
effective farmers had more appeal than some form of
compulsory crop control.(13) With the failure of the
Board reduction campaign, Secretary Hyde emphasized a
land withdrawal scheme and land utilization became
popular with many farm spokesmen. The Board wanted to
withdraw acreage from cultivation and to restore the
wood lot. Some even adopted the domestic allotment
concept which increasingly represented the movement
toward some form of compulsory reduction program.(14)
Hoover felt that reduction was inevitable but it must
come through the process of education--the voluntary
decision by the individual farmer guided by his
cooperative leaders.

As farm leaders, except for some of the
McNary-Haugen people, prepared themselves and their
followers to accept forced reduction of production,
prices on most farm crops had collapsed with wheat
bringing about one-third of its pre-crash price.
Farmers were storing grain on the ground, leaving it
in the fields or destroying crops they could not sell,
while starving people were rummaging through garbage
cans and city dumps for enough to survive.(15)

Not many made the leap of reconciling the
"paradox of want in the midst of plenty" by providing
food to the needy. Herbert Hoover, before the
President's Agricultural Commission in 1925, had
emphasized "increased domestic consumption" as a
possibility for reducing the agricultural surplus.
This could only be achieved through "a higher general
buying power" and a "higher standard of living of the

whole population." Hoover believed that there was
room for a 20 to 30 per cent increase in
consumption.(16)

Farm leaders remained more concerned about
reducing production to raise prices than feeding the
hungry, but some farmers seemed more aware of the
paradox and talked about the "millions of unemployed
that cannot buy" or the "wrath of God if I should
slack my best effort to supply food." Some spokesmen
seemed convinced that there was an unlimited need for
all the food they could supply to feed the always
starving Chinese as well as the hungry Americans if
only some way could be found to get the food where it
was needed. Few Americans voiced the view that the
greatest productivity of American farms was a
potential blessing rather than a growing curse. One
observer compared Hoover to the ancient Pharaoh: "What
a pity our Herbert lacked the wisdom of that old
Egyptian king! He could have found a Joseph who would
have known what to do with that pesky surplus."(17)
In contrast, a prominent Hoover correspondent
complained that farmers who had been "the backbone of
this country" were being foreclosed and proposed that
the Farm Board should buy "from one hundred to two
hundred million bushels of wheat and dump it into the
Gulf of Mexico, the Atlantic and Pacific Oceans and
into the Great Lakes. This will do away with the
visible supply absolutely."(18) The issue of food for
hungry Americans became significant politically in the
fall of 1930 with the major drought adding millions to
the Depression caused hungry. The question quickly
developed as to federal responsibility to feed the
hungry.

In the summer of 1930 the greatest drought in
modern history (prior to 1934) hit much of the country
but centered in the Ohio and Mississippi River
Valleys. By the end of July crop failure was
widespread, hungry livestock were being sacrificed,
wells were going dry, streams and even the Mississippi
River were slowing to trickles, heat and perhaps
hunger brought human death. Mark Sullivan reported
that President Hoover turned to the drought with
something akin to eagerness. His success in the
Presidency had not been spectacular, but this was the
kind of disaster he knew and had handled many times in
the past. He cancelled his vacation and turned to the
drought. He ordered investigations of the conditions,
he met with John Barton Payne, president of the Red
Cross. He called the drought state governors to

163.

Washington and then established a National Drought
Committee headed by Arthur Hyde of the Agriculture
Department.(19) Governors were instructed to
establish drought committees, the railroads were asked
to lower rates and he told the country that the crisis
would be handled. Newspapermen and much of the
country agreed that no better man could be in charge
of such a disaster. The great opportunity for Hoover
to demonstrate his capacity, to rally the country, to
turn attention from the previous lack of success
resulted in the first major battle over relief.

The Hoover program emphasized credit expansion,
lower transportation rates, farm loans for livestock
and crop production in 1931, with the relief of human
suffering left to the Red Cross. The question of food
for hungry drought victims became the controversial
aspect of the program. Local committees made up of
bankers, prominent farmers, county agents, and Red
Cross representatives, with the state drought
committees drawn from the same types were to
investigate and report needs and supervise the relief.
Two conferences were held in Washington in the late
fall to discuss federal assistance. The State
Commissioners of Agriculture and the state drought
chairmen reported needs for food, feed, and seed that
might reach 120 million dollars; but, after
consultation with Congressman James B. Aswell of
Louisiana and Secretary Hyde, the request was set at
60 million dollars. Aswell declared that Hyde checked
with Hoover and was told to go ahead with the request.
After Aswell introduced the measure, the
Administration immediately brought forth a measure
that called for only 25 million dollars and excluded
any food for humans. Aswell charged that food was
"eliminated by a scheme, a political trick." He
considered C.W. Warburton, agriculture extension
director, to be in large part responsible and insisted
that Warburton had his mind made up before any of the
evidence was presented. This, he charged, "is the
cheapest, political pinhead action I have ever had
thrust in my face." While Warburton insisted that he
had always doubted the granting of government loans,
Hyde declared that he:

> personally regard[ed] loans by the Federal
> Government upon security that is so thin, in
> many cases, that it approaches the vanishing
> point as a dangerous step toward the dole
> system in this country. If we make loans to
> farmers for food and clothing, then by the

same token we should make loans to laboring
men who are unemployed or otherwise in
distress.

Aswell felt betrayed and questioned the political
integrity of both Hoover and Hyde. The Administration
apparently became concerned about the security of
loans--Hyde often expressed concern about the
repayment record and ability of farmers. More
important, perhaps, the Administration worried about
the drought aid providing a precedent for general
depression relief.

While unemployment bread and soup lines attracted
attention, and many questioned the ability of private
charity and local governments to feed the hungry, the
drought victims provided a clearer case for the
advocates of federal relief. A bitter debate
continued for weeks in Congress and the press.
Letters to the Administration described extreme need
and questioned the reluctance of Hoover to provide
aid. Newspapers sent reporters into the drought area
and printed descriptions of need that many Americans
found difficult to accept. Southern Congressmen,
joined by Insurgent Republicans, questioned the Hoover
knowledge of conditions, compared his great
humanitarian concern for the European victims of
hunger and his reputation as the world's "greatest
relief" expert. They pointed to the inadequacy of the
Red Cross aid, and successfully branded Hoover with
inhumanity if not stupidity. Hoover later recalled
that they made him appear "heartless."(21) From
Arkansas came reports of a food riot and possible
deaths from hunger; from Missouri came the description
of a "soup line in our school" because it was
discovered that children came with only a turnip for
lunch "and some not even that." In the drought area
the Red Cross had distributed turnip seeds and a
bumper crop was produced. In Arkansas and Missouri
the terms "Hoover hogs" (rabbits) and "Hoover apples"
(turnips) became popular. Some complained that their
blood was turning to turnip juice. One survivor
reported that the milk and everything else they ate,
drank, and touched, tasted or smelled like
turnips.(22)

The Red Cross food assistance was meager, in some
cases providing less than 7 cents per day against 85
cents for prisoners in the Little Rock (Pulaski
County) jail. Even the Red Cross admitted that this
assistance might be considered by some a "cruel jest"

but then defended itself by insisting that "it gave
the recipient all the food he needed of the kind to
which he had been accustomed."(23)   The Red Cross had
pledged five million dollars to food relief, but the
national officials did not want to publicize that it
had the money or that the national organization would
come into the relief.   From September through December
the organizastion emphasized self-help, it supplied
garden seed and it urged local responsibility.   There
were major efforts by local communities but with the
virtual collapse of the entire economy in states such
as Arkansas, the efforts were of limited value.(24)

        Congressmen expressed doubt that five million
dollars would provide enough relief for the one to two
million needy persons.   Senator Elmer Thomas of
Oklahoma charged that the Red Cross had a fund of 44
million dollars which it could use and wondered why
the organization was so miserly.   Others argued that
no human should be required to survive on the measly
provision of the Red Cross when the federal government
provided eight dollars a month to feed a mule in
Mississippi for a month, while the Red Cross provided
only $11.67 to feed a family of five for a month.   An
Arkansas congressman questioned the moral character of
an Administration that "would feed Jackasses but
wouldn't feed starving babies."   Senator Tom Connally
of Texas warned that during the French Revolution some
of the ministers, when told that the people were
hungry had said, "'Let them eat grass'.   We are going
to buy hay for animals, and the attitude of the
Administration undoubtedly is that if the people are
really hungry let them eat hay. . . ."   Connally then
compared the Hoover relief in Europe:

        true these people were not living in
        America; they were not of our flesh and
        blood; they were not our own kinsmen; they
        were not our own constituents; they were not
        citizens who had some right to look to this
        government for generous treatment; they were
        people living in Russia.

Hoover, he charged, thought it "sound and safe" to
give money to Russians but not to loan to Americans.
Hoover, said Connally, appeared before a congressional
committee to advocate an "appropriation of $20,000,000
to feed hungry Russians, hungry Bolsheviks, hungry men
with long whiskers (laughter) and wild ideas."   Hoover
wanted and got money to feed hungry Russians suffering
from drought but he refused to feed hungry

Americans.(25)

Senator Royal Copeland of New York touched
the same note:

When I hear it suggested that a man who did
so much for the relief of starving people in
other countries in any way whatever
interfering with the relief of American
citizens who are starving, I simply can not
believe it possible. There must be some
mistake.

Senator Thomas J. Helfin of Alabama raised the return
by the treasury of some 160 million dollars in tax
refunds with one estate in Massachusetts getting some
16 million dollars and questioned the reaction of
drought victims when they see the rich getting money
of this quantity and:

they see their loved ones starving, sick and
dying, it is enough to make Bolshevists out
of them, it might make communists out of
them, worse than that, it is enough to drive
them mad.

The same points were made in letters to the President
for the next three years. People were simply not able
to understand how "the great humanitarian" could set
idly by and let his people starve. Some suggested
that if the Americans would move to Russia, or half
way round the world, Hoover would be eager to feed
them.(26)

Senator George Norris of Nebraska asked "are we
going to let people die of starvation because it may
establish a precedent that will be difficult to
overcome in the future? Norris blamed Hoover for the
situation: "We can not get an appropriation for food
for human beings because of the power and influence of
the President of the United States." The Hoover view
prevailed in the House of Representatives and blocked
the 60 million dollar loan which provided food aid.
Subsequent attempts failed to provide food from
federal funds either through separate federal grants
of food money to the Red Cross or direct federal loans
to individuals. Hoover sent his friend, Mark
Sullivan, to Senator William Borah to seek his
assistance. Sullivan met limited success. He
reported that Borah suggested that Hoover talk to
Senator Joe T. Robinson of Arkansas. Soon a

167.

compromise was worked out between Hoover and Robinson
which permitted a 20 million dollar loan for
rehabilitating in addition to the earlier 45 million
dollar seed and feed loan which was not supposed to be
used for food. After two and one-half months of
bitter and devisive debate Congress had appropriated
65 million dollars to aid drought victims instead of
the original Aswell proposal of 60 million dollars.
The value of the program to the poorest was
negligible. Farmers with adequate security could get
loans. The poor tenant farmers, the share-croppers
and other poor farmers remained dependent upon Red
Cross charity. President Hoover subjected himself to
several months of humiliating and disastrous attack
upon his prestige and highly acclaimed concern for
suffering humanity. He gave way ultimately to much
that his opponents had wanted but with every
appearance of poor grace, and he "forfeited the relief
issue."(27)

     The press also debated the Hoover program. From
almost universal praise and expression of high
expectation in August, 1930, there developed bitter
criticism by late winter. Paul Anderson, a respected
commentator for the Nation, suggested that only a
"mining engineer" such as Hoover could "dig a home as
deep" as Hoover over the food relief issue. The
conflict, said Anderson, degenerated into a "blood
feud." Some questioned the distinction Hoover made
between national relief as a dole and private or local
government aid as the traditional American way:

     Bread lines and soup kitchens, according to
     Mr. Hoover nourish and sustain self-respect
     and dignity, provided private and local
     public philanthropy alone finance these
     authentic American institutions. Such
     reasonings cannot be taken seriously.

     The Memphis Commercial-Appeal editorialized, "If
starvation is such now that only doles can prevent
disease, suffering and starvation, then let us have
them," and warned that the President might bring about
the very thing he sought to prevent. Another
journalist charged that Hoover "had no sense of
actuality. Facts and statistics, when unpleasant,
leave him, the engineer and economist cold and
indifferent. No wonder his tools and hirelings doctor
and manipulate statistics and distort painful facts."
Heywood Broun expressed the view of many: "No hungry
man has ever been denied the benefit of an optimistic

Presidential statement."(28) Denial of food was a
"no-win" situation no matter the reason. The drought
victims provided a ready and easy group to portray.

From the hills of Appalachia in the middle of the
drought debate came a protest that miners had asked
the Red Cross for "bread and were given a stone."
Drought on top of depression, strikes and the decline
in the industry had brought disaster. Children, it
was reported, were begging on the highways. Grace
Abbott, head of the Children's Bureau, reported that
conditions were appalling. Her group told the
President's Emergency Committee on Employment (PECE)
that "many people are suffering a slow form of
starvation . . . even the partially employed can not
earn enough to feed their families . . . . But the
towns are too poor to do anything about it." An
investigator reported that "probably one-third of the
families are living on starvation rations." In one
town, a store owner said that "half the people were
living on beans, bread and syrup."(29) By late 1930
it became clear that local relief where it existed was
virtually exhausted. Members of PECE, created by
Hoover in October 1930 to arouse local spirit and
local responsibility, began to pressure the Red Cross
and the President for some action. One PECE
memorandum remarked:

> Within our committee and in the minds of
> every group outside with whom I have
> conferred, the feeling is unanimous that the
> poor law machinery of states and local
> communities is with the exception of very
> few cities and counties wholly inadequate .
> . . .

In February another memorandum urged that the
Agriculture Department liberalize its loan policy and
that the Red Cross end its concern about why people
were hungry and start feeding them. In March, Fred C.
Croxton of PECE warned:

> Public sympathy is easily aroused by hungry
> people anxious to work but unable to secure
> work, and the time is sure to come when
> local food supplies will be taken possession
> of by hungry folk unless conditions can be
> improved.(30)

Within weeks after its creation, representatives
of PECE urged a takeover of food relief by the only

national charity, the Red Cross, and talked about
federal money to assist in food relief. In early
February, 1931, Arthur Woods, head of PECE, met with
Hoover and Payne. The President asked the Red Cross
to assist in the hunger situation among coal miners.
Payne refused but agreed to quietly look at the
problem. The Red Cross bureaucracy again opposed aid
and Hoover turned to the American Friends Service
Committee. Clarence Pickett, director of the Friends,
reported that Grace Abbott was sent to the Friends.
Hoover supplied approximately 225,000 dollars left
from the American Relief Administration Children's
Fund. Within five months the Friends were feeding
some 40,000 children in 563 communities. The state
and local communities had exhausted their funds, said
Pickett.(31)

Hoover continued his efforts to get the Red Cross
to give aid or to supply funds to the Friends. The
Red Cross, the President argued, was the only agency
that could meet the needs:

> likely to be formulated as a charge that
> the Red Cross is not taking care of the
> whole of the people. . . . In fact we have
> no other agency to turn to at the present
> time to take care of these segments of our
> distress problems.(32)

James Fieser, vice-chairman of the Red Cross, in a
confidential memorandum to Payne warned against the
involvement. The PECE group led by Croxton, Fieser
said, had been trying for months to involve the Red
Cross:

> In fact some of our people felt that he was
> leading the agitators of the question. . . .
> We have had repeated discussions with Porter
> R. Lee, Mr. Croxton, Frank Bane and others
> of Colonel Wood's organization, pointing out
> the unwisdom of nationalizing the . . .
> relief situation.

The idea of nationalizing hit home for both Payne
and Hoover. Fieser argued that the Red Cross
committees and donations came from the best people of
each neighborhood, and he warned that some committee
chairmen had already threatened resignation if the
organization provided aid to hungry miners. Donations
would probably suffer and they feared involvement in
the labor dispute between owners and miners.(33) The

Red Cross refused any real involvement and the
Friends, with limited funds, restricted their aid to
some feeding programs for school children. One
Friends worker reported that adults were not receiving
relief from any source and at a:

> "little colored school" . . . "the teacher"
> reported "that every day after lunch has
> been served to the children some of the
> adults . . . come in and beg for what is
> left over. . . ."

Apparently there was a growing distress in the
PECE organization centered on the belief that the
President was mistaking words for accomplishments.
Woods left PECE and wrote Hoover that the states were
at the "limit of resources" and urged that something
must be done for local resources were unable to bear
the burden of relief.(34) Again the President had
sought to use local sources, arouse a spirit of
neighborly giving, called upon the national charity
organization--with little success--and then brought
the American Friends into the relief situation. The
Friends, unable to raise adequate funds, provided
limited stop-gap aid but accomplished little. Hoover
did not get as much political heat from the mining
situation as the drought but the pleas for aid, the
protests and the hunger marches continued to the end
of his Administration.(35)

"It burns me up," a North Dakotan wrote the
President in late summer of 1930, "That we should
produce an over supply of wheat and still part of the
world should be starving to death." The writer
insisted that wheat growers were ready to give up to
20 per cent of their bounty for charity:

> The American farmers are at heart the most
> generous people in the world. A nation wide
> Christian act would lift the rural life
> above the present discontent and unrest.(36)

This was the spirit that the President sought to
arouse but he failed to take advantage of it. Many
people in that first Great Depression winter urged
that he use the vast store of surplus wheat to feed
the hungry. Governor Huey Long of Louisiana, Governor
John Pollard of Virginia, Senator Joe Robinson,
William Gibbs McAddo and a host of others now saw the
use of surplus wheat as a logical and appropriate way
to resolve the paradox of "want in the midst of

plenty." Pollard added that all it would take would
be a word from the President. Alexander Legge of the
Farm Board announced that the Board would be willing
to sell the wheat at a good price or on the credit to
any of the charity organizations. Others presented a
variety of worthy or "crackpot" ways to use the wheat.
One group argued that the wheat, without any
processing, made the most nearly perfect of foods.(37)

There is no evidence that the President ever gave
consideration to relief use of surplus farm
commodities. As Governor Pollard said, it would only
take one word from the President. He did not give it.
The government printed a bulletin advocating that
farmers feed the lower price wheat to their livestock
instead of corn. Measures to distribute Farm Board
wheat to the needy appeared in Congress in late 1930
but the distribution was delayed until the spring of
1932 when Congress turned over some 85 million bushels
to the Red Cross for the hungry. Although Senator
Robinson suggested that this might be considered a
federal dole and that everyone knew the President
opposed the measure, Hoover could not afford to veto
so limited a relief measure at that late date. Five
years later, Larry Richey, secretary and friend to
Hoover, claimed that the Hoover Administration bought
85 million bushels of wheat and distributed it "as a
gift" to the starving.(38) In essence this was
untrue. As in the previous food relief issues, Hoover
managed to avoid either political or humanitarian
credit.

In mid-1932 an acquaintance of White House staff
member French Strother, questioned whether the
Administration truly understood the human suffering in
the land. Why had President Hoover, who had
demostrated more awareness "to the sufferings of
humanity" than any man alive, failed to get across to
the nation that his eyes have seen and his ears heard
"the cause of humanity." Hoover, she urged, should
"take the side of the forgotten millions. . . .   Will
not the fine true man in Washington, of whom we all
hoped so much, take the lead?"(39)   It was impossible
to plead ignorance. Hoover had every access to the
information. Strother replied:

> I would stake my life on it that nobody in
> the world is more concerned over the human
> problems of the hour, and that nobody in the
> world understands better their human meaning

in terms of the individual person in
distress than he. I am also convinced that
nobody has a better understanding of the
practical means by which to provide the
maximum of effective relief.(40)

If ignorance of the conditions is not the answer,
historians must still ask the question. Why did the
"master of emergencies" fail first and most completely
in precisely that area where experience, knowledge and
desire best equipped him to achieve success? Why did
he remain adamant that the policy followed must be his
policy even when it clearly was not working? This is
seen in farm policy, the drought and the other food
relief issues. The easy answer of political
philosophy--that the President was above the easy,
political or pragmatic action--can not be considered
adequate. In 1920 he advocated practicality and
accepted the nomination of Warren G. Harding to the
presidency. In 1932 he sent Secretary Hyde to the
northern plains to "stage a little drama" for the
farmers in hope it might bring political benefit. The
compromise with Senator Robinson also indicates that
when he felt it essential Hoover could act in a
pragmatic fashion.(41) It could be argued that Hoover
failed to comprehend the nature of the crisis until
too late. This is clearly true in the drought and
almost certainly the broader Depression. It became
clear during the drought issue that both Hoover and
the Red Cross had difficulty adjusting their concept
of the nature of the drought problem. They tended to
think in terms of a traditional disaster such as a
flood or earthquake. The slow, creeping pervasive
nature of this disaster which ultimately weakened and
virtually destroyed many of the bases of the affected
communities made the drought and the Depression
something very different from the Mississippi flood
crisis that Hoover had handled with more skill. While
this may explain the early attitude of the President,
it does not provide a complete answer.

In his effort to integrate the farmer into his
"New Era," Hoover sought to perpetuate agriculture as
a "calling." Agriculture developed as no other
economic activity, "strong individualism,
independence, character, initiative, and resources."
The farmer was in "close contact with nature" and was
thus "free from a certain artificiality of urban life"
and was thus less likely to submit "to the insidious
forces of moral degeneration."(42) This ideal farm
life Hoover tied to the small family farm; it may also

be traced to his own rural boyhood. He insisted that
it must be preserved as the farmer was guided and
educated in business-like methods.

It could be argued that the Hoover farmer did not
exist even during his rural boyhood and certainly not
in the twenties. It is impossible to see how the
Hoover program would do much if anything to preserve
the viability of the small subsistence farmer.
Commercial farmers might talk in terms of the superior
nature of their way of life but by the time of the
Depression, indeed much earlier, their primary concern
was economic improvement not reform and not some
romantic vision of their "calling." Hoover's farm
plan faced failure even before the crash; it was
inevitable with the 63 per cent drop in farm prices.
As the Depression brought economic collapse,
bankruptcy, the inability to get food from the farm to
the hungry, Alexander Legge, Hoover's first chairman
of the Farm Board, moved on to the domestic
allotment--but not Hoover.(43) The President was so
devoted to his mythical concept of the farmer and the
values of family farm life that he was unwilling to
risk any subversion of that dream. In his refusal to
go beyond his established plan, he forgot something he
said in 1925:

> The higher qualities of human nature, the
> qualities of character which we hold the
> choicest attributes of humanity, flowered
> when man met a measure of success in his
> economic struggle. Starvation does not
> produce these things.(44)

The farmer--for the most part--suffered starvation
only in the figurative sense but the call "to duty"
which Hoover made to him and to all Americans in the
midst of the Depression met the reality of
"starvation," in the sense of the economic
deprivation, for the society.

The hunger problem existed before and outside the
drought of 1930-31, but the drought projected it upon
the national stage. The President met the problem as
he had met previous emergencies. He sought to arouse
the psychology of self-help, the selfless spirit of
giving. He created a bureaucracy of committees from
Washington down to the local community, manned by
those successful types who could give the right
guidance. He called upon the Red Cross to provide
assistance to those who could not help themselves.

When he created the President's Emergency Committee
for Employment in October, 1930, he designed the
organization in the same way for the same ends. He
told the people that as a nation we must prevent
"hunger and cold to those of our people who are in
honest difficulties."(45) He would use the same
refrain as he sought to block federal food aid and to
arouse the people to the call of that duty:

> It is unthinkable that any of our people
> should be allowed to suffer from hunger or
> want. The heart of the nation will not
> permit it. . . . It is a call to
> citizenship and to generousity in time of
> trial. . . .(46)

He insisted that the battle with Congress was not over
whether the country would "maintain the spirit of
charity and mutual self-help through voluntary giving"
or impair and perhaps destroy something "infinitely
valuable" to the life of Americans. He pledged that
"if the time should ever come that the voluntary
agencies . . . together with the local and state
governments" were unable to feed the hungry he would
use every resource of the federal government. There
was, however, "no such paralysis" among the American
people. This was a period when "character and courage
are on trial, and where the very faith that is within
us is under test." If Americans would hold to their
traditions and the ideals of the American system, they
could come out of this test "stronger in character, in
courage, and in faith."(47)

An exchange between Hoover and Perry Davidson, a
correspondent, revealed something of the personality
and beliefs of the President. Davidson wrote that the
federal government must take over relief, for the
"communities are impotent; statement governments are
shot through with politics and political motives;
local charities are jaded, discouraged, bankrupt,
disorganized, discredited. Their task is too great.
Their support is gone." A three and one-half page
response was drafted which was bitter and almost
vicious in nature. "This nation," it said, "did not
grow great from feeding upon the malignant pessimist
of calamity mongers or weeping men, and prosperity for
all our people will not be restored by the voluble
wailings of word-sobbers nor by any legislative
legerdemain proposed by theorists who are without
responsibility. . . ." The letter which actually went
to Davidson was only one page in length but equally

nasty in tone. Hoover suggested that Davidson had lost his "nerve." "Many of the best soldiers," the letter continued, "that we have sent to the front have given way for an instant and yet have proved themselves the staunchest and most courageous of men." The President concluded that he had more faith in Davidson's "better second thought." Hoover could not accept that the better qualities, the superiority he found in Americans, had faltered. William Allen White was correct when he described the President as "a hundred percenter in his passionate almost bigoted belief in America." Hoover's belief that his method was the ony one consistent with the American System was, as Craig Lloyd said, "virtually ingrained."(48)

Hoover was not alone in his conviction, as William Appleman Williams has said, "that you let the system come apart at the seams rather than violate the principles by saving the system for the people." The supporter who urged, "Roman nation and civilization fell when they fed the mob from the public crib. History will call you savior of our institutions and civilization," was not unique.(49) Hoover clearly believed that the people must save their own system through traditional institutions.

The Hoover program failed in part, because starvation does not produce "the higher qualities of human nature" and because, as one of Hoover's correspondents warned, the rich "have not been voluntary nor liberal" in their giving to feed the hungry. Too, the issue became political. The President charged that his opponents were "playing politics with human misery" but his opponents felt he was playing a deceitful brand of politics. His administration violated what some considered an agreement on drought aid. He used the Red Cross to perform what some considered a governmental responsibility and in the process he made that organization a political issue.(50) More fundamentally, Hoover and the Red Cross failed in a practical sense to meet the need. The President never accepted the warning that "this is a condition and not a theory" the country faces and thus both he and the Red Cross made a basic under-estimation of the crisis.

If the drought had occurred under prosperous conditions, local credit institutions and local charity might have fulfilled the duties as Hoover saw them. Instead, local credit institutions either collapsed or refused to make loans and local charity

was quickly exhausted. The federal loans were
surrounded by so much red tape, delay and banker types
that it caused many problems. The Red Cross
assistance was so limited that it provided less than
the "hard-hearted" landlords in their provisioning,
and, the Red Cross permitted itself to become a tool
of the planter aristocracy. With planters and bankers
dominating the local committees, they restricted aid
and forced blacks, in particular, to work for aid.
Hoover apparently considered attacking his
congressional opponents for serving as the tools of
southern planters to maintain their workers in a state
of peonage. The charge probably had validity for
Senator Robison, but it was also true of the Red Cross
and the Hoover program.(51)

     Hoover failed to heed the warning of Will Rogers
who helped to raise money for the Red Cross drought
effort, ". . . you let this country get hungry and
they are going to eat, no matter what happens to
budgets, income taxes, or Wall Street values.
Washington mustn't forget who rules when it comes to a
showdown." Hoover cited the budget as a reason for
not spending money on relief as early as December
1930. This would be used more and more frequently.
Del Papa suggests that Hoover first used the word
"dole" as a fright tool and later used the budget to
prevent relief money.(52) While there may have been
some political use of the idea of an unbalanced
budget, Hoover was sincerely fearful of the effects,
and the Democrats were as devoted to the idea of a
balanced budget. Many, however, felt that Hoover's
priorities were wrong. While he insisted that relief
funds would endanger the budget, the government spent
money on other things thus ignoring the warning of
Rogers.

     The President put his reliance on the Red Cross
to back up local charity. Use of the Red Cross fitted
perfectly his concept of the proper use of individual
responsibility and avoidance of statism. His faith
was misplaced. The Red Cross contained many of the
bureaucratic evils he feared in the development of
statism. The organization was also reluctant to go
beyond what Payne and Fieser considered to be its
traditional boundaries. It feared a large drought
program would drag it into general Depression relief
and it feared the effects of such aid on donations.
The leaders were as devoted to the American System
concept as Hoover. By the spring of 1932 the Red
Cross would be prepared to undertake a larger role in

relief activities but the structural change came
slowly and with considerable reluctance.(53) The
leaders were as eager to delude themselves as the
President.

Joan Hoff Wilson, Craig Lloyd and others have
pointed to a lifetime history on the part of Hoover at
self-delusion. Some have gone so far as to cite
intentional deceit as a part of the Hoover character.
Wilson goes back to his business career. Pete Daniel,
in a study of the Mississippi flood, suggests that
Hoover submitted false information on drowning
victims.(54) It is, of course, natural for any man in
or out of presidential politics to seek to put his
record in the best light. In the food issue there is
a record of careful selection of what was to go on the
public record, a number of instances of apparent
self-delusion and even what might be considered
twisting of the facts. Early in the drought crisis
James P. Goodrich of Indiana wrote the President that
the drought had been greatly exaggerated. The
President responded:

> Your report is much as I suspected . . . a
> great deal of it will recover
> psychologically after the first shock. I
> have always found that when you set up
> assurances in these matters, it tends to
> decrease the load. People begin to consider
> then what they can do for themselves.(55)

Hoover wanted to believe that the drought reports were
greatly exaggerated and that a little assurance from
him would have a major influence. He insisted that
the demands came more from selfish economic and
political motives than from need. In spite of reports
of great need, even after January, 1931, from the Red
Cross, he questioned that conditions were as bad as
they said. The same attitude is found in his
continued insistence that no one had starved and that
human health was better than before, In the third
winter of the Depression he responded to Walter
Gifford, head of the President's Organization on
Unemployment Relief who had told him that most of the
states could get through the winter with little
difficulty, the suggestion that "if we could have the
sum of five to ten millions of dollars placed at your
disposal . . . we could certainly avoid all the
infinite evils of the Federal Government entering into
this problem." He suggested that Gifford, whose
reputation as an expert in the problems of need was

clearly suspect, should contact some of the
"substantial men" to raise the fund.(56) Del Papa
points to the first effort to make a statistical study
of the unemployment problem. The report, completed by
experts, was subjected to reinterpretation by the
President so as to cut by over half the number of
unemployed. Although Hoover insisted upon a reliance
of scientific fact gathering and the creation of
bodies of experts to provide guidance, he had a
tendency to ignore reports which did not conform to
his judgment. Thus the drought committees and the
state commissioners of agriculture knew less than he
did about the needs. The PECE desire for stronger
action was wrong. The reports that the Red Cross aid
was failing and that the drought loans were inadequate
were ignored.(57)

     Hoover demonstrated throughout his public career
a bitter suspicion of Congress and a questioning of
the motives of individual congressmen. He sought in
the drought relief issue to operate without or outside
of Congress which was his customary pattern. He
apparently believed that his committee structure with
its voluntary spirit, its arousal of grass roots
involvement brought a more true expression of the
American spirit than the politicized constitutional
structure. This was true, of course, for his entire
system which would remove everything of importance
from the inefficient and corrupting influence of the
political arena. Even so he was ready to ignore his
own structure when it differed from his wishes.

     Although Hoover emphasized the idea of
traditional relief methods and certainly a majority of
the country agreed with him in the early stages of the
Depression, Congress, press and others pointed to a
120 year history of federal appropriations for
emergencies such as the drought. Even if the Hoover
tradition was the more accurate one for prolonged
disaster, Hoover, with his record for humanitarian
relief, could have secured almost any action he wanted
in the winter of 1930-31. Hoover, as Jordan Schwarz
makes clear, maintained basic control over Congress at
least until the spring of 1932.(58) Thus, the
President was responsible for the lack of food relief.
In the process he forfeited the relief role to the
Democrats and Congress and set the tone of debate over
the issue which lasted until he left the presidency.

     Hoover had alternatives which stayed within the
tradition as he outlined it. In the fall of 1930 he

considered a great private fund drive which would be used by the great charity organizations for relief. He and PECE officials talked to the Red Cross and the Community Chests about such a joint drive. Some of the charity leaders feared the effects of a national drive upon local fund raising and he retreated. There was also the great voluntary effort found in the donation of some 623 carloads of food and other goods for the drought. Throughout the period the President was urged to sponsor a vast donation of surplus agricultural commodities to the needy. There were various gleaning efforts that might have received more encouragement.(59) All of these--as complex as implementation might have been--stayed within the boundaries set by the President.

The overall effects of such efforts might be questioned but the sponsorship would have contributed to that spirit Hoover sought and would have represented an effort to do something. But the President proved timid, particularly in the fund drive, when he might have been better served with the more traditional stubbornness.

The Hoover personality influenced his refusal to change course on both farm and food policy. His life experience convinced him that he understood the American System as few others did, that he could rise above self-interest and look to the long term value structure. Opponents seemed socialistic or pork-barrel politicians. The Hoover drive to succeed as the leader into a "New Era" contributed to the Hoover reluctance to admit that he was wrong about food relief needs. To admit failure where he should have had the greatest success came too close to questioning his concept of himself and the American Society. Theodore G.Joslin, secretary to the President, wrote: "Figuratively, he was the father protecting his family against the troubles impending, shouldering their burdens for them, keeping the 'bad news' to himself."(60) Human character and human value systems were the base of the Hoover system. He refused to participate in any action that might weaken the character and destroy the system.

FOOTNOTES

1. The volume of historical material on Hoover and
    the Hoover Presidency has exploded in the last
    fifteen years. Among the works of greatest
    importance to this study have been: Joan Hoff
    Wilson, Herbert Hoover; Forgotten Progressive
    (Boston: Little, Brown and Company, 1975); Ellis
    W.Hawley, The Great War and the Search for a
    Modern Order: A History of the American People
    and their Institutions, 1917-1933 (New York:
    St.Martin's Press, 1979); Albert U. Romasco, The
    Poverty of Abundance; Hoover, the Nation, the
    Depression (New York): Oxford University Press,
    1965); J.Joseph Huthmacher and Warren I. Susman,
    eds., Herbert Hoover and the Crisis of American
    Capitalism (Cambridge, Massachusetts: Schenkman,
    1973); Martin L. Fausold and George Mazuzan,
    eds., The Hoover Presidency: A Reappraisal (New
    York: State University of New York Press, 1974);
    Jordan A. Schwarz, The Interregnum of Despair:
    Hoover, Congress, and the Depression (Urbana:
    University of Illinois Press, 1970). There is
    one unpublished study of considerable value to
    this study: E. Del Papa, "Herbert Hoover and the
    Struggle for Relief, 1930-1933" (Ph.D. Diss.,
    Miami University, 1974). The word starvation
    raises certain questions about whether there was
    true starvation or only a little hunger. Hungry
    will be used more frequently throughout this
    paper than starvation. It matters little in the
    political arena whether it was starving Americans
    or hungry Americans. The perceived situation is
    often more important than the real situation. In
    at least two instances the situation does reach
    the point of starvation--the drought of 1930 and
    the coal mining communities in the winter of
    1930-1931.

2. Henry A.Wallace, New Frontiers (New York: Reynal
    and Hitchcock, 1934): 182-183; Edmund Wilson,
    The American Earthquake: A Documentary History of
    the Twenties and Thirties (Garden City, New York:
    Doubleday and Company, 1958): 462-464; Louise V.
    Armstrong, We Too are the People (Boston: Little,
    Brown and Company, 1938): 10. Del Papa gives an
    extensive coverage of the need as do a host of
    contemporary anbd semi-scholarly studies.

3. Gary H. Koerselman, "Herbert Hoover and the Farm
    Crisis of the Twenties: A Study of the Commerce

Department's Efforts to Solve the Agricultural
Depression, 1921-1928" (Ph.D. diss., Northern
Illinois University, 1971): 25-31; Ellis W.
Hawley, "Herbert Hoover, The Commerce
Secretariat, and the Vision of an 'Associate
State', 1921-1928," Journal of American History
61 (June 1974): 117-135; Joan Hoff Wilson,
"Hoover's Agricultural Policies, 1921-1928,"
Agricultural History 51 (April 1977): 338-358.
Among studies of agriculture in the twenties and
the Hoover Presidency that have contributed to
this study are Gilbert C. Fite, George N.Peek and
the Fight for the Parity (Norman: University of
Oklahoma Press, 1954); William D. Rowley, M. L.
Wilson and the Campaign for the Domestic
Allotment (Lincoln: University of Nebraska Press,
1970); David Bruce Miller, "Origins and
Functions of the Federal Farm Board," (Ph.D.
diss., University of Kansas, 1973); Ronald Eldon
Mickel, "Patterns of Agrarian Self-Consciousness
in the 1920's" (Ph.D. diss., Wayne State
University, 1961); William R. Johnson, "Farm
Policy in Transition: 1932, Year of Crisis"
(Ph.D. diss., University of Oklahoma, 1963);
Joan Hoff Wilson, "Hoover's Agricultural
Policies, 1921-22,"; Martin L.Fausold,
"President Hoover's Farm Policies, 1929-1933,";
Gary H. Korselman, "Secretary Hoover and National
Farm Policy: Problems of Leadership,"
Agricultural History 51 (Spring 1977); C.Roger
Lambert, "Herbert Hoover and Federal Farm Board
Wheat," Heritage of Kansas 10 (1977).
Fundamental to the Hoover view on agriculture and
relief is Herbert Hoover, American Individualism
(Washington: Herbert Hoover Presidential Library
Association, reprint, first published 1922).

4.   Henry A, Wallace, "Stabilization of Farm Prices
     and the McNary-Haugen Bill," Annals of the
     Academy of Political and Social Sciences CXLII
     (March 1929)) 404; Fite, Peek gives a complete
     coverage to the McNary-Haugen movement.

5.   Hoover to C. C. Teague, 1 December 1924, CDP, FM,
     HHP. Hoover was engaged in a bitter struggle
     with the Agriculture Department over farm policy.
     He employed W. H. Walker, paying him with
     Department funds and apparently his own, to
     discuss cooperative marketing, the Hoover plan
     with farm groups and others. Walker may not have
     pushed Hoover the man but he did report on how

much favor the Secretary had with the various groups. Hoover to Theodore D. Hammatt, 13 December 1921, Hoover to W. H. Walker 4 September, 14 October, 20 November, 13 Deember, 1924, Harold P. Stokes to W. H. Walker 20 November 1924, W. H. Walker to Herbert Hoover 22 October 1924, Draft, Proposal to Create a Federal Agriculture Marketing Board 19 March 1924, Hoover to Arthur B. Williams 29 March 1924, ˋCDP FM, HHP. Hoover to E. D. Funk 31 May 1924, Hoover to Dean J. H. Skinner 18 May 1923, CDP, FM, HHP Wilson, "Hoover's Agricultural," 340-349.

6. Herbert Hoover, 2 November 1928, St. Louis, Public Statements, HHP.

7. W. R. Bayless to Editor, Wallaces Farmer, 21 January 1925, Henry A. Wallace Papers, University of Iowa Library, Iowa City, Iowa. Wilson, "Hoover's Agricultural," 338, 347-57; Lambert, "Hoover and Farm Board Wheat," 22-23; Miller, "Origins and Functions," Chap. 5.

8. Lambert, "Hoover and Farm Board Wheat," Kansas City Star 2 July 1930; Federal Farm Board Minutes 22 October 1930, Presidential Papers, Farm Board, HHP; United States Department of Agriculture, Yearbook of Agriculture, 1933 (Washington, GPO, 1333) 3-4, 404. The Yearbooks changed the statistics on prices, production, yield, and acreage every year between 1929-1933.

9. Wilson, "Hoover's Agricultural," 343; Lambert, "Hoover and Farm Board," 24-26; Romasco, Poverty of Abundance 115-116; Miller, "Origins and Functions," 2-6-220.

10. Lambert, "Hoover and Farm Board Wheat," 25-27; quotation in Miller, "Origins and Functions," 223; Sam R. McKelvie to Walter H. Newton, 2 April 1930, Presidential Papers, Farm Board, HHP; New York Times 22 July 1930; Kansas City Star, 23 July 1930.

11. Lambert, "Hoover and Farm Board Wheat," 26.

12. Farmer-Labor Party Platform, 4 July 1930, Wallace Papers; Kansas City Star 6 August 1930; Rowley, M. L. Wilson, 72-73, 82-84.

13. Johnson, "Farm Policy," 135-162; Rowley, M.

L.Wilson 107-117; Henry A. Wallace to Joseph
Flynn, 18 August 1930, Wallace Papers; Malcolm
O. Sillars, "Henry A. Wallace's Editorials on
Agricultural Discontent, 1921-1928," Agricultural
History (26 October 1952): 133-136.

14.   Ibid., Mickel, "Patterns of Agrarian," 224.
      Federal Farm Board Press Release 22 January 1930,
      Haugen Papers, Iowa State Historical, Iowa City,
      Iowa;   Statement by Secretary of Agriculture,
      Arthur M. Hyde, 18 February 1923, PP, FB, HHP.

15.   Fite, Peek 243-249;   Johnson, "Farm Policy,"
      190-212.   The evidence here is widespread and can
      be found in numerous contemporary sources.   Del
      Papa does a good job of bringing together much of
      this information.   John Beemster to Herbert
      Hoover 27 August 1930, PP, HHP.   Beemster
      provided an early warning of the hunger problem
      outside of the drought situation.

16.   Herbert Hoover, Before President's Agricultural
      Commission, 20 January 1925, CDP, FM, HHP.

17.   L. B. Hanna to Herbert Hoover 28 September 1932,
      Joseph Rothschild to Herbert Hoover, 21 July
      1931, PP, HHP.   It might be worthy of note that
      these correspondents came from the prominent
      banking, investing, and political world rather
      than agriculture.

18.   There are two published works on the 1930
      drought;   Robert Cowley, "The Drought and the
      Dole," American Heritage 23 (February 1972) and
      C. Roger Lambert, "Hoover and the Red Cross in
      the Arkansas Drought of 1930," Arkansas
      Historical Quarterly 20 (Spring 1970).   There are
      two more recent and more extensive unpublished
      studies: David E. Hamilton, "The Hoover
      Administration, Congress and the Gret Drought of
      1930."   Masters Essay, Department of History,
      University of Iowa (February 1978) and Nan
      Elizabeth Woodruff, "The Great Southern Drought
      of 1930-31;   A Study in Rural Relief," (Ph.D.
      diss., University of Tennessee, 1977).   Hamilton
      makes the important point that the drought
      contributed to the widespread bank failure
      throughout the drought stricken South and may
      have renewed the Depression.   Woodruff offers a
      detailed study of the drought and drought relief.
      She describes Hoover as a "prisoner of his own

ideology." Except for some minor errors, incorrect bibliography citations and quoting Henry C. Wallace five years after his death, this is a valuable study. The press tended to look with high expectation to the Hoover take over of the drought and considered it a boon for his Presidency. New Republic, 64 20 August 1930 "It gives him a chance to do something that he can do well. In organizing relief for present distress he has confidence and experience. Here he does not fumble and compromise. . . ." p. 1. Cowley, "The Drought and the Dole," 18. Arthur M. Hyde, "Drouth," PP, Drouth, HHP; Harris G. Warren, Herbert Hoover and the Great Depression (New York: Oxford University Press, 1959) 179.

19. Cowley, "The Drought and the Dole," 18.

20. Report of the National Drought Conference, Washington, D.C., 20 November 1930, PP, Drought, HHP. House of Representatives, 71 Cong., 3rd sess., Hearings Before the Committee on Agriculture, Drought and Storm Relief: Agriculture Experiment Station Work in Puerto Rico (Washington, 1930); 9, 17, 18, 20, 57, 61.

21. Lambert, "Hoover and Red Cross," 3-19; Cowley, "The Drought and the Dole,"; Hamilton, "The Great Drought,"; Woodruff, "The Great Southern Drought," Herbert Hoover, The Memoirs of Herbert Hoover: The Great Depression, 1929-1941 (New York: MacMillan Co., 1952) 55.

22. New York Times, 29 Januarey 1931; W. B. Farris to Herbert Hoover 21 January 1931; House of Representatives of the State of Missouri to Herbert Hoover, 21 January 1931, Paul Pinkerton to Herbert Hoover, 19 January 1931; Clipping, St. Louis Post Dispatch 5 January 1931. F. W. Greenwood wrote Hoover cn 31 January 1931 quoting Will Rogers' report that Hoover had quoted to Rogers the Grover Cleveland veto message in which Cleveland insisted tha the government did not support the people, the people supported the government. He urged Hoover to relent, PP. Drought, HHP; Lambert, "Hoover and Red Cross," 16-19.

23. Congressional Record, 71 Cong., 3 sess., 74: 44-33-4436; Official Report of Operations of the American National Red Cross, Relief Work in the

Drought of 1930-31 (Washington: ARC, 1931): 47;
Wilson, Earthquake, 249-266; Edgar Kirk,
Interview with Author, 16 September, 1976.

24. DeWitt Smith to James Fieser, 20 September 1930;
    Confidential Memorandum to Members of the Central
    Committee, 10 October 1930, PP, Red Cross, HHP;
    Relief Work in the Drought, 18-24.

25. Congressional Record, 71 Cong., 3 sess., 74:
    3372, 2143-2144, 2152-2153, 33-74-3375; New
    Republic (11 February 1931) 336; LXVI (25
    February 1931) 38.

26. The citations here are numerous. Hoover sought
    to answer the charge on 3 February 1931. He
    pointed to the total collapse in Europe:

    There is no such paralysis in the United
        States and I am confident that our
        people have the resources, the
        initiative, the courage, the stamina
        and kindliness of spirit to meet this
        situation. PP, Public Statements, HHP.
        This clearly reflects the feeling of
        American superiority and the higher
        expectations which were fundamental to
        Hoover, Americans were unique and the
        American System was superior. To
        preserve that one could and must demand
        more of them than could be expected of
        other people.

27. Congressional Record, 71 Cong., 3 sess., 74:
    2141-2142: Mark Sullivan, Memorandum, 17 January
    1931, Presidential Personal, Sullivan, HHP.
    Woodruff says that Harvey Couch, chairman of the
    Arkansas Drought Committee was instrumental in
    convincing the President to compromise.

28. Memphis Commercial Appeal, Editorial, 17 January
    1931; Heywood Broun, "It seems to Heywood
    Broun," The Nation 130 (25 June 1930): 723; Paul
    Y. Anderson, "Food and Drink in Washington," The
    Nation 132 (11 February 1931): 150; Paul Y.
    Anderson, "A Washington Honor Roll," The Nation
    132 (28 January 1931): 93; Andrew Fairfield,
    "Mr. Hoover's Credo," The Nation (30 September
    1931): 331-332.

29. Charles Finley to Herbert Hoover 1 April 1931;

William Turnblazer to Herbert Hoover 31 March 1931, PP, Unemployment, Coal, HHP; Del Papa, "Herbert Hoover and the Struggle," 88-98; Grace Abbott, "Improvements in Rural Public Relief: the Lesson of the Coal-Mining Communities," Social Service Review, 6 (June 1932): 189-196.

30. Herbert Hoover to John Barton Payne, 4 April 1931; Porter R. Lee to Arthur Woods 14 January 1931; Fred C. Croxton, Memorandum to Col. Arthur Woods, 17 March 1931, PP, PECE/POUR, HHP; Del Papa, "Herbert Hoover and the Struggle," 95-98; Clarence E. Pickett, For More Than Bread (Boston: Little, Brown and Company, 1953): 20-26.

31. Ibid.

32. Herbert Hoover to John Barton Payne 4 April 1931, PP, PECE POUR, HHP.

33. James C. Fieser to Judge Payne, 7 April 1931, PP, PECE/POUR, HHP.

34. Memorandum: Conversation with Herbert Hoover and John B. Payne by Col. Arthur Woods, 11 February 1931; Larry Richey to Fred C. Croxton: Memorandum describing conversation between Hoover and Payne, 2 June 1931: Arthur Woods to Herbert Hoover 2 August 1931; Reports of American Friends Workers, Office Files of Fred Croxton 1 March 1931, PP, PECE/POUR, HHP; Craig Lloyd, Aggressive Introvert: Herbert Hoover and Public Relations Management (Columbus: Ohio State Univerity Press, 1972): 159-161.

35. No One Has Starved," Fortune 6 (September 1932): 19-28.

36. V. Villiallair to Mrs. Ellis A. Yost, 8 October 1931, U. S. Stone to Herbert Hoover, 6 September 1930, Glenn I. Matthews to Herbert Hoover, 17 October 1930, PP, Grain, HHP.

37. Huey Long to Herbert Hoover, 12 November 1930, Joe T. Robinson to Wm. G. McAddo 29 November 1930, Clipping, Chicago Tribune 23 October 1930, John Garland Pollard to Herbert Hoover, PP, Grain, HHP; Gilbert Haugen to James Murch, 1 February 1932, Haugen Papers, Iowa State Historical, Iowa City, Iowa; Congressional Record, 71 Cong., 3 sess., 74: 2137: Commercial

and Financial Chronicle 29 November, 20 December
1930, 24 January, 26 September 1931; USDA,
Feeding Wheat to Livestock (Washington, D.C.,
Miscellaneous Publication No. 96, September
1930); Lambert, "Hoover and Farm Board Wheat,"
28-29.

38. Larry Richey to Arthur M. Hyde, 4 December 1937,
Post Presidential Papers, HHP; New York Times 5
June 1932.

39. Mrs. Harold T. Clark to Frank Strother, 4 July
1932, PP, Unemployment, HHP.

40. French Strother to Mrs. Harold T. Clark, 13 July
1932, PP, Unemployment-POUR, HHP.

41. Herbert Hoover to Arthur M. Hyde, 29 July 1932,
PP, Secretary, HHP.

42. Herbert Hoover, William Penn College, Oskaloosa,
Iowa, 12 June 1925, Public Statements, HHP.

43. Louis H. Bean, "Agriculture and the World
Crisis," in Yearbook of Agriculture 1933
(Washington, GPO, 1934): 93; Agricultural
Adjustment Administration, Industry's Production
and the Farmer, C-44 (Washington: GPO, September
1935): 1. Rowley, M. L. Wilson, 148.

44. Herbert Hoover, William Penn College, Oskaloosa,
Iowa, 12 June 1925, Public Statements, HHP.

45. Press Release 17 October 1930, Public Statements,
HHP.

46. Radio Address from White 22 January 1931, Public
Statements, HHP.

47. Press Statement, 3 February 1931, Radio Address
12 February 1931, Public Statements, HHP.

48. Perry Davidson to Herbert Hoover, 20 August 1931,
PPF, Unemployment, HHP. Draft, 29 August 1931,
letter 1 September 1931, PPF, Unemployment, HHP.
William Allen White, "Herbert Hoover--the last of
the Old Presidents or the First of the New?"
Saturday Evening Post 205 (4 March 1933): 54.
Lloyd, Aggressive Introvert, 159-160.

49. William Appleman Williams, Some Presidents from

<u>Wilson to Nixon</u> (New York: New York Review Book, 1972): 27; C. H. Williams to Herbert Hoover, 3 February 1931, Farm Matters, HPL.

50. Walter J. Calverley to Herbert Hoover, 9 January 1931, PP, Unemployment, HHP.

51. Hamilton, "The Hoover Administration" makes a strong case for the failure of the banking system of the South, especially in states such as Arkansas. Woodruff, "The Great Southern Drought" illustrates clearly the failure of the traditional credit institutions throughout much of the drought region in particular the more rural South. <u>Jonesboro Tribune</u>, 8 January 1931; Woodruff, "The Great Southern Drought," 290-291.

52. C. Roger Lambert, "Hoover, the Red Cross and Food for the Hungry," <u>Annals of Iowa</u> 44 (Winter 1979): 538; Del Papa, "Hoover and the Struggle," 207-208 makes the argument that in the early debates on relief Hoover used the word dole to stigmatize; but then turned to budget balancing and used the term "pork barrel." There is obviously some truth in this but Hoover was concerned about the budget from the winter of 1930.

53. Lambert, "Hoover, the Red Cross and Food," 530-540.

54. Wilson, <u>Herbert Hoover; Forgotten Progressive;</u> Pete Daniel, <u>Deep'n as it come: The 1927 Mississippi River Flood</u> (New York: Oxford University Press, 1977): 87-89, 138-141.

55. Herbert Hoover to James P. Goodrich, 25 August 1930, PP, Drought, HHP.

56. Lambert, "Hoover and Farm Board," 70.

57. Del Papa, "Hoover and the Struggle," 115. James S. Olson in a series of studies makes the point that Hoover essentially dropped his reliance upon voluntarism and turned to a more interventionist policy. See: "The End of Voluntarism: Herbert Hoover and the National Credit Corporatiopn," <u>Annals of Iowa</u> (Fall 1972); "Gifford Pinchot and the Politics of Hunger, 1932-1933," <u>Pennsylvania Magazine of History and Biography</u> (October 1972). Olson makes a strong argument but as he states

the spirit and administration of the relief loans raises some question. It could be argued that Hoover turned to relief activity not out of changed beliefs but out of pragmatic avoidance of something worse.

58. Members of Congress traced back to 1827 or 1803 federal appropriations for purposes comparable to the drought. Lambert, "Hoover and the Red Cross." Schwarz, The Interregnum of Despair; Jordan A. Schwarz, "Hoover and Congress: Politics, Personality, and Perspective in the Presidency," in Fausold, The Hoover Presidency.

59. E. E. Hunt to Col. Arthur Woods 27 October 1930, Hopkins Papers, Franklin D. Roosevelt Library, Hyde Park, New York; Cowley, "Drought and Dole," 93. It is not completely clear who or what decided against the great drive. Cowley believes it was the local leaders who balked out of fear of loss of local fund drives. Relief Work in the Drought: 90, Appendix VII. Some 623 carloads of commodities were donated during the drought crisis. This came about without any strong encouragement from either the government or the Red Cross.

60. Theodore J. Joslin, Hoover Off the Record (Garden City, N.Y.: Doubleday, Doran and Company, 1934): 3.

THE FEDERAL FARM BOARD AND THE ANTECEDENTS
OF THE AGRICULTURAL ADJUSTMENT ACT 1929-1933

by Dr. Bernard M. Klass

Since the 1930's, historians have debated the
issue of whether the New Deal was evolutionary or
revolutionary. A growing trend of interpretation in
current historiography is to emphasize the former
view. In this broader context, the Hoover
Administration is seen, not only as a continuation of
many elements of the Progressive Era, but the
precursor of the New Deal. Instead of viewing the
Hoover and Roosevelt Administrations as diametrically
opposed, many contemporary historians have stressed
the basic continuities between the two.(1) This paper
will focus on a comparison of the agricultural
policies of both. The Federal Farm Board and the
Agricultural Adjustment Administration will be
analyzed in detail as case studies. Were there
significant antecedents of the Agricultural Adjustment
Act during the Farm Board's existence from July 1929
to May 1933? Was the Triple-A, as many historians
have interpreted it, a radical departure from previous
farm policy? These are two of the key questions to be
answered in this study. Therefore, the Farm Board's
major stabilization programs and its voluntary acreage
reduction program for selected commodities form a
major portion of this paper. The Board's own Economic
Staff played a major role in developing the Voluntary
Domestic Allotment Plan which later formed the core of
the AAA's production adjustment programs.   The
Board's two chief economists, Joseph S. Davis and John
D. Black, plus staff member Mordecai Ezekiel (Black's
former student) were the principal figures in this
development.

While stressing the continuities between Hoover
and Roosevelt, many contemporary historians
differentiate Hoover's corporatist approach from
Roosevelt's. Corporatism meant that government was to
be administered by non-political experts who were
impervious to pressure groups or Congressional
interference. These experts would help businesses
help themselves through promoting voluntary trade
associations, and in agriculture, by encouraging
cooperatives which were farmer owned and controlled.
At the outset of his Administration, Hoover stated
that the farm problem was the most urgent facing the
nation.(2) Ironically, the Agricultural Marketing Act
of 1929 representing the culmination of his

corporatitst approach, became the first major failure
of his corporatist-associationist philosophy.
Conflicting personalities and ideologies, disputes
within the Federal Farm Board, the unprecedented
length and severity of the depression, and the
pressures exerted by the farm organizations to adopt
their favored plans, left Hoover's proposed
corporatist solution in ruins. In response to these
conditions, the Farm Board often adopted programs and
policies that directly contradicted Hoover's earlier
philosophy. They experimented with devices, such as,
price fixing, government surplus storage, nation-wide
commodity marketing agreements, recommendations for
land-use planning, and acreage reductions. Many of
these would later become common-place under the AAA.
Despite some protestations, however, Hoover did not
interfere wih the Farm Board. Why he abandoned his
earlier philosophy will be subsequently explored.

BACKGROUND OF THE AGRICULTURAL MARKETING ACT

Hoover's administrative experiences during and
immediately after World War I made him a vigorous
opponent of price-fixing for solving farmers'
problems. He concluded that it contributed to
inflation, politicization, and post-war surpluses. He
believed that agricultural cooperatives, through the
promotion of long-term efficiency and the elimination
of waste, offered the best solution. Agriculture
during the 1920's, however, more than any other "sick
industry", seemed to defy his "New Era Corporatist"
theories. Hoover admitted that it was nearly
impossible to integrate agriculture into his overall
plans for eliminating contradictions between foreign
and domestic policies. He blamed the farmer's extreme
individualism for the wasteful competition with
existing cooperatives. The individual farmer lacked
sufficient capital to build powerful local, regional,
and national cooperatives.(3) Hoover's ideas for a
Federal Farm Board during the 1920's were based on the
assumption that adequate government loans could
overcome this defficiency. In short, the farm problem
could be solved by using the same methods as
successful business and trade associations. Hoover's
ingrained beliefs were confirmed by his California
experiences where cooperatives had been successful in
stabilizing markets for citrus, grapes, dairy
products, and other specialized crops.

During the 1920's, Secretary of Agriculture,
Henry C. Wallace, and the major farm organizations

192.

favored a program opposite to Hoover's.   Wallace and
Hoover had clashed during World War I over the issue
of price supports. After the war, their conflict
centered on whether Agriculture or Commerce should
have exclusive authority to send agriculture attaches
abroad for promoting expansion of farm exports.
Hoover lobbied in Congress for enactment of the
Jones-Winslow bill providing Commerce with such
authority, but the Wallace supporters defeated it in
June, 1924. This bitter jurisdictional conflict
remained unresolved throughout the 1920's. The two
departments often duplicated each other's foreign and
domestic functions in direct conflict with the
Hooverian tenet of efficiency.(4)

     The Wallace and Hoover forces also clashed on the
issue of the effectiveness of agricultural
cooperatives. The former did not believe that they
were an adequate solution to the immediate farm
problem. Wallace argued that the Department of
Agriculture's traditional policy of supplying
information to farmers about cooperatives was
sufficient. He accused Hoover of confusing farmers'
problems with those of commerce and industry. In 1924
he campaigned successfully against Hoover's plan for
new legislation to create a Federal Marketing Board
and a system of marketing cooperatives. Wallace
concluded that a hierarchy of farm boards would lead
to wasteful expenditures, since Agriculture was
already performing these functions. He contended that
these federally sponsored farm boards, representing
regions on a commodity basis, would not gain the
individual farmer's support.(5)   These predictions
proved remarkably accurate when compared with the
actual experience of the Federal Farm Board from 1929
through 1933.

     Perhaps the best known clash between the Hoover
and Wallace forces was over the McNary-Haugen bills.
This protracted controversy demonstrated strong
support for immediate price-raising plans and Hoover's
adamant opposition to them. The McNary-Haugenites
campaigned for the equalization fee or the
export-debenture which required establishing complex
systems for separating the domestically consumed
portion of selected commodities from the export
surplus. Both involved creation of a government
corporation for export dumping of the surplus in order
to make the tariff effective.   This would secure a
higher domestic price for farmers. Economists and
historians have long debated their feasibility, but

Hoover argued that they were unconstitutional. He
believed that they would lead to overproduction of
selected crops and demands by other special interests
for similar favors. He viewed all such devices as
destructive of his non-political, corporatist solution
of the farm problem.(6)

Despite these fundamental conflicts between the
Hooverites and the McNary-Haugenites, they agreed on
many points. After Coolidge's 1928 veto of the 1928
McNary-Haugen Bill, Congressman Gilbert Haugen did not
despair. He refused to abandon his support for most
Republican farm policies and Herbert Hoover. Since
neither Smith nor Hoover supported the equalization
fee during the 1928 campaign, Haugen remained loyal to
the Republicans and Hoover. George N. Peek , another
leading McNary-Haugenite, by conrast, had bolted the
Republicans to support Al Smith. With the exception
of the equalization fee, the McNary-Haugen bills were
remarkably similar to Hoover's cooperative marketing
legislation, especially the 1929 Agricultural
Marketing Act. The McNary-Haugen bills encouraged
cooperatives providing financing and promoting the
orderly marketing of commodities. They recommended
elimination of excessive speculation in marketing and
reducing wasteful practices of middlemen.(7)

Part of Haugen's support for Hoover rested on the
assumption that the Federal Farm Board would later use
the equalization fee as one method for market
stabilization. He demonstrated a willingness to
compromise when the Marketing Act was being debated in
Congress. Since he felt that it was impossible to
secure the equalization fee immediately, he, the Farm
Bureau, the Farmers' Union, and the National Grange,
agreed that the Farm Board be given broad discretion
for adopting its' own farm relief mechanisms. After
the Board had been operating for several months,
however, and made no use of the equalization fee,
Haugen became very critical of it.(8)

Thus, in its final form in June, 1929, the
Agricultural Marketing Act was a compromise between
Hoover's cooperative marketing plans and the demands
of the McNary-Haugenites for immediate price-raising
legislation. Hoover succeeded in his efforts to
eliminate the equalization fee and the export
debenture plans from the bill. As a concession to the
McNary-Haugenites, however, the law contained a pledge
to place agriculture on an equal basis with other
segments of the American economy. It also provided

194.

that under certain conditions, the federal government
could purchase farm surpluses as part of major
stabilization operations. This proved to be the most
controversial portion of the Act during the Farm
Board's existence.(9)

An examination of Section 1 of the Agricultural
Marketing Act illustrates that it was a broad tapestry
for appeasing conflicting Presidential and
Congressional interests. It declared that it was
Congressional policy to promote effective
merchandising of agricultural commodities in
interstate and foreign commerce, placing farming on an
equal basis with other industries. To that end, the
law described the need for controlling and stabilizing
agricultural commodities and processed foods in
interstate and foreign commerce. This was to be done
by minimizing speculation; preventing inefficient and
wasteful methods of distribution; encouraging
producers to organize associations or corporations;
and through financing a system of farmer-owned and
controlled cooperatives. There was a vague reference
to production control in that surpluses would be
avoided through orderly production and distribution.
This would stabilize price fluctuations in domestic
markets. The law, however, did not specify how the
Federal Farm Board would implement these impressive
objectives.(10)

Almost immediately after the law's enactment,
Hoover began naming the eight members of the Federal
Farm Board. While the act provided for a six-year
term for each appointee, the first appointments were
for terms ranging from one to six years so that the
entire Board would not be reappointed at the same
time. The Board was provided with maximum
independence. Hoover selected his long-time friend
Alexander Legge as chairman. During World War I,
Legge served Bernard Baruch as Vice-Chairman of the
War Industries Board. In his business dealings as
president of the International Harvester Corporation,
Legge had traveled world-wide. He shared Hoover's
vision of a long-term corporatist solution for the
farm problem. In spite of later differences over
stabilization policy, Legge and Hoover remained
friends. This continued even in the face of strong
criticism of Legge for having profited at the expense
of debt-ridden farmers while President of
International Harvester. Conflict-of-interest charges
were made against him during his term as Farm Board
chairman.

Among the other most prominent members of the Board were C.B. Denman of Farmington, Missouri, past president of the National Livestock Producers' Association; James C. Stone of Lexington, Kentucky, former head of the Burley Tobacco Growers' Association; and Charles C. Teague of Santa Paula, California, who led powerful citrus and walnut cooperatives in that key agricultural state. Another key member was Samuel McKelvie, then living in South Dakota, who had been a Nebraska Governor. He was a rival of Senator Norris and was active in several grain cooperatives. These men all represented wealthy farmers opposed to immediate price-raising plans through government controls. Teague, for example, opposed the stabilization and clearinghouse provisions of the Agricultural Marketing Act. He initially refused Hoover's appointment to the Board on those grounds. Hoover, who by June, 1929 had accepted limited government stabiliztion of agriculture, finally persuaded him to accept. He explained that the stabilization and clearinghouse provisions might be useful under emergency conditions. Apparently, Hoover was willing to make some temporary concessions for dealing with an emergency situation similar to that he had encountered during World War I.(12)

While Hoover claimed that he was trying to represent all major farm groups in his Farm Board appointments, much dissatisfaction was expressed. Southern states, from Virginia to Texas, complained through their Congressmen about the lack of a cotton representative familiar with their problems. Farmer organizations in the Dakotas and Minnesota were not satisfied with McKelvie. While nearly all members of the Board came under heavy criticism during their tenure, Legge, Denman, Williams, and McKelvie were targets of unusually heavy fire. Hoover, writing to Iowa Governor, John Hammill (who was upset about the lack of an Iowan on the Board) conceded that it was impossible to represent all geographic areas on the Board. He wrote: "As you doubtless know, the Farm Bill requires that members of the Board be representatives of different sections of the agricultural industry. They cannot be chosen geographically because there are twelve or fourteen geographical areas from an agricultural point of view and only eight members of the Board."(13)

Shortly after the Board's appointment, Hoover issued a Memorandum on Board Organization recommending

196.

five operating divisions. They were: [1] Cooperative Marketing to be transferred from the Department of Agriculture; [2] Legal; [3] Financial, as Hoover conceived it, in charge of making and supervising loans to cooperatives; [4] Economic--in charge of assisting the Board in its analysis of domestic and foreign conditions affecting agriculture. Hoover specified that this Division be headed by an economist acceptable to him; and [5] Educational--in charge of preparing and disseminating advice to farmers. In his basic organizational structure Hoover achieved most of his goals, but his recommendations on Board operations were not closely followed.(14)

The Memorandum also called for advisory committees representing selected commodities. Hoover wanted them chosen carefully to represent "the constructive and not the political side of agriculture." He believed that wheat should be the first of these commodities and the second, cotton. Quoting from the Memorandum:

> In some commodities, particularly grain, it may be desirable to erect a central marketing concern at an early date--something of the title of Farmer Owned Grain Corporation would convey the psychology rather than use the word 'stabilization', which is coming in the minds of many to convey an element of gambling.(15)

The most controversial area of the Board's operations was clearly in stabilization. Section Nine of the Marketing Act provided authority to conduct such operations, but left wide discretion in implementation. During the first months of its existence the Farm Board recognized four primary groups of stabilizing measures: [1] the normal development of cooperatives which it believed would lead to long-term market stabilization; [2] emergency surplus control, either by the cooperatives themselves, or with the Board; [3] major stabilization operations in the form of stabilization corporations; and [4] surplus control measures preventing excessive future production or curtailing existing crops. The Board's definition of stabilization would be the crucial factor governing which options it would use.(16)

The Board's first use of its stabilization powers

was in its $1.5 million loan to the Sunmaid Raisin
Cooperative. That amount had to be matched by a group
of California banks and would be used to purchase
white grapes from California growers. This would
enable the Board to make advances on their 1929 raisin
crop. Charles C. Teague, the California member of the
Farm Board, had played a key role in this decision.
Other Board members were critical of Teague for
favoritism to his home state.(17) The issue of which
commodities to stabilize, plagued the Board throughout
its existence. Unfortunately, the length and severity
of the world-wide depression, which few recognized in
the early 1930's, created an impossible climate for
stabilization operations.

    Despite their internal disagreements, Legge,
Teague, and the other Board members agreed that major
stabilization operations, in the form of Stabilization
Corporations, were only to be used as emergency
measures. While Hoover privately reiterated that
philosophy, he publicly supported the Board's decision
to use major stabilization operations in early 1930.
He continued to voice his misgivings in correspondence
with Alexander Legge. He believed that the only
acceptable stabilization method was through the
long-term process of building farmer owned and
controlled cooperatives. This would avoid direct
federal intervention in agriculture.(18)

    The Board's decision to undertake major
stabilization operations came after several months of
trying other alternatives. From July to October,
1929, it had tried to check the decline in wheat
prices by advising farmers to delay marketing their
wheat. By October, 1929, however, it began making
loans to a few wheat cooperatives in an amount it
determined would be the ultimate market price. The
basic loan value was $1.25 per bushel for No. 1
Northern Spring Wheat. Since prices temporarily
advanced during November and December, 1929, this
limited section misled the Board into thinking more
loans were necessary. By January, 1930, however, a
steep decline in wheat prices occurred which was
aggravated by the Stock Market Crash and the
world-wide glut of wheat. Responding to growing
pressures from the major farm organizations, the
cooperatives, and the recommendations of its wheat
Advisory Committee, the Board decided in February,
1930 to undertake major stabilization operations.(19)

    Why did the Farm Board make this fateful decision

despite its earlier reluctance? One intriguing
explanation was offered by the Washington based
<u>Kiplinger Farm Board Newsletter</u> of February 25, 1930.
Kiplinger argued that the former supporters of the
equalization fee and export debenture plans were also
the strongest advocates of the Stabilization
Corporation provisions of the Marketing Act. By
February, 1930, Hoover was deeply alarmed by the
Senate's insistence upon retaining the Export
Debenture Plan in the current Tariff Bill. The
Newsletter concluded that he was willing to support
major stabilization operations in return for the
abandonment of the Export Debenture Plan by the Senate
Agricultural bloc. The Farm Board believed that it
could curtail over production through voluntary means
in cominbinaion with major stabilization actions.
This proved to be a serious misjudgement.(20)

The Board also based its decision on the
assumption that the depression would be short-lived.
Hence a temporary stabilization effort would prevent
chaos in the wheat markets and stabilize rural
banking. In his correspondence with Hoover, Legge
justified the Board's decision arguing that it was an
emergency measure to strengthen cooperatives for
undertaking their own long-range stabilization. He
admitted that great pressures were building on the
Board due to the unprecedented severity of the
depression. Hence, it was shifting from long-term
measures supporting cooperatives to emergency
stabilization.(21)

The Stabilization Corporation which provided the
core of the Farm Board's major stabilization
operations was supposed to be controlled by its member
wheat cooperatives. In reality though, it was
governed by the Farmers' National Grain Corporation.
Samuel McKelvie, the wheat member of the Farm Board,
had played a major role in organizing the Farmers'
National on July 30, 1929. It served as a central
marketing agency absorbing existing wheat pools and
grain elevators. Since not all of the existing
cooperatives were represented in the Farmers'
National, the issue of which ones would become the
regional representatives was crucial. Recognition by
the Farmers' National was a requirement for
cooperatives to receive Farm Board loans. In regions
such as the Dakotas and Minnesota, where there had
long been intense competition among cooperatives, the
recogntion issue was laden with political dynamite.
Since neither the Farmers' National nor the Board was

able to resolve this issue, some of the most intense criticism of the Farm Board came from that region between 1930 and 1933.(22)

Critics also attacked several key personnel of the Farmers' National and the Stabilization Corporation. William Kellogg, the manager of the Farmers' National also headed the Grain Stabilization Corporation. Since the Farm Board controlled major decisions by both the Stabilization Corporation and the Farmers' National, critics could attack them as if they were criticizing the Board itself. The situation was exacerbated by serious conflict-of-interest charges against Kellogg who was forced to resign. He was replaced by George Milnor. Milnor, formerly the general manager of a small milling company in Alton, Ilinois, was criticized for lacking the experience to administer nation-wide stabilization. He alienated the Farm Board by attempting to dump surplus wheat stocks abroad. Legge had forced him to desist his activities by May, 1930. Two other key personnel who came under heavy fire were Clarence E. Huff and M. W. Thatcher. Huff of Salina, Kansas became president of the Farmers' National in April, 1930 and remained in that post until the organization's demise. Thatcher of Minneapolis was one of the directors of the Farmers' National.(23)

In the midst of this growing controversy, the Board's major stabiliztion operations seemed to work for a short time. Between February and May, 1930 net stabilization purchases totaled 65 million bushels of wheat and kept American prices from falling as rapidly as those in Liverpool. The Board contended that its stabilization operations keep Kansas City prices, for example, well above the market prices for wheat prevailing during the first half of 1931. Unfortunately, for wheat growers and the Board, however, the latter's wheat stocks rose from just over 50 million bushels in July, 1930 to more than 250 million bushels by April, 1931.(24)

Even when Board stabilization seemed to be working, growing pressures from private grain traders and President Hoover forced the Board to abandon its major operations in this area by April, 1930. At that time, the Board's vacillating policies led to a storm of controversy. Hoover continued to argue publicly that the Board was an independent agency and that he could not exert his authority to override its decisions. The President, however, was sharply attacked for his attempts to disassociate himself from the Farm Board's decisions. An editorial in the Central City Nebraska Republican criticized him for the conflict between his no government in farming philosophy and his support of contrary Board policies, such as buying, selling, and price-fixing. The editorial concluded: "It is Mr. Hoover who disclaims any responsibility in this connection, not because he is bothered by bureaucracy and domination, but because the Farm Board is in such a mess that he must to save his skin deny any connection with its methods."(25)

The private grain traders, seeing their vital economic interests threatened by the competing regional cooperatives and the Farmers' National, unleashed a torrent of criticism against the Board. One of the most effective and persistent critics was Frederick B. Wells. Wells, a leading grain trader and member of the influential Minneapolis Chamber of Commerce, began his campaign as early as November, 1929. His grievances were typical of those emanating from the private grain trade in the key wheat growing regions. He accused the Board of using the same tactics as the radical Non-Partisan League. The League had attempted to replace the private grain trade with government owned and controlled marketing institutions. Wells denounced stabilization loans as socialism and attacked Board member Carl Williams. Williams had previously denounced private grain dealers as gamblers and speculators. Wells also blamed the confusing stabilization policies for unsettling the market. The growing stocks of unsold grain in storage held a proverbial sword of Democles over the private market. He was also alarmed by Milnor's plans to acquire grain elevators and related marketing facilities. He lashed out at Milnor for lacking marketing experience, and warned Hoover that if the Board continued its policies the private grain trade would completely repudiate the Administration. They were already deeply distressed by Hoover's signing of the Hawley-Smoot Tariff, which they saw as a major threat to their export trade.(26)

While the Board was being condemned for its massive stabilization operations, the major farm organizations, small producers, and cooperatives were incensed when it abandoned its initial stabilization program in April, 1930. Kansas wheat grower, John Vesecky, writing to Alexander Legge on November 3, 1930 expressed a common grower sentiment when he argued that stabilization was the key to gaining

farmer support against the powerful grain traders. If
the Board did not renew its stabilization program, it
would lose the support of its allies. Vesecky also
criticized the Board for its failure to consult with
cooperatives before making decisions in the vital area
of stabilization. This failure would cost it support
that it could ill-afford to lose.(27)

When he defended the Farm Board, insurgent North
Dakota Senator, Gerald Nye, expressed arguments
similar to those of Vesecky. He placed it on the side
of the small farmer against the special interests,
especially the middlemen, who had taken undue
advantage of the producers over the years. He
contended that it was the larger grain dealers,
holding seats on the major exchanges and controlling
the big elevators, who were leading the campaign
against the Board. However when the Board abandoned
its wheat stabilization program, Nye, like Vesecky,
became critical of it. These sentiments were echoed
by Congressman Clifford Hope, representing the
nation's largest wheat growing district in Kansas.
Kansas Senator, Arthur Capper, joined with Hope. Hope
in 1930 was favorable to the Farm Board, but by early
1932 had switched his support to the Voluntary
Domestic Allotment Plan and wanted the Board ended.
The Levand Brothers, publishers of the Wichita Kansas
Beacon were consistent Board critics, particularly of
Board chairman Legge and James C. Stone. Much of
their anger was generated by the Board's failure to
implement a consistent and sufficient wheat
stabilization program and its attack on Kansas wheat
growers for overproduction.(28)

The Board, in partial response to the
unprecedented depth and severity of the depression and
the virtual collapse of the foreign wheat market began
to reconsider stabilization purchases by August, 1930.
An overly optimistic forecast by the Bureau of
Agricultural Economics (then under Department of
Agriculture rather than Farm Board control) could have
easily misled the Board into thinking that short-term
emergency stabilization would alleviate the
agricultural depression. In its October 15, 1930
Report the BAE stated:

> The world's consumption in the 1930-31
> marketing season probably will exceed
> production, and carryover at the end of the
> season is likely to be reduced to a normal
> level. Shorter feed crops and lower wheat

prices probably will increase the
consumption of wheat in the United States
and in Europe to the extent of 250 million
bushels, leaving the world's carryover of
wheat on July 1931 about 150 to 200 million
bushels less than on July 1, 1930. This
would reduce the recorded world's stocks to
about 350 to 400 million bushels, somewhere
between the stocks of July 1, 1927 and July
1, 1928.(29)

The Board had apparently ignored the figures
provided by its own Chief Economist, Joseph S. Davis.
Davis in a Memorandum to the Board dated July 18,
1930, indicated that total wheat supply in all forms
as of July, 1930, that is, in processing mills, the
carryover, and on farms was the largest of any year
since the World War. Davis' assessment proved more
accurate than the Bureau of Agricultural Economics'.
The collapse of the wheat market was aggravated by
Soviet Russia's decision to dump wheat on the European
market. Nearly all of the importing countries took
retaliatory measures to protect their growers.
Germany, for example, raised her tariffs to $1.62 a
bushel and France limited her imports to the amount of
exports with her trading partners. Henry A. Wallace,
then a leading farm journalist, economist, and Hoover
critic, was quick to blame the foreign moves on the
Hawley-Smoot Tariff. He urged a gradual lowering of
tariff barriers to restore trade.(30)

The Farm Board took its fateful plunge into
renewed massive stabilization in the late summer of
1930. It began on a small scale by purchasing limited
amounts of future wheat contracts. As early as
November, 1930, however, it was evident that this
policy had failed to stem sharp price declines. There
were massive bank failures in several of the key farm
states. On November 14, 1930 the Board announced that
its future policy was to liquidate gradually its
accumulated stocks. In order to cushion price
declines, it decided to limit sales in the open market
to a total of 60 million bushels of wheat for 1931 at
a rate of 5 million bushels per month. The Board also
attempted to liquidate its carryover through foreign
sales. While some stabilization wheat was sold to
Brazil, China, and Germany this represented special
circumstances. Long-term credits were granted to
China and Germany and coffee was exchanged for wheat
with Brazil. While these sales did not make a major
impact in the total carryover stocks, they indicated

some future potential if foreign trade could be freed from tariffs and other barriers. The total Chinese sale of 15 million bushels, for example, represented most of the surplus of the Pacific Northwest region.(31)

By the Spring of 1932 it was apparent that the Board's second attempt at major stabilization had failed. Its days as an independent agency were numbered. With increasing pressures on Hoover, he lost interest in the Farm Board shifting his attention to the Reconstruction Finance Corporation. The latter was given major responsibility for agricultural loans combined with its other functions. With a $2 billion appropriation for the RFC and Hoover's emphasis upon retaining the gold standard through balancing the budget, the Board and other existing agencies sustained major cutback.(32)

The Board's doom was imminent when it began losing support from its remaining friends in Congress, sympathetic farmers, and the major farm groups. These groups renewed their efforts to gain long-sought immediate price-raising measures. The Board did manage to survive a motion to abolish it by Georgia Congressman Carl D. Vinson. He proposed transferring most of its functions to the Department of Agriculture, but his motion was soundly defeated by a margin of 152 to 23. Nevertheless, the Farm Board suffered a massive budgetary cutback for fiscal 1933. Its administrative budget under the Independent Agencies Appropriation Bill was $800,000. That represented a 40 percent cut compared to the Board's actual administrative expenditures of about $1.4 million for fiscal 1932. While other agencies suffered cutbacks, none was as proportionately severe as the Board's. This indicated that its opponents had succeeded. The balance of its $500 million revolving fund had been appropriated for fiscal 1932. There were no appropriations for that purpose for fiscal 1933. The Board would be crippled in making loans or in retaining its staff.(33)

In summation, the Board's Congressional opponents had plenty of ammunition for attacking it during the budgetary debate of 1932. Among the most serious charges were: [1] the ineffectiveness of its major stabilization programs; [2] its failure to achieve voluntary production control; [3] the high salaries of Board members, the general counsel, the economic staff, and the managers of the Grain and Cotton

Stabilization Corporations; and [4] alleged
incompetence and corruption in the operations of the
Stabilization Corporations. Its most vociferous
opponents in the House included John D. Clark of New
York, Henry T. Rainey of Illinois, Marvin Jones of
Texas, Clifford Hope of Kansas, Carl D. Vinson of
Georgia, and Clifton A. Woodrum of Virginia. In the
Senate the opposition was led by George Norris of
Nebraska, Peter Norbeck of South Dakota, and James
Byrnes of South Carolina.(34)

    The Congressional critics and outside opponents
disregarded the novelty of the Board's stabilization
operations in the worsening depression. New Republic
editor, A. C. Hoffman, was hardly objective when he
labeled the experiment a total failure. While Hoover
might well be criticized for using stabilization as a
sop to those demanding more comprehensive action, his
reluctant support of it marked a major departure from
his previous farm policies. Other critics, such as
Charles Crandall, president of the Central Cooperative
Exchange, were on firmer ground when they attacked
Hoover for the Hawley-Smoot Tariff. His signing of it
wiped out whatever gains might have been realized from
stabilization.(35) Here was one fundamental
difference between his policies and those of
Roosevelt.

    Perhaps the fairest evaluation of stabilization
came from two of the sources closest to it. Charles
C. Teague admitted that no member of the Farm Board
believed effective stabilization could be accomplished
with available funding. He contended though that he
and his colleagues decided that direct actions were
required once demoralized wheat and cotton markets
created panic. Bank failures in the wheat and cotton
belts made it imperative for the Board to stabilize
markets, and this was done for a time. It was
apparent that Teague had changed some of his views on
farm policy during his tenure on the Board. As noted
earlier, he had almost turned his appointment down
because of his initial opposition to the stabilization
and clearinghouse provisions within the Agricultural
Marketing Act.(36)

    While admitting serious problems with the
stabilization operations, the Board's Economic
Division defended them as necessary emergency
measures. Its Report stated:

    It is quite true that world prices of wheat

and cotton have declined since these
operations were inaugurated. So are the
prices of almost all other raw materials,
including many on which the Board has no
influence, however remote. Students of
wheat and cotton markets can find abundant
reasons for price declines in these products
without charging them to the Federal Farm
Board. The Board accepts that fact that the
operations did not, and probably could not,
under the circumstances that were faced,
indefinitely prevent a tide of price decline
that was caused by extremely powerful
forces, worldwide in scope.(37)

The report concluded that no direct link could be
established between the Board's stabilization policies
and the price declines. It argued that these
operations cushioned the drop and prevented it from
being even worse in the domestic markets.(38)

With the end of its stabilization programs, the
Board shifted its emphasis toward voluntary production
control. It began a concerted effort in that
direction between April and November, 1930. Joseph S.
Davis, the Board's first Chief Economist, responding
to Kansas Senator Capper, recommended that growers cut
their acreage if they expected prices to rise. Capper
had been urging the Board to purchase additional wheat
supplies. The Farm Board's efforts for voluntary
production control proved a marked failure, however,
since they did not offer direct financial incentives
to growers. Moreover acreage cutbacks ran counter to
the farmer's strongly individualistic traditions and
his belief that there were millions of starving people
who needed American food.(39)

Dissatisfied with the results of voluntarism,
some members of the Farm Board's economic staff began
to develop specific production control alternatives.
The economic staff was given broad responsibilities in
this area under Section 5 of the Agricultural
Marketing Act. It authorized them to advise the Board
on crop prices, future trends, existing domestic and
foreign supply and demand. They were empowered to
investigate conditions of crop overproduction, their
prevention, and to conduct land-utilizatiopn analyses.
They were also assigned to study domestic and foreign
market expansion. This included methods for
developing by-products and new uses for agricultural
commodities as well as transportation conditions and

their effects upon marketing.(40)

The Board's two chief economists, Joseph S. Davis and John D. Black along with staff economist, Mordecai Ezekiel, played major roles in formulating production control alternatives. Davis, the Board's first chief economist from September, 1929 to September, 1931 persuaded many outstanding agricultural economists, such as John D. Black, Mordecai Ezekiel, George C. Hass, and Charles F. Sarle to join the Board's staff. Davis believed that his primary responsibility was as administrative expert and organizer creating a first-rate staff for developing policy options. Although he had strong policy views, he kept these out of his work. He strongly disagreed, for example, with Hoover's signing of the Hawley-Smoot Tariff in 1930 and his unyielding attitude on the war debt settlements. Davis felt that he could not publicize his views then, because he saw them as conflicting with his role as an impartial adviser to the Board.(41)

An excellent summary of Davis' view of his functions and that of the economic staff was contained in his February 25, 1930 Memorandum to the Board. Its major recommendations were: [1] to increase the size of the staff for organizing commodity information. Individual staff members could then specialize on particular crops and maintain data gathered by other government agencies on a more current basis; [2] the staff should be responsible for advising the Board on current policy issues directly related to its functions; [3] the staff should analyze future trends and the Board's response to them; and [4)] it should conduct follow-up studies on existing policies keeping the Board informed on their effectiveness. In addition the staff should conduct studies of broad policies, such as land utilization, taxation, speculation, and production control. Outside experts were recommended for use on a temporary consulting basis.(42)

While the Board agreed in principle with Davis' recommendations, they favored a more gradual development of them. Unfortunately, the accelerating chaos of the depression would not wait for this gradualistic approach. When Davis resigned in September, 1931 he felt that the economic staff needed more size and expertise to function effectively as the Board's policy adviser. The most serious limitation was the severe shortage of broadly-trained agricultural economists.(43)

Acting upon Davis' recommendation, the Farm Board
appointed Professor John D. Black as its second Chief
Economist effective October 14, 1931. Black, who was
generally considered the leading farm economist of
that era, was a native of rural Wisconsin. He had
gone on to an outstanding career as a teacher and
researcher at the University of Minnesota and Harvard.
He and Davis were close friends since 1925 when both
served on the Agricultural Advisory Committee of the
Social Science Research Council. Despite their
different policy views, they remained close friends
into the 1930's. Then they collaborated on several
studies of New Deal farm programs. Davis kept Black
fully informed on Farm Board developments and problems
in organizing his economic staff. Two of Black's
former students, Mordecai Ezekiel and Chares F. Sarle,
were recruited by Davis from the Department of
Agriculture's Bureau of Agricultural Economics.(44)

Unlike Davis, Black did not hesitate to publicize
his views for resolving the deepening agricultural
depression. In addition to formulating and then
campaigning for the Voluntary Domestic Allotment Plan
as an immediate price-raising method, he favored
comprehensive and long-term land-use planning. The
latter, he believed, offered the best long-range
solution and could become the basis for a permanent
agricultural policy. While Agriculture Secretary Hyde
also advocated land-use planning, Black was quite
critical of his approach. He believed that Hyde's
plans were based on inadequate research and a failure
to examine alternatives. A clearer conception of
Black's views on land-use planning can be seen in his
role in the abortive Christgau bill.(45)

Victor Christgau of Minnesota, a former Black
student and the first farm economist to serve in
Congress, introduced a bill in the summer of 1930
containing many of Black's ideas. It represented a
major alternative to the Board's voluntary crop
reduction program. The Board's program was criticized
by Black and other leading farm economists, such as
Howard L. Tolley and Milburn L. Wilson, as crude and
inadequately researched. Their alternative was the
Christgau bill which provided the Department of
Agriculture with increased funding and the authority
to conduct cooperative research with agencies outside
of government. These agencies included agricultural
experiment stations and regional farm management

research councils, such as Wilson's Fairway Farms Incorporated in Montana. Based upon this research, recommendations would be made to individual farmers for producing the most profitable crops. Production would thus be harmonized with existing demand and as changes occurred production methods would be readjusted.(46)

Land-use planning was an integral part of the Christgau bill. It authorized the Department of Agriculture to make recommendations for regional and national land-use adjustments and for acreage limitations of specific crops. These could be implemented, for example, by federal, state, or local governments purchasing sub-marginal lands in accordance with their best regional and national uses. The Farm Board would assist the Department of Agriculture in conducting land-classification studies.(47)

While the Chritgau bill provided for acreage reductions based on thorough research, it relied, like the Farm Board's program, on a long-term educational appeal. It did not provide for strong adminstrative controls. The Bill never got out of committee, since Christgau's disagreements with Hoover deprived it of the necessary support. Although Black continued to support the bill as a basis for long-range planning, he recognized its limitations for solving immediate agricultural problems.(48)

During the rest of 1931, and well into 1932, Black urged the Farm Board to support the Voluntary Domestic Allotment Plan as an immediate price-raising device. He and the economic staff carefully analyzed the numerous bills containing some form of the domestic allotment plan, gave M. L. Wilson and his supporters direct access to the Board, and helped draft later versions of the plan in the form of the Hope-Norbeck bill in the summer of 1932. Black kept in constant communication with M. L. Wilson who sought his counsel at every stage of the campaign.(49)

The story of Wilson's conversion of Rexford G. Tugwell to the domestic allotment plan is well-known. Although Roosevelt did not directly endorse it during the 1932 campaign, he supported many of its key concepts in his major farm address at Topeka, Kansas in September, 1932. Among these were production controls with financial incentives for compliance. Roosevelt strongly attacked the Farm Board during the

1932 campaign, and it was obvious that the Board's existence as an independent agency would end if he won.(50)

Hoover did not support the Farm Board either during the 1932 campaign. The continuing decline in farm prices during the spring and summer 1932 made the Board a political liability. The Farmers' Holiday strike, in usually conservative and Republican Iowa, was an excellent example of the farmer's desperation and anti-Hoover bitterness during that campaign.(51)

During the Interregum Period, Hoover adamantly refused to support any legislation containing the domestic allotment plan. Hyde was in the process of formulating a plan for long-term leasing of marginal lands by the federal government, but Hoover could not implement it. During this crucial period, Mordecai Ezekiel advised the Board to replace its stabilization plans and voluntary crop reduction efforts with the Voluntary Domestic Allotment Plan. The Board finally yielded to Ezekiel when faced with erosion of its political support. In December, 1932 it endorsed the domestic allotment plan as an amendment to the Agricultural Marketing Act.(52)

Following Roosevelt's inauguration, the Federal Farm Board was abolished as a separate agency. That was done under authority granted the new President by the Economy Act of 1933. It provided broad powers for eliminating agencies like the Board without resorting to specific legislation. Although the Farm Board was abolished, many of its functions were retained. These were incorporated, along with those of other existing farm credit agencies, into the new Farm Credit Administration. The powerful National Cooperative Council's defense of remaining Board functions during late 1932 and early 1933 contributed to FDR's recognition of the importance of its cooperative and credit functions.(53)

Despite its rather sudden demise as an independent agency, the Federal Farm Board contributed much to its successor the Agricultural Adjustment Administration. Antecedents for the Triple A can be found in underlying philosophy, marketing agreements, stabilization, the need for production control, and several key Farm Board personnel who continued in advisory or administrative roles during the New Deal.

Joseph S. Davis contended that the Federal Farm

Board and the Triple A were essentially the same in their underlying philosophies and operations. Agriculture was considered a fundamental industry and farmers a class of paramount importance in American Society. The objective of national farm policy, therefore, was to raise farmers' icomes since they had not obtained their fair share. This required special aid from the federal government. When the Federal Farm Board proved unable to accomplish this, the farm organizations demanded new and more potent relief measures from the national government.(54)

Mordecai Ezekiel also saw significant antecedents for the Agricultural Adjustment Administration in the Farm Board experience. He believed that the Farm Board marked a major departure from past programs, since it was the first significant example of federal intervention in agriculture. Former New Deal brain-truster, Rexford G. Tugwell agreed with Ezekiel and carried it one step further. In 1974 he stated that while reluctant to admit it earlier, nearly the entire New Deal was derived from programs begun during the Hoover Administration. In his Memoirs, Hoover admitted that after the Stock Market Crash of 1929 and the European financial panic of 1931, his administration turned the Farm Board into a depression remedy.(55)

A number of significant antecedents can be found in specific areas as well as underlying philosophy. The Agricultural Adjustment Act of 1933 authorized its administrative agency to enter into marketing agreements with producers and middlemen for stabilizing farm prices. The Board's stabilization operations had involved government loans, storage, and purchase of selected commodities. They also involved price fixing, that is, attempting to establish a floor under farm prices. All of these devices, although on a larger scale, and as part of a longer term commitment, would be used in the New Deal farm programs. The comprehensive marketing section of the Triple A was used for commodities, such as citrus, dairy products, and tobacco.

Charles C. Teague, former Farm Board member, recognized the importance of marketing agreements under the AAA. Writing to his long-time friend and former Farm Board counsel, George Farrand, he concluded:

For years the orange growers, members of the

Exchange, prorated and regulated markets
themselves without any help from outside
shippers. A time came, however, when the
Exchange could no longer do this and the
industry was brought under the Agricultural
Marketing Agreement Act in 1933. Since that
time, there has been an industry prorate and
all shippers have borne their fair share of
surplus removal to stabilize the market.(56)

In spite of their obvious differences over the
methods and scope of production control, both the Farm
Board and the AAA agreed that overproduction was a
major cause of the farm problem. Although the Board's
voluntary production control program had failed, it
marked a drastic departure for that era. In August,
1931, for example, it surprised Southern governors
with a telegram urging farmers to plow under every
third row of cotton. Hoover not only favored the
plan, but urged farmers to kill off their baby pigs as
well.(57) Ironically, that was precisely the approach
used by Agriculture Secretary, Henry A. Wallace during
the first year of AAA operations.

The AAA appeared to be a major departure from the
Federal Farm Board since it used direct acreage
allotments. There were financial incentives for
compliance contained in contracts with individual
growers. A virtual army of federal agents was
required to advise farmers and check on compliance.
Charles C. Teague recognized these similarities and
differences conceding that Farm Board stabilization
had involved some federal intervention and
expenditure. He argued, however, that the Board did
not create a huge bureaucracy to regulate directly
every phase of agricultural production. The AAA spent
far more on production control and market
stabilization than the Farm Board had ever dreamed
of.(58)

The failure of the Board's stabilization and
voluntary production control programs led the major
farm organizations to accept reluctantly the AAA's
more comprehensive programs in these areas. The heart
of the production control mechanism of the
Agricultural Adjustment Act was the Voluntary Domestic
Allotment Plan. This was developed by Farm Board
economists John D. Black and Mordecai Ezekiel.
Ezekiel was a primary participant in the final
drafting process of the AAA between March and May,
1933. Both Black and Ezekiel continued to have

significant advisory roles during the New Deal. They were close friends and consultants of Secretary of Agriculture, Henry A. Wallace. Black's close friend, M. L. Wilson became an Undersecretary of Agriculture during the New Deal. He had been a close outside adviser of the Federal Farm Board.(59)

Stanley Reed, the Farm Board's second general counsel, served Roosevelt as Solicitor General from 1933 through 1936. He represented the government in many cases before the U.S. Supreme Court arising out of the NRA, the AAA, the Wagner Act, and TVA. In early 1938 Roosevelt appointed him as an Associate Justice of the Supreme Court.(60)

Whether the AAA was more successful than the Federal Farm Board in solving the agricultural dilemma has often been debated by economists and historians. Black and Wilson who had experience with both were not satisfied with either. They had supported the AAA on the assumption that it was the start of a comprehensive long-range plan. They were sorely disappointed by the mid 1930's, however, since they believed that the AAA merely concentrated on immediate price-raising. They were upset about its lack of long-term land-use planning and continued to favor the Christgau Bill as a start toward achieving that goal.(61) Although it was never enacted into law that bill represented the culmination of their experience during the Federal Farm Board's existence.

FOOTNOTES

1. David Burner, <u>Herbert Hoover: A Public Life</u> (New York: Alfred Knopf and Co. 1979), pp. 329-331; Maury Klein, "The New Deal: End of a Beginning" in <u>Readings in American History: Reconstruction Through the Present</u>, Vol. II (Guilford, Conn.: Duskin Press, 1980), pp. 118-129; Ellis W. Hawley, <u>The Great War and the Search for Modern Order</u> (New York: St.Martin's Press, 1979), pp.213-226; William Appleman Williams, <u>Americans in A Changing World: A History of the United States in the Twentieth Century</u> (New York: Harper and Row, 1978), pp. 237; David A. Shannon, <u>Twentieth Century America: The Twenties and Thirties</u>, Vol.II (Chicago: Rand McNally, 1977), pp.154-155; Joan Hoff Wilson, <u>Herbert Hoover: Forgotten Progressive</u> (Boston: Little, Brown and Co. 1975), pp. 152-158; and <u>Agricultural History</u> (April, 1977), Vol. 51, No. 2, especially the articles therein by Martin L. Fausold "President Hoover's Farm Policies, 1929-1933," pp. 362-37, and Joan Hoff Wilson "Hoover's Agricultural Policies, 1921-1928," pp. 337-338.

2. Gilbert C. Fite, "The Agricultural Issue in the Campaign of 1928," <u>Mississippi Valley Historical Review</u>, Vol. 38 (March, 1951), pp. 661.

3. Joan Hoff Wilson, "Hoover's Agricultural Policies, 1921-1928," op. cit., p.338; and Edward L. and Frederick H. Schapsmeier, <u>The Wallaces of Iowa: The Agrarian Years, 1910-1940</u> (Ames, Iowa: Iowa State University Press, 1968), pp. 71-73.

4. Herbert Hoover to Henry A. Wallace, March 10, 1925, Henry A. Wallace Papers, Reel 1, Frame 108, University of Iowa Library, and Joan Hoff Wilson, "Hoover's Agricultural Policies, 1921-1928," op.cit., 340-41.

5. Wilson, op.cit.,. pp. 340-41.

6. Murray R. Benedict, <u>Farm Policies of the United States,</u> 1790-1950 (New York: Twentieth Century Fund, 1953), pp. 225-226.

7. Gilbert N. Haugen to Robert F. Lee, October 28, 1928 in Folder 4 of the Haugen Papers "Campaign Correspondence," Iowa State Historical Society;

and George N. Peek to Edward G. Campbell in
Folder on 1928 Campaign Materials in Hoover
Papers, Hoover Presidential Library.

8. Box 33 of the Haugen Papers, "General Legislative
    Correspondence."

9. David Miller, "Origins and Functions of the
    Federal Farm Board," (University of Kansas:
    Unpublished Doctoral Dissertation, 1973), pp.
    133-34; and the Second Annual Report of the
    Federal Farm Board (1931), pp. 81-87.

10. Ibid., pp. 84-5.

11. For an excellent discussion of the organization
    of the Federal Farm Board refer to folder marked
    "Farm Matters: The Agricultural Marketing Act,
    1929-1930," Box 126 of the Hoover Presidential
    Papers, Subject File and Herbert Hoover to
    Alexander Legge, March 15, 1930 in folder
    "Federal Farm Board Correspondence, March 1-15,
    1930," Box 128 of the Hoover Presidential Papers,
    Subject File.

12. "Farm Matters: The Agricultural Marketing Act,
    1929-1930," of the Hoover Presidential Papers,
    Subject File; Charles C. Teague to Herbert
    Hoover, June 27, 1929 in Box 6 of the Teague
    Papers, UCLA Special Collections Library; and
    Herbert Hoover to Charles C. Teague, June 29,
    1929 in Box 6 of the Teague Papers.

13. New York Times, October 3, 1929, p. 4, and
    Herbert Hoover to John Hammill, April 24, 1929,
    "Federal Farm Board Correspondence, March-May,
    1929.

14. Hoover's Memorandum on Farm Board Organization in
    "Federal Farm Board Correspondence, July 1-15,
    1929," Box 128 of the Hoover Presidential Papers,
    Subject File.

15. Ibid.

16. First Annual Report of the Federal Farm Board
    (1930), pp. 24-25.

17. Ventura (California) Free Press, August 30, 1929,
    p. 6, at the Ventura County Historical Museum,
    Ventura, and Charles C. Teague to Ralph P.

Merritt, October 28, 1929 in Box 3 of the Teague
Papers.

18. Herbert Hoover to Alexander Legge, March 15, 1930
in Box 128 of the Hoover Presidential Papers,
Subject File.

19. Second Annual Report of the Federal Farm Board
(1931), p. 39.

20. Kiplinger Farm Board Newsletter, February 25,
1930 in Box 3 of the Teague Papers.

21. Alexander Legge to Herbert Hoover, March 10, 1930
in "Federal Farm Board Correspondence, March
1-15, 1930," Hoover Presidential Papers, Subject
File.

22. A. C. Hoffman, "After Two Years of Farm Relief,"
New Republic, Vol. 67, (July, 1931), pp. 168-170.

23. David Miller, "Origins and Functions of the
Federal Farm Board," op.cit. pp. 177-179 and
366, and the comprehensive articles by the
Nation's associate editor Mauritz A. Hallgren,
"Farm Relief Scandals, I and II, Nation, Vol.
133 (December 2 and 9, 1931), pp. 593 and 641.
Hallgren criticized Clarence E. Ruff as a
business failure in Kansas who lacked farming
experience. Professor Francis Schruben in his
Kansas in Turmoil, 1930-1936 (Columbia, Missouri:
University of Missouri Press, 1969), p. 52
indicated that Huff served simultaneously as
president of the Farmers' Union and the Farmers'
National. Schruben also indicated that Ralph
Snyder, head of the Kansas Farm Bureau,
considered Huff honest and well qualified.
Hallgren also condemned M. W. Thatcher as an
incompetent auditor who had worked for several of
Dakota and Minnesota cooperatives. The failure
of one of these had led to criminal proceedings
against him.

24. Third Annual Report of the Federal Farm Board,
(1933), pp. 78-79.

25. Central City, Nebraska Republican, November 1,
1930 in "Federal Farm Board Correspondence,
September-December, 1930," Box 129 of the Hoover
Presidential Papers, Subject File.

26. Frederick B.Wells to Walter H. Newton, November 9, 1929 in "Federal Farm Board Correspondence, November 1-9, 1929," Box 128 of the Hoover Presidential Papers, Subject File and Frederick B. Wells to Walter H. Newton, June 16, 1931 in "Federal Farm Board Correspondence, June, 1931," Box 130 of the Hoover Presidential Papers, Subject File.

27. John Vesecky to Alexander Legge, November 3, 1930 in "Federal Farm Board Correspondence, September-December, 1930," Hoover Presidential Papers, Subject File.

28. Max and Louis Levand to Herbert Hoover, July 10, 1930 in "Federal Farm Board Correspondence, July, 1930," Hoover Presidential Papers, Subject File.

29. Report of the Bureau of Agricultural Economics of the U.S. Department of Agriculture, October 15, 1930 in Box 3 of the Teague Papers.

30. Joseph S. Davis, "Memorandum to the Federal Farm Board, July 18, 1930," Box 5 of the Teague Papers and Henry A. Wallace to Alexander Legge, November 18, 1930, Reel 4, Frame 211, Henry A. Wallace Papers, University of Iowa Library.

31. Third Annual Report of the Federal Farm Board, pp. 65 and 67.

32. David Miller, "Origins of the Federal Farm Board," op.cit., p.256.

33. Congressional Record, 72 Congress, 1st Session, pp. 7588-7590 and p. 13972.

34. Ibid, pp. 7588-7590.

35. Minneapolis Tribune, February 10, 1932 in "Federal Farm Board Correspondence, January-March, 1932" in Hoover Presidential Papers, Subject File.

36. Charles C. Teague, Fifty Years a Rancher (Los Angeles: Ward Ritchie Press, 1944), pp. 180-181.

37. "Memorandum of the Economic Division of the Federal Farm Board, March 31, 1931," in Box 3 of the Teague Papers.

38. Ibid.

39. Miller, "Origins of the Federal Farm Board,"
    op.cit., p. 256.

40. Joseph S. Davis Interview, October 11, 1967,
    Herbert Hoover Oral History Program, p. 2, Hoover
    Presidential Library.

41. Ibid., p. 20.

42. Joseph S. Davis, "Memorandum to the Federal Farm
    Board, February 25, 1930," in Box 5 of the Teague
    Papers.

43. Joseph S. Davis to John D. Black, August 4, 1931,
    Box 4 of the Black Papers, Wisconsin State
    Historical Society.

44. Joseph S. Davis, "Memorandum on the Economics
    Division of the Federal Farm Board," in Box 42 of
    the Black Papers, Wisconsin State Historical
    Society, and Minutes of the Federal Farm Board,
    Vol. 3, p. 434, Hoover Presidential Library.

45. Bernard M. Klass, "John D. Black: Farm Economist
    and Policy Adviser, 1920-1942," (UCLA:
    Unpublished Doctoral Dissertation, 1969), p. 73.

46. Richard S. Kirkendall, Social Scientists and Farm
    Politics in the Age of Roosevelt (Columbia:
    University of Missouri Press, 1966), p.18.

47. Ibid., p. 19.

48. Klass, "John D. Black: Farm Economist and Policy
    Adviser," op.cit., pp. 74-75.

49. Ibid., pp. 81-82.

50. Miller, "Origins of the Federal Farm Board,"
    op.cit., p. 326.

51. David A. Shannon, Twentieth Century America,
    op.cit., p.160.

52. James C. Stone to Herbert Hoover, February 18,
    1933 in "Federal Farm Board Correspondence,
    1933," Hoover Presidential Papers, Subject File,
    and Miller, "Origins of the Federal Farm Board,"
    op.cit., p. 326.

53. James Guth, "The National Cooperative Council and Farm Relief, 1929-1942," <u>Agricultural History</u>, Vol. 51, No. 2 (April, 1977), pp. 441-458.

54. Burner, <u>Herbert Hoover: A Public Life</u>, op.cit., p. 243-44.

55. <u>Herbert Hoover's Memoirs</u>, Vol. II, p.255, and Burner, op.cit., p. 244.

56. Charles C. Teague to George Farrand, October 5, 1940, Box 10 of the Teague Papers.

57. Burner, <u>op.cit.</u>, p. 243.

58. Teague, <u>Fifty Years a Rancher</u>, <u>op. cit</u>, p. 181.

59. Klass, "John D. Black: Farm Economist and Policy Adviser," <u>op.cit.</u>, p. 87.

60. <u>Current Biography</u> 1942, p. 690.

61. Klass, <u>op.cit.</u>, pp. 97-98.

THE PERILS OF WESTERN FARM POLITICS:
HERBERT HOOVER, GERALD P. NYE, AND AGRICULTURAL REFORM
1926-1932

by David A. Horowitz

Although the Republican party dominated both the
Presidency and Congress in the 1920s, party unity was
threatened repeatedly by a vocal minority of
Progressive insurgents in the United States Senate.
Acrimony within the Republican party reached
particularly bitter levels over the issue of
agricultural reform. Nevertheless, by 1929 two of the
most virulent antagonists in the farm policy debate,
Herbert Hoover and Senator Gerald P. Nye, found
themselves in surprising agreement over the
establishment of a highly controversial federal farm
board. By 1932 their alliance once again collapsed.
This essay traces the curious political relationship
between the two between 1926 and 1932, when farm
policy played a major role in Republican party
politics. A focus upon agricultural reform provides
the opportunity to explore the features and
contradictions of both the New Era political
philosophy espoused by Hoover and the Progressive
insurgency set forth by Nye.

As Secretary of Commerce under Presidents Warren
G. Harding and Calvin Coolidge, Herbert Hoover
promoted the idea that economic efficiency and
national prosperity depended upon wise management in
large corporations and private bureaucracies. Hoover
had advanced this view in <u>American Individualism</u>, a
skillful treatise published in 1922. The energetic
commerce secretary argued that private firms and
organizations could foster efficiency in production
and distribution through voluntary cooperation,
concerted efforts to eliminate waste, and a sense of
service. Although Hoover warned that marketplace
power should not result in actual control of
government, he believed that administrative agencies
such as the Department of Commerce could assist the
private sector in promoting an equitable and efficient
marketplace. He promised that voluntary interaction
between governmet and private bureaucracies could
sustain a "tempered" individualism among the American
people -- a synthesis of collective expertise,
democratic pluralism, and personal initiative.(1)

Hoover's notion of the "associative state"
received ample scrutiny by several Republicans

representing western and agricultural constituencies
in the Senate. Led by Robert M. La Follette, Jr. of
Wisconsin, Hiram Johnson of California, William E.
Borah of Idaho, and George W. Norris of Nebraska, a
small but influential band of Senate Progressives
often dissented from policies associated with the
Harding and Coolidge administrations. The
Progressives accused the Republican White House of
endorsing corporate monopoly, eastern privilege,
financial imperialism and military adventurism
overseas. The insurgents vehemently protested that
friendliness to corporate capital at home and abroad
did nothing to meet the needs of independent
entrepreneurs in trade and agriculture. Hostility to
concentrated financial power in large corporations and
banks also led these dissenting Republicans to
distrust government agencies and bureacracies which
appeared to implement the wishes of big business and
high finance. Occasionally the "anticorporate"
Progressives combined radical denunciation of class
and regional privilege wih a faith that farmers, small
businessmen, and workers might use the state to
counter concentrated economic power.(2)

As Secretary of Commerce in the Harding and
Coolidge administrations and later as President,
Herbert Hoover was compelled to address the plight of
the independent western farmer. A postwar depression
in much of American agriculture, characterized by
shrinking markets, declining farm prices, and rising
costs contributed substantially to the harsh tones of
western insurgency in the 1920s. Progressive demands
for agricultural reform tested Hoover's contention
that voluntary cooperation and marketing efficiency
were the best solutions for beleagured producers.
Western Progressives frequently expressed the opinion
that the White House had abandoned the farmer once the
government had cancelled grain purchases following
World War One.(3)

Facing western distrust of administration farm
policy, Commerce Secretary Hoover began to address the
farm issue early in the Harding administration.
Consistent with his emphasis on efficiency in
distribution Hoover called for the creation of a
government farm marketing board in 1921. Through this
plan experts would assist farmer-controlled
cooperatives in the formation of central sales
organizations. Five years later Hoover added another
feature to his proposal. The farm board, he
suggested, could lend funds to federally-licensed

cooperatives so that agricultural products could be efficiently marketed and distributed in an expert manner.(4)

Secretary of Commerce Hoover viewed federal sponsorship of marketing cooperatives as an alternative to government involvement in either price-fixing or the purchase of agricultural surplus. "I do not think we have been neglectful of the notion that the farmer is in a position of inequity," he responded to a complaint in 1923. To demonstrate his preference for non-statist solutions to farm problems, Hoover chaired a President's Conference on Northwestern Agriculture and Finance in 1924 and pushed for crop diversification.(5) But Hoover's emphasis on cooperative marketing was not shared by Secretary of Agriculture Henry C. Wallace, who resented the Commerce Secretary's meddling in agriculture, or by congressional representatives from the farm states. Both Wallace and the farm congressmen pressed for government programs to purchase agricultural surplus. Under proposals embodied in the McNary-Haugen bills of 1924, 1927, and 1928, a government marketing corporation would buy surplus commodities and sell them overseas at reduced rates. Government losses would be compensated by an "equalization fee" levied on each farmer's surplus. Commodity prices would be sustained because the government would be willing to dump price-depressing surpluses in foreign markets. With Hoover's advice and consent, however, President Coolidge twice vetoed McNary-Haugen legislation in 1927 and 1928, objecting both to the questionable constitutionality of the equalizaton fee and to government interference with buying and selling.(6)

The rejection of McNary-Haugen infuriated western progressives with large agricultural constituencies. Prominent among them was Republican Gerald P. Nye of North Dakota. Nye launched his political career through the auspices of North Dakota's Nonpartisan League, a farmer's alliance founded in 1915 by Arthur C. Townley, a former socialist. Like the farmers of the midwestern Populist states of the 1880s and 1890s, North Dakota's frontier grain producers found themselves vulnerable to market control by outside forces. Distribution centers in the Twin Cities, Duluth, and Chicago fixed agricultural prices, while high-interest loans, exorbitant elevator fees, and burdensome railroad rates made life oppressive for the independent farmer. The Nonpartisan League hoped to

provide farmers with control of transportation and
marketing through state-owned facilities, services,
and stringent regulatory commissions. Within the
first six months of its existence, Townley's
organization spread to 40,000 North Dakota farmers and
won the governorship in 1916. By 1918 the antiwar
Nonpartisan movement had expanded membership to more
than 120,000 farmers in Minnesota, Nebraska,
Wisconsin, South Dakota, and Montana.(7)

    Nye entered politics when the Nonpartisan League
asked him to run as an independent for Congress in
1924. Speaking to farmers and townspeople who felt
victimized by banks, railroads, and middlemen, Nye
echoed Robert La Follette's concern over the
monopolies of the "money power." The North Dakotan
lost the 1924 campaign by a few hundred votes but
received a gubernatorial appointment to a vacant seat
in the United States Senate the following year. Nye
won the seat in his own right in 1926 as a candidate
who received Nonpartisan endorsement but ran on the
Republican ticket.(8)

    Once in the Senate Nye joined ranks with the
western Progressives. He opposed United States
participation in the World Court because he feared the
tribunal would become a collection agency for
international bankers. He denounced the dispatch of
marines to Nicaragua in 1927 as "Financial
Imperialism." He criticized tax reductions introduced
by Treasury Secretary Andrew Mellon as a gift to "the
favored few at the expense of masses." He argued that
the use of money in electing public officials and
controlling the government was a greater threat to the
well-being of the nation than "all the reds
combined."(9)

    Nye remained particularly adamant about the
plight of North Dakota's grain farmers. His 1926
senatorial campaign had stressed that one-third of the
state's farm acreage was operated by tenants and that
the percentage was increasing. National farm
indebtedness, he indicated, had risen 300 per cent
since 1911. Nye continued to insist that the
agricultural depression of the 1920s was a result of
deliberate financial and tax policies pursued by the
federal government. Farmers had been victimized by
deflationary credit policies following World War One,
he argued, pointing to insistence by the Federal
Reserve System that wartime farm loans be repaid.
Forced to sell produce in a declining agricultural

market to repay their debts, farmers faced bankruptcy
and foreclosure while the "money power" gained. For
Nye, a central irony lay in the fact that government
loans to the Allies had been renegotiated through the
Dawes Plan of 1924, but that government loans to
farmers had not. The Senator's solution was not "any
radical change in the system," but the assumption of
control over money and credit by a government imbued
with "character and honest administration."(10)

Nye connected government disdain for the
independent farmer to the inferior status of the West
in national politics and finance. He compared
westerners to a colonial people who dedicated their
labor and energy "to the profit of the American who
remains in the East." The Senator described the
Capitol as "a great nurse bottle." While farm
assistance was dismissed as "class legislation," he
complained, Washington attracted railroad interest,
manufacturers, and bankers who were fed "to their
hearts' content."(11) Nye simply wished to apply the
mechanisms of federal assistance to western farmers.

The North Dakotan's emphasis on the problem of
credit did not allow him to see the McNary-Haugen
proposals as a cure-all. But Nye was under intense
pressure from his constituents to work for federal
assistance to the troubled Farmer. "We want Frazier
and Nye to insist upon farm relief legislation first,"
the North Dakotan Nonpartisan bluntly announced after
Coolidge vetoed McNary-Haugen for the first time. One
of Nye's political mentors predicated that the farm
issue would "rise up to confound the Coolidge
administration" and that without relief, North Dakota
would experience "a political revolt more spectacular
than any we have ever had." Nye believed that
although McNary-Haugen would "not accomplish
everything desired, it will at least serve as an
entering wedge for more helpful legislation in the
future." The Senator even threatened to support an
outright subsidy for farmers if Coolidge vetoed the
farm bill a second time.(12)

Nye saw Coolidge's veto of McNary-Haugen as still
another example of regional discrimination against the
West. In the fall of 1927, the North Dakotan publicly
called for the formation of a "militant" progressive
bloc among Senate Republicans. Unlike the "farm bloc"
of the early 1920s, Nye's program of congressional
insurgency went beyond farm reliefs. It included
federal flood control and public power, abolition of

branch banking, restrictions on the Federal Reserve
Board, equitable freight rates, inland waterway
improvement, and reduction of government debt. In a
speech before the national Chamber of Commerce, Nye
warned that if the East continued to ignore the needs
of the West, sectional prejudice would produce a new
party alignment. Another address before the
Westchester County Bankers Association prophesied a
new political alliance between West and South if farm
relief was persistently blocked by the East.(13)

Although western Progressives could not hope to
constitute a Senate majority, their strategic
importance to the Republican party placed them in the
role of potential power brokers in congressional
politics. Consequently, Nye met with Senators Borah,
Norris, Lynn Frazier of North Dakota, and Smith W.
Brookhart of Iowa in October 1927 to plan for
congressional rule by a progressive coalition. But
the power bloc failed to materialize. Borah believed
that the equalization tax in the McNary-Haugen bill
was unconstitutional and refused to support the
proposal. At the same time, Norris and Brookhart
pushed for emphasis on Senate committee assignments
for Progressives, and objected to a discussion of
legislative programs. Only Frazier, Brookhart, La
Follette, and John J. Blaine of Wisconsin finally
joined Nye in a December letter to the Republican
party which demanded endorsement of McNary-Haugen.
Thus, Progressive commitment to McNary-Haugen was
tenuous. Newspaper reports even suggested that
western insurgents were prepared to give up the
equalization fee to win the support of Borah. Nye and
the other Progressives also rejected the presidential
candidacy of former Illinois Governor Frank C. Lowden,
who had won considerable midwestern support for his
endorsement of McNary-Haugen. The insurgents prefered
George Norris, a Progressive whose concern for western
interests went beyond his farm relief. But Norris had
little enthusiasm for McNary-Haugen.(14)

Agricultural politics played a role in the
controversy surrounding the Republican nomination of
Herbert Hoover for the presidency in 1928. Strong
anti-Hoover sentiment emanated from the Corn Belt
Committe, a pro-McNary-Haugen federation of
twenty-eight midwestern farm organizations first
created in 1926. The Committee had generated press
attention at that time with a resolution which
supported a congressional investigation of the
influence of Hoover's Commerce Department on

agricultural policy. Shortly after Coolidge's second
veto of the farm relief bill in May 1928 the Corn Belt
Committee met in Des Moines to warn that Republicans
must nominate a candidate sympathetic to agricultural
goals or lose the midwest. The Hoover forces publicly
discounted the Committee's influence.
McNary-Haugenism, claimed the chairman of Hoover's New
York State campaign, is "vigorously advocated by only
a few fanatics who are hangovers from the Populist
days or who more recently were wrecking the Northwest
with Townley's Non-Partisan League. The influence of
these men is negligible. They are just noisy."
Despite such glib dismissal of the Corn Belt Committee
threat, however, Hoover's administrative secretary had
taken the trouble to request information concerning
the political background of A.W. Rickner, the
Committee's secretary, from the government's own
Bureau of Investigation. Bureau Director J. Edgar
Hoover personally responded to the request, noting
that Rickner was an "Ultra Radical" who was "known
amongst farm leaders as a communist..."(15)

While the Corn Belt Committee tried to build
support for Lowden, Governor Adam McMullen of Nebraska
called for 100,000 farmers to protest the Coolidge
veto of McNary-Haugen at the Republican Convention.
Hoover's supporters countered these efforts by
soliciting enthusiastic support for their candidate
from leaders of the American Farm Bureau Federation.
When the McMullen demonstration fizzled and farm
dissidents failed to unify, Hoover easily won the
presidential nomination at the summer convention.(16)

Hoover's victory only aggravated the divisions
within the uneasy coalition of western progressives.
Norris and Blaine supported the Democratic nominee, Al
Smith. Although a Hoover supporter attempted to
convince Robert La Follette, Jr. that the candidate's
cooperative marketing system would eliminate the
middlemen and speculators denounced in 1924 by the
elder La Follette, the heir to Wisconsin Progressivism
refused to support the Hoover ticket. Shipstead of
Minnesota also expressed no interest in the Hoover
candidacy. Yet Charles McNary, Brookhart, Frazier,
Johnson, and Borah all supported the Republican
standard bearer.(17)

Gerald Nye initially vacillated on the Hoover
nomination. "This man Hoover," he told the press in
June, "whom some are trying to drive down our throats,
believes that agriculture is improving: if

226.

agriculture is improving it is dying of improvement."
But Smith had only promised to appoint a committee to
study the agricultural problem. In a postcard survey
of public leaders conducted by the Republican National
Committee in August, Nye responded that farmers could
expect more from Hoover than from the Democratic
candidate. Noting the commerce secretary's handling
of postwar business problems, Nye wrote that Hoover
"can be a great aid to agriculture and I believe he
will so apply himself." The North Dakotan publicly
endorsed Hoover a week later, following a conference
with the candidate on the day Al Smith accepted the
Democratic nomination. But although Nye expressed a
conviction that Hoover was determined to solve the
farm problem, North Dakota Nonpartisans failed to
endorse the Republican ticket. And when the
Nonpartisan League supported a pro-Smith Democrat for
governor, Nye felt compelled to do likewise. He also
bridged the gap between party loyalty and insurgency
by campaigning for Shipstead, the Farmer-Labor party
Senator from Minnesota who remained neutral in the
presidential campaign.(18)

As Hoover prepared to assume the presidency early
in 1929, Nye's position was paradoxical. Regular
Republican newspapers in Bismarch and Fargo continued
to portray the North Dakota insurgent as the "ranting
and reason-roaming senator, and paramount publicity
seeker;" as an "adolescent" junior senator who
confused reform with revolution.(19) But Nye
established a working relationship with the
president-elect when Hoover suggested that the Senator
send him suggestions from farm leaders in the Midwest.
Nye passed on several strong letters to Hoover in
January, hoping to provide the newly elected president
with "some opportunity to ascertain the frame of mind
existing at the present time." In general, the
letters and newspapers clippings which Nye chose to
forward expressed reservations about the federal farm
board which Hoover proposed to oversee cooperative
marketing. One Farmers Union official conveyed
discomfort with "a super machine at Washington" which
would not be directly responsible to farmer
organizations and cooperatives. Another correspondent
supported govement credit to aid marketing
associations, but objected to the unwarranted control
which might be placed in a national farm board. And
Nye forwarded an editorial from the Farmers Union
Herald which stressed that farmers wanted equal credit
and tariff policies, not "an autocratic farm board
whose members conceivably might do more harm than

good."(20)

These views were remarkably close to Nye's public positions on agricultural reform. Yet the Senator moved closer to Hoover's program during the special session of Congress devoted to farm relief in the spring of 1929. After toying with a scheme to allow farm cooperatives to use government capital to administer the equalization fee, Nye met with Hoover and endorsed the president's Agricultural Marketing Bill. Satisfied that Hoover would name an agricultural board that was "farm-minded," the North Dakota insurgent warned Senate colleagues against wasting time and announced that "we ought to support a bill that is practical."(21)

Nye took to the Senate floor in early May to record his support for Hoover's farm bill. "I do not greatly enthuse over the proposed legislation now before us," he confided. But Nye explained that although the Agricultural Marketing Bill did not afford all that he hoped "would be provided to meet the farm need," he would not apologize for his support of Hoover and his farm program. The test of the bill, the Senator stressed, would come with the naming of the Federal Farm Board and he was confident that the President would make "friendly" choices. Nye repeated the Hooverian view that the agricultural problem was "mainly a question of marketing." But the insurgent from North Dakota liked the farm bill because it offered credit resources to cooperatives and thereby promised to liberate independent agriculture from the stranglehold of eastern and regional financial centers. Nye's May 3rd speech singled out the Minneapolis grain merchants, ominously suggesting that there could be no effective administration of farm legislation "which does not infringe upon the opportunities and favors which accrue to those who utterly control the marketing machinery under the prevailing order."(22)

Having set forth these general principles, Nye went on to list the advantages of the Agricultural Marketing Bill. Three of them substantially reflected the president's point of view. First, Nye noted that government aid to marketing cooperatives would increase net income for farm producers by lessening distribution costs and providing farmers with "collective bargaining power" in the market. Second, he suggested that aid to cooperative purchasing agencies would have the same effect. And third, Nye

praised the bill's provisions for clearinghouse
associations to route perishable supplies more
efficiently. The North Dakotan also supported the
more controversial provision for stabilizing
corporations to buy up or remove surplus commodities
from the market.(23)

Farmers were "especially skeptical of boards to
administer laws which have been passed in behalf of
agriculture," the North Dakotan told the Senate in
May. But in August, two months after the President
signed the Agricultural Marketing Act with great
fanfare, Nye expressed qualified approval of Hoover's
nominees for the Federal Farm Board, including
Chairman Alexander Legge, former head of International
Harvester and wartime food planner. In a radio
address to North Dakotans, Nye insisted that the law
"was the best thing available at the present stage."
When the President's eight choices for the farm board
came up for Senate confirmation in October, Nye
supported all of them. Here he parted company with
western Progressives such as Brookhart, Norris, La
Follette, and Burton K. Wheeler, who voted against
Legge, Samuael R. McKelvie, and Carl Williams.
Nevertheless, Nye was safely within the Senate
majority, since Legge won confirmaion by a 67-11 vote,
McKelvie of Nebraska by a 50-27 margin, and Williams
of Oklahoma by 57-20. There was no division in the
Senate on the other five nominees for the Federal Farm
Board.(24)

Despite Nye's belief that the Hoover farm program
was inadequate, the North Dakotan continued to support
the farm board through its most bitter controversies.
Even before passage of the marketing act, grain
dealers and millers in Minneapolis had expressed
anxiety over the prospects of government assistance to
selected farm marketing cooperatives. In October 1929
the farm board recognized the Farmers National Grain
Corporation in Minnesota as the central marketing
agency for northwest grain cooperatives. This
qualified the giant agency for government marketing
loans. Private grain dealers in Minneapolis and
Chicago mounted a vociferous campaign against such
favoritism. "The establishment of loan values and the
pronouncements of the Board," one Minneapolis Chamber
of Commerce representative protested to the White
House, "are more socialistic than any governmental
action with which I am familiar, excepting only the
manifestoes issued by Mussolini." National Chamber of
Commerce chairman Julius H. Barnes, a Hoover friend

who had directed wheat distribution fo the government
in World War One, led the Chamber into a full-scale
crusade against farm board policies. In Chicago,
small vegetable and fruit distributions objected to
cooperative marketing in that field, protesting to the
president against "the entry of our Government into
business within this industry in competition with
private capital and private citizens."(25)

For Nye, the Minneapolis situation clarified the
farm bill controversy. "The fight now being made upon
the Farm Board by influences which have built a little
world of their own in the grain-marketing field." he
told the Senate in December 1929, "is the best
possible indication of sympathetic administration of
the farm bill." If the farm board would "succeed in
eliminating from the market machinery of the country
that crowd of leeches and giants who have caused all
the misery to American agriculture out in our
section." Nye continued, "it will have accomplished a
wonderfully worth-while thing." When Senator Peter
Norbeck of South Dakota protested that Nye's defense
of the administraion might delay passage of the
equalization fee, the North Dakotan conceded
limitations in the agricultural program, but said it
was essential to defend the farm board "when all they
are bearing is the damnation of the grain trade."
Nye's pro-farm board views were not merely public
postures. A note in a briefly-kept diary revealed the
depth of the North Dakotan's position: "That board is
playing on the square. What a victory it would be if
they go straight through."(26)

Nye's passionate support of Hoover's farm board
stemmed from the Senator's assessment of northwestern
grain economics. He maintained that private elevators
customarily controlled the market and dominated
farmers by checking grades, inspecting crops, and
providing selective market information. The private
elevators, in turn, were controlled by commercial
firms holding seats on grain exchanges operated by
boards of trade and chambers of commerce in
Minneapolis, Duluth, and Chicago. If
farmer-controlled cooperatives operated their own
terminals and elevators, Nye asserted, the grain trade
would lose the opportunity to collect its "unearned
tolls from producers of grain." For Nye, a "war of
propaganda" had been mounted by selfish interests
aginst "genuine farm relief." Despite its rejection
of McNary-Haugen, the Hoover administration had
produced "farm-controlled marketing machinery."(27)

The debate over farm board policy reached fervor
pitch with the creation of a government Grain
Stabilization Corporation in February 1930. Directed
by the farm board to begin the direct purchase of
wheat at a fixed price, the stabilization corporation
marked a concession to western supporters of the
equalization fee. But to the dismay of private
elevator and commission men in the northwest, the
agency only would offer the cherished $1.25 a bushel
to cooperatives and elevators affiliated with the farm
board grain program. Even Nye received telegrams from
private elevator operators in North Dakota which
protested the board's policy on grain purchases. The
Senator's response was to lash out more fervently at
grain merchants. He inserted another telegram into
the Congressional Record. "No justification for any
protest from elevator companies," a cooperative
marketing official wired. "Chairman Legge has proven
himself a champion for the farmers and an American
statesman."(28)

Following conferences between Legge and Chicago
grain dealers in late February, however, the farm
board announced that its stabilization corporation
would only buy at market prices, not the pegged loan
prices which had benefitted the cooperatives.
Confidence in the board quickly began to wane among
cooperative supporters. On March 3rd, Nye submitted a
Senate resolution which called for an investigation of
the farm board issue. Resolution 221 asked the
Committee on Agriculture to ascertain whether the
Federal Farm Board had fairly interpreted the
Agricultural Marketing Act, whether the grain
merchants had "conspired" to destroy the purpose of
the law and to depress world wheat prices, and whether
grain trade interests were being assisted by banking
and credit institutions. Once again, Nye had managed
to connect issues of banking and credit to the farm
problem. But Agriculture Committee Chairman McNary
chose to sidetrack the Nye resolution and hearings
were postponed. Several months later, when he called
for an investigation of the activities of the American
Boards of Trade and Chambers of Commerce in foreign
grain markets, Nye still believed that sale of cheap
grain overseas was "part of the program to depress
agricultural prices in order to discredit the Farm
Board."(29)

Although the farm board ended its grain purchase
program in March 1931, opposition to federal farm
policy escalated among northwest commodity dealers. A

controversy over closing the Chicago Board of Trade
and the threat of massive unloading of government-held
wheat convinced private distributors that the
president's farm board was in competition with private
enterprise. "The trouble with men like Senator Arthur
Capper, La Follette, Nye and Norris, to say nothing of
Brookhart," a Chicago dealer wrote President Hoover in
mid-1932, "is that they know nothing whatever about
the science of political economy." As far back as
1922, Hoover angrily had insisted that it was "rank
nonsense" to believe that cooperative marketing was
socialistic. But by the summer of 1931 Minneapolis
grain dealers were complaining about "Communistic rule
applied to agricultural marketing." The grain trade
particularly objected to the farm board's recognition
of the Farmers National Grain Corporation as the sole
agent for cooperative marketing in wheat. As the
Farmers National absorbed northwest cooperatives such
as the Farmers Union Terminal Association and the
Northwest Grain Association, charges of monopoly, as
well as fresh allegations of fraud and intimidation,
received widespread coverage in the Twin Cities
press.(30)

By 1931 and 1932, the failure of the
stabilization program to stop the disastrous decline
in agricultural prices opened the farm board to
criticism outside the grain trade. A polemic
published in Minneapolis, J.W. Brinton's Wheat and
Politics (1931), attempted to portray the exploitation
of the defenseless farmer "up to the Federal Farm
Board with Sam McKelvie's Chain Store system for
marketing grain through a Delaware Corporation
[Farmers National Grain Corporation] financed from the
Public Treasury." A Nebraska weekly claimed in March
1932 that farmers in eighteen surrounding counties
opposed the farm board by a ten-to-one margin. Seven
months later, the chairman of the Republican State
Committee wired the White House that there was
"widespread bitter opposition in Nebraska" to the farm
board and that he was sure the attitude prevailed
through the central west. The Farmers Union remained
nominally loyal to the board in North Dakota,
Minnesota, Wisconsin, Missouri, and Kansas. But in
1930, control of the national organization shifted to
anti-farm board leaders who worked with the Corn Belt
Committee in demanding new forms of farm relief.(31)

In the face of increasing criticism toward the
farm board, Nye attempted to defend its actions
against the northwest grain trade while keeping up

pressure for more extensive relief. In a Senate speech on another matter, Nye paused to note that the farm board controversy with grain trading interests would not have occurred if the Federal Trade Commission had been able to stop attempts to crush the farm cooperative movement of the early 1920s. He placed into the Congressional Record a 1932 radio address by the head of the Farmers National Grain Corporation. A Nye amendment to the independent office appropriation of 1932 attempted to raise the limit on farm board office spending to $1 million, but was defeated 33-12. "I am just as severe a critic...of some of the practices of the Federal Farm Board as others," the North Dakotan declared in one debate, but urged that the board not be starved to death. When a colleague questioned whether farm board loans would ever be repaid, Nye dryly responded that recovery of outstanding loans to cooperatives would "be as large as...the recovery by the Reconstruction Finance Corporation from those to whom it loans money."(32)

Despite his delight in the discomfort of Minneapolis grain interests, Nye fought to move beyond farm board policy. He continually insisted in the spring of 1932 that the Senate refuse adjournment until it had considered two agricultural relief bills before it. The first consisted of three amendments to the Agricultural Marketing Act introduced by Agriculture Committee Chairman McNary. The amendments called for an equalization fee, a debenture plan, and the domestic allotment scheme proposed by the Farmers Union. "I am not personally a believer in price-fixing programs," Nye explained in defense of his endorsement of the allotment plan, which proposed to create another board to determine the production cost of surplus as a basis for a fixed price. But Nye told a radio audience that the agricultural emergency demanded a solution which went to the root of the farm problem. The amendment, said Nye, could mark the "turning point in the legislative battle for the American farmer."(33)

The second bill that Nye promoted was the Frazier Debt Moratorium, which promised to refinance farm indebtedness with new government loans. With the support of Blaine, Brookhart, Frazier, and Norris, Nye had tried to insert a one-year moratorium for farm obligations in the European Debt Moratorium Bill of 1931. When it appeared that few Senators besides the western Progressives desired such an extension of the debt moratorium principle, Nye had quipped that farmers would benefit more "if they would pledge themselves to spend what they would be excused from paying immediately for battleships." The Frazier Bill of 1932, which Nye saw as a measure to destroy the power of those who controlled money, was referred to committee in July, one month after the McNary amendments were recommitted over the protests of western Progressives and some Democrats.(34)

Amidst such reversals, Nye could only reassert persistent arguments. Economic prosperity, he insisted, was impossible unless agriculture was healthy. Second, falling farm prices and increased bankruptcy called for "drastic change." The longer the Senate put off the task of extending relief, Nye warned, "the more drastic will need be the means resorted to, to accomplish the desired ends." And third, the only solution to the farm depression was a cancellation of private loans and their substitution by low-interest government loans. Campaigning in North Dakota in June, 1932, Nye once again lashed out at bankers who had "squeezed" not only the profits from agriculture but the capital as well. "Ultimately," he concluded, "a radical readjustment of national wealth will be necessary."(35)

Nye had supported Hoover in 1928 because of the Commerce secretary's promises to assist agriculture, the candidate's defense of Prohibition, and the disarray of western Progressivism. Like most representatives of farm states, the North Dakotan had rallied behind the Agricultural Marketing Act of 1929 because there was no politically workable alternative. Once the Federal Farm Board began to assist northwestern farm associations in capturing the market machinery from the grain trade, Nye had overcome a distrust of government farm agencies and become one of the prime defenders of the controversial board. It was certainly ironic that President Hoover, who detested government intervention in the private market, had sponsored a radical experiment in political control of commodity distribution. Between 1929 and 1933 Nye of North Dakota remained one of the most unlikely farm allies from whom Hoover won political support. Yet by continually calling for further agricultural relief and the revamping of credit sources, the Senator also kept his distance from Hoover during the Depression years.

In supporting Hoover's approach to cooperative

marketing, Nye walked a tightrope between radical
agitation and viable reform, between sensitivity to
constituent issues and cooperation with the
administration, between support for independent
farmers and willingness to use federal bureaucracy,
between free-market economics and adherence to
national planning. A Progressive deeply committed to
small producers, Nye initially had rejected government
agencies as statist tools of financial capitalism.
But as a spokesman for the independent grain farmers
of the northwest, he found himself supporting the one
aspect of Hoover's program which placed more emphasis
on coercion than voluntarism.

Although the North Dakotan endorsed important
aspects of Hoover's farm policy, Nye's agrarian
radicalism made it increasingly difficult to support
the troubled President as the 1932 elections neared.
The Senator had asked Hoover to make a North Dakota
speech during the President's summer tour of the West
in 1930. But once the Republicans lost congressional
strength in the November elections, Nye blamed the
results on inadequate farm relief and hostility toward
the electric power trusts. The West had shown
"extreme displeasure with the administration and the
operation of the farm act," he announced in 1940. Like
other western Progressives, the North Dakotan also
objected to the high duties on manufactured goods
embodied in the Smoot-Hawley Tariff of that year.
During 1931 the White House received newspaper
clippings and a report from a Fargo banker that
indicated that Nye "pounded President Hoover in every
speech he made in North Dakota."(36)

Both Hoover and Nye faced re-election in 1932.
North Dakota politics demanded that Nye make amends to
Nonpartisan insurgents as well as Republican regulars.
Early in the year the Senator issued a stinging attck
on the administration's Depression policies. It was
intolerable, he reported, to "sit and listen to more
of this urge which we have had blown at us for years
that all we need in America is more confidence;
...that we must beware of paternalism, of socialism,
of bolshevism, of the dole." Without mentioning
names, Nye condemned current pleas "to have confidence
in the old order which has all but destroyed us." Not
surprisingly, the Senator won re-election support from
the Nonpartisans in February. The next month he told
the press that he did not plan "to campaign on a
Hoover platform in view of the Hoover Administration's
failure to respond adequately to the needs of

agriculture and to give agriculture the same play given to business and the railroads." But despita a growing reputation as an anti-Hoover Republican, and despite sharp criticism of the Reconstruction Finance Corporation's aid to banks and railroads, Nye insisted that he would not make "anti-Hooverism" the issue of his re-election. While the White House received continuing reports of Nye's infidelity to the administration, the Senator took great pains to explain to North Dakotans that his differences with Hoover had "been upon the highest ground." There had "often been no opportunity to stand by the President on farm bills," he told campaign audiences, "and remain true to the farm people." Running as a Republican Independent, Nye professsed neutrality in the presidential race between Hoover and Franklin D. Roosevelt. Nye and the North Dakota Nonpartisans carried both the Republican primary and the election of 1932. Ironically the Senator's 70 percent plurality over his Democratic opponent matched Roosevelt's margin over Hoover in North Dakota.(37)

Since his emergence into political life in 1924 Gerald Nye had attempted to build an insurgent progressivism which occasionally touched base with the regulars of the Republican party. In his desire to use federal power to promote independent farming and business, Nye found himself endorsing the Federal Farm Board of the Hoover administration. The farm board's sponsorship of agricultural marketing cooperatives provided a clear example of the associative state long envisioned by President Hoover. But in its disruption of traditional marketing arrangements among entrepreneurs in the grain trade, the federal agency may have implemented the most radical program of the Hoover presidency. Despite reservations over the limitations of the Hoover farm program, Nye was pleased with the federal government's effort to use bureaucratic power to discipline grain distributors. Yet he never budged from the basic tenet of his anticorporate progressivism: that the problems of farmers and small businessmen were rooted in the monopoly of capital and credit exerted by the private banking community.

Herbert Hoover, the nation's leading strategist of New Era business philosphy, and Gerald P. Nye, one of its most radical critics, were not likely political allies. For a short time between 1928 and 1932, however, the interests of the two Republicans met in support of the controversial farm board. To Hoover,

236.

the board represented a long-awaited attempt to use
the auspices of the federal government to assist
producers in the creation of cooperative marketing
associations. This was consistent with the effort to
develop efficiency in the nation's distributive
process. For Nye, the board represented a
long-awaited attempt to use the auspices of the
federal government to free small producers from the
tyranny of bankers and monopolistic distributors.
Although the alliance appeared tenuous and
uncomfortable to both, the two men cooperated to
fashion an unusual chapter in the history of business
progressivism and reform. The subsequent opposition
of each to the statism of Franklin D. Roosevelt's New
Deal would only add another twist to this most unusual
alliance between two wildly dissimilar American
reformers of the twentieth century.

FOOTNOTES

1. Herbert Hoover, American Individualism
    (Washington, n.d.), 4-5 13, 17, 19-21. For a
    description of the Associative State see Ellis W.
    Hawley, The Great War and the Search for a Modern
    American Order: A History of the American People
    and Their Insitutions, 1917-1933 (New York: St.
    Martin's Press, 1979), 53-55, 80-97, 100-04.

2. David P. Thelen, Robert M. La Follette and the
    Insurgent Spirit (Boston: Little Brown, 1976);
    LeRoy Ashby, The Spearless Leader: Senator Borah
    and the Progressive Movement in the 1920s
    (Urbana: University of Illinois Press, 1972);
    Richard Lowitt, George W. Norris: The
    Persistence of a Progressive, 1913-1933 (Urbana:
    University of Illinois Press, 1971). The
    congressional farm bloc of the 1920s is described
    by Theodore Saloutos and John D. Hicks,
    Agricultural Discontent in the Middle West,
    1900-1939 (Madison: University of Wisconsin
    Press, 1951), chap. XI and Russel Nye, Midwestern
    Progressive Politics: A Historical Study of its
    Origins and Development, 1870-1950 (East Lansing:
    Michigan State College Press, 1951), 323-47.

3. Henry R. Willging, "Herbert Hoover, the
    McNary-Haugenites, and American Agricultural
    Policy, 1920-1929," (M.A. diss., University of
    Wisconsin, 1967), 85-105.

4. Ibid. See "Agriculture--Addresses by Mr. Hoover,
    1924-1925," Commerce Papers, Herbert Hoover
    Presidential Library (hereafter, HHPL); and
    Hoover, "My Plan for Eliminating Waste in the
    Farming Industry," Capper's Farmer (March, 1925).

5. Hoover to Nicholas Doyle, 18 May 1923,
    "Agriculture, 1923," Commerce Papers;
    "Agriculture--Northwestern Agriculture,
    1923-1924," Commerce Papers, HHPL.

6. Willging, 80-82.

7. Saloutos and Hicks, chap. VI; Nye, 310-20. See
    Robert L. Morlan, Political Prairie Fire: The
    Nonpartisan League, 1915-1922 (Minneapolis:
    University of Minneapolis Press, 1956).

8. Wayne S. Cole, Gerald P. Nye and American Foreign

Relations (Minneapolis: University of Minnesota
Press, 1962), 37-46; Nye Platform, "Campaign of
1924;" Campaign Address, "Addresses, 1924,"
Speeches and Articles, Nye Papers, HHPL.

9. "The World Court," 23 January 1926, "Addresses,
1926, Campaign Speech," Speeches and Articles; "A
Program for Progressives," 27 November 1927,
"Addresses, 1927," Speeches and Articles;
Address, n.d., "Addresses, 1928," Speeches and
Articles; Campaign Speech, "Addresses, 1926,"
Nye Papers, HHPL.

10. Campaign Speech, "Addresses, 1926," Campaign
Speech, Speeches and Articles; Radio Address,
n.d., "Addresses, 1936, Campaign Speech,"
Speeches and Articles; Campaign Address,
"Addresses, 1924," Speeches and Articles, Nye
Papers, HHPL.

11. "Friendly Advice to Reactionaries," n.d.,
"Addresses, 1928;" "The World Court," 23 January
1926, "Addresses, 1926, Campaign Speech," Nye
Papers, HHPL.

12. "Advice to Our Senators," North Dakota
Nonpartisan, reprinted in Dunn County Farmers,
Journal, 1 December 1927, "Clippings, 1927;"
Thomas H. Moodie to Nye, 22 January 1927,
"Correspondence, 1927;" Nye to Judge W.S.
Lauder, 20 January 1927, "Correspondence, 1927,
Nye Papers, HHPL; New York Times, 5 December
1927.

13. New York Times, 15, 20 September, 19 October
1927; Sioux City Sunday Journal, 29 January 1928,
"Clippings, January-February, 1928," Nye Papers,
HHPL.

14. New York Times, 4 December 1929; Baltimore Sun,
21 October 1927. See Ashby, Chap. 8.

15. St. Paul Pioneer Press, 21 July 1926; New York
Evening Post, 12 May 1928; "Townley's
Non-Partisan League," Press Releases, June 1928,
Campaign and Transition, 1928-1929; Memorandum
from the Director, in re A.W. Ricker, 13 April
1928, and J. Edgar Hoover to Lawrence Richey, 13
April 1928; "Corn Belt Committee, 1928,
Agriculture, 1928, October-November,
Misrepresentations File, HHPL. See Gilbert C.

Fite, "The Agricultural Issues in the
Presidential Campaign of 1928," Mississippi
Valley Historical Review, 37 (March 1951),
653-72.

16. Fite, 653-72; "Agriculture, 1928, March-April,"
    Misrepresentations File; "Campaign Literature:
    Press Releases, March 12, 1928, Farm Speech,"
    Campaign and Transistion, 1928-1929, HHPL.

17. B.F. Yoakum to La Follette, Jr., 29 October 1928,
    "Campaign Literature: Press Releases, 29 October
    1928," Campaign and Transition, 1928-1929, HHPL.

18. New York Times, 23 September 1928; Nye postcard,
    14 August 1928, "Campaign Literature: National
    Who's Who Poll," Campaign and Transition,
    1928-1929; New York Times, 23 August 1928;
    Devil's Lake Journal, 23 August, 6 September
    1928, "Clippings and Scrapbooks," Nye Papers,
    HHPL.

19. Bismark Capitol, 26 February 1929, "Clippings,"
    Nye Paper, HHPL. See also the description of Nye
    as "political clown extraordinary," Fargo Forum,
    2 December 1927, "Clippings."

20. Nye to Hoover, and attachments, 17 January 1929,
    "General Correspondence, 1928-1929, Nye,"
    Campaign and Transition, 1928-1929, HHPL.

21. New York Times, 15 March, 28 April, 14 May 1929.
    Nye introduced a Senate resolution to assure farm
    relief first priority in the special session.
    See Congressional Record, 71st Cong., spec.
    sess., 18 April 1929, p. 352.

22. Congressional Record, 71st Cong., spec. sess., 3
    May 1929, p. 835

23. Ibid., 836-38.

24. Ibid., 839; "The Farmer and Pending Legislation,"
    Radio Address, 24 August 1929, "Addresses, 1929,"
    Speeches and Articles, Nye Papers, HHPL. See
    Congressional Record, 71st Cong., spec. sess., 16
    October 1929, pp. 4610-11. For an account of the
    controversies surrounding farm board
    appointments, see the correspondence in "Farm
    Matters--Federal Farm Board Endorsements,"

Subject File, Presidential Personal File, HHPL.

25. Baltimore Sun, 9 December 1929; Saloutos and
    Hicks, Chap. 14; Frederick B. Wells to Walter H.
    Newton, 9 November 1929, "Farm Matters--Federal
    Farm Board, Correspondence November 1-15, 1929,"
    Subject File, Presidential Personal File; J.D.
    Houton to Hoover, 30 December 1929, "Farm
    Matters--Cooperative Marketing, 1930-1933,"
    Subject File,Presidential Personal File, HHPL.
    For grain trade opposition to cooperative
    marketing in the months preceding passage of the
    Agricultural Marketing Act, see the various
    folders under "Farm Matters--Federal Farm Board,"
    Subject File, Presidential Personal File, HHPL.

26. "The Federal Farm Board and the Farmer,"
    Congressional Record, 71st Cong., 2nd sess., 9
    December 1929, pp. 301-04; 4 January 1930,
    "Diary, 1930," Subject File, Nye Papers, HHPL.

27. Congressional Record, 71st Cong., 2nd sess., 9
    December 1929, pp. 303-04.

28. Ibid., 26, 27 February 1930, pp. 4280-81;
    4606-08.

29. New York Times, 4, 5 March, 28 September 1930.
    For an account of the stabilization program, see
    Saloutos and Hicks, 417-24. For the politics
    behind stabilization attempts, see Martin L.
    Fausold, "President Hoover's Farm Policies,"
    Agricultural History, 51 (April, 2977) 362-77.

30. C. C. Millett to Hoover, 29 July 1932, "Farm
    Matters--Federal Farm Board, Correspondence,
    June-July, 1932;" Frederick B. Wells to Walter H.
    Newton, 7 August 1931, "Farm Matters--Federal
    Farm Board, Correspondence, August 1-15, 1931;"
    Julius H. Barnes to Hoover, 28 April 1932, "Farm
    Matters--Federal Farm Board, Correspondence,
    April-May, 1932;" C. A. Wallingford, 25 July 1932
    to Henry J. Allen, "Farm Matters--Federal Farm
    Board, Correspondence, June-July, 1932," Subject
    File, Presidential Personal File, HHPL;
    Minneapolis Tribune, 5 August 1931. See the
    outpouring of grain trade protest against the
    farm board in the Farm Board correspondence of
    the Presidential Personal File. For Hoover's
    early defense of cooperative marketing as "the
    exact antithesis of socialism," see "Why

Cooperative Marketing Should Receive United
Support," Country Gentleman, 21 October 1922,
"Agriculture, 1919-1922," Commerce Papers, HHPL.

31. J. W. Brinton, Wheat and Politics (Minneapolis,
1931); Central City Republican, 29 March 1932;
Robert Smith, telegram to Walter H. Newton, 1
October 1932, "Farm Matters--Federal Farm Board,
Correspondence, October-December, 1932," Subject
File, Presidential Personal File. See Brinton's
promotional pamphlet, "Wheat and Politics," "Farm
Matters--Federal Farm Board, Correspondence,
September-December, 1931," Subject File,
Presidential Personal Hile, HHPL. For an account
of increasing farm frustration with Hoover's
agricultural program, and farm organization
proposals for an equalization fee, export
debentures, or cost-of-production price-fixing,
see Saloutos and Hicks, 429ff.

32. Congressional Record, 71st Cong., 3rd sess., 24
January 1931, p. 3063; 72nd Cong., 1st sess., 6
May, 26, 27 June 1932, pp. 9711-12, 14,030,
14,037, 14,039.

33. Ibid., 72nd Cong., 1st sess., 26, 27 May, 13 June
1932, pp. 11,260, 11,360, 12,768; "What
Progressives Hope for in 1932," 7 January 1932,
"Addresses, 1932," Addresses and Speeches, Nye
Papers, HHPL.

34. Congressional Record, 72nd Cong., 1st sess., 13,
15 June, 11 July 1932, pp. 1120-21, 12,769-71,
13,000, 14,997. The Nye amendment to the
European Debt Moratorium Bill of 1931 was
defeated by a decisive 60-15 margin, but the vote
to recommit the McNary amendments in 1932 was a
far closer 38-28.

35. Ibid., 13 June 1932, pp. 12,768-70; Press
Release, June, 1932, "Campaign of 1932," Campaign
File, Nye Papers, HHPL.

36. Nye to Hoover, 20 May 1930, "Nye," Secretary's
File, Presidential Personal File; New York Times,
8 November 1930; William Stern to Walter H.
Newton, "Nye," Secretary's File, Presidential
Personal File, HHPL. For Nye and tariff policy
see "The Farmer and Pending Legislation," 24
August 1929, "Addresses, 1929," Speeches and
Articles, Nye Papers; New York Times, 17 November

1929; Press Release, Democratic National
Committee, 14 March 1930, "Nye," Secretary's
File, Presidential Personal File, HHPL.

37. "What Progressives Hope for in 1932," "Addresses
and Speeches," Nye Papers; <u>Minneapolis Weekly
Mirror</u>, 2 April 1932. See L. B. Hanna to Hoover,
28 September 1932, "Nye," Secretary's File,
Presidential Personal File, HHPL.

THE IOWA CONGRESSIONAL DELEGATION
AND THE GREAT ECONOMIC ISSUES
1929-1933

By David L. Porter

Historians writing about the Great Depression
have paid relatively little attention to the response
of the rural, agrarian Middle West to vital economic
legislation. For example, how did Iowa, the state in
which President Herbert Hoover was born, view crucial
national economic problems? This essay describes the
reaction of the Iowa Congressional delegation during
the Republican Hoover administration to major measures
aiding business, benefiting organized labor, providing
federal unemployment relief, and expanding government
competition with private industry.(2)

In this essay, five basic themes are stressed.
[1] Between 1929 and 1933, the Iowa Congressional
delegation usually supported bills helping business
and organized labor; [2] On the other hand, it usually
resisted federal unemployment relief and increasing
government control over private enterprise; [3]
Economic considerations prevailed among Iowa Senators
and Representativesd, with political motivations
playing a subordinate role; [4] The Iowa Congressional
delegation comprised a mixture of progressives,
moderates, and conservatives, who clashed fairly often
on fundamental economic measures; [5] Iowa Senators
and Representatives were less conservative than
anticipated, frequently demonstrating more
progressivism than President Hoover on the great
economic issues.

Republicans dominated the Iowa Congressional
delegation, which comprised the following members:(3)
(Table 1)

Between 1929 and 1931, Hoover's party held all
eleven House seats and one Senate position.
Republicans continued to prevail the next two years,
occupying ten House and both Senate seats. Democrats
wielded negligible power, with Senator Steck and
Representative Jacobsen the only party members in the
Iowa delegation.

Despite serving a moderately populated,
predominantly rural state, the Iowa Congressional
delegation had considerable political clout on Capital
Hill. In the Senate, the flamboyant Brookhart

vigorously defended agriculture and organized labor
and often made vitriolic attacks on big business.
Representative Haugen, serving in Congress since 1899,
chaired the prestigious Agriculture Committee and
sponsored numerous farm measures. House colleagues
regarded Congressmen Dickinson and Ramseyer as
financial experts and Representative Cole as an
authority on international affairs. Congressman
Swanson belonged to the influential Judiciary
Committee, while Representative Thurston served on the
powerful Rules Committee.(4)

The Iowa Congressional delegation resoundingly
adopted the Smoot-Hawley Act of 1930 aiding big
business. Besides raising business tariff duties to
an unprecendented 40 percent level, the Smoot-Hawley
measure nearly doubled protection for agricultural
commodities.(5) With the exception of Representative
Campbell, Iowa Congressmen welcomed the rate chnges.
(Table 2) Ramseyer even battled in the Ways and Means
Committee to increase protection for Middle West
farmers, while Cole urged President Hoover to "make
very speedy disposition" of the tariff measure. "If
there is too much delay," Cole warned, "it will get on
the nerves of the people and create unlimited
propaganda which may be quite as embarrassing as the
senatorial debates have been."(6)

Excitement about potential economic benefits for
Iowa farmers induced the state's Representatives to
endorse the Smoot-Hawley bill. The tariff measure
dramatically increased duties on corn, beef, pork,
fruits, poultry, eggs, lard, wool, and other farm
products, better safeguarding agricultural interests.
"It gives agriculture," Congressman Letts boasted,
"the best rates the farmer has ever had."(7)   The
Smoot-Hawley legislation, Iowa Representatives argued,
sheltered American producers against foreign
competition and perhaps saved the jobs of native
workers. "To keep the home market in large part for
the home producer," Congressman Robinson stressed, "is
a very vital thing." An ardent protectionist,
Representative Haugen asserted, 'It has restricted the
importation of foreign merchandise into this country
and kept American plants going."(8) Politically, the
nearly unanimous Republican delegation gladly
empowered President Hoover to raise duties. "We have
in the White House," Congressman Ramseyer contended,"
a President who understands the needs of the country
and is especially well equipped to deal with the great
economic and moral problems that must be solved."(9)

By contrast, Senators Brookhart and Steck, along with Representative Campbell, denounced the economic ramifications of the Smoot-Hawley bill. (Table 3) The trio protested that the tariff measure benefitted eastern industrialists at the expense of midwestern farmers. "'Big business,'" Brookhart charged, "has garnered extortionate profits, but it has ruined the general prosperity of the country."(10) Campbell condemned the legislation as "one of those political monstrosities" placing "heavier burdens" upon the farmer and feared that it "increased protection for many of those industries" already "making fortunes." Any agricutlrual benefits, Steck warned, would "be more than absorbed in the increased prices the farmer will have to pay because of additional duties on the things he must buy." In addition, they insisted tha tariff increments would harm American foreign trade and sharply curtail agricultural exports. "I favor a protective tariff as an established American institution," Steck declared, "but cannot support a prohibitive tariff."(11)

Similarly, the business-oriented Reconstruction Finance Corporation Act of 1932 attracted wholehearted backing from the Iowa delegation. All Iowa Representatives and Senator Dickinson, who had defeated Steck in the 1930 election, strongly favored the creation of the powerful Reconstruction Finance Corporation. (Tables 2, 3) The comprehensive measure allocated the R.F.C. $500 million to rescue and revive depressed banks, railroads, and building and loan associations.(12)

As on the tariff issue, economic considerations persuaded the Iowa delegation to defend the Reconstruction Finance Corporation Act. The R.F.C. they predicted, would rescue collapsing business institutions and spark national economic recovery. According to Congressman Campbell, "the two million dollar Corporation, with General (Charles) Dawes at its head, will be a great help to the country at large."(13) The Iowa delegation also insisted that the measure would benefit midwestern farmers by revitalizing America's distressed financial institutions and railroads. Representative Haugen, the dean of the Iowa delegation, vowed that the R.F.C. would "give renewed support to business, industry and agriculture." Congressman Cole, an ardent champion of big business, declared, "I hope this gigantic corporation does help the railroads - it will help us all."(14)

Of the entire Iowa Congressional delegation, spirited Senator Brookhart alone resisted the Reconstruction Finance Corporation Act. (Table 3) During floor debate, Brookhart denounced the measure as a "bolshevik bill" advantageous to large business and financial interests."The same bankers who howl about putting the Government into business," he protested, "never hesitate to put it in for their own benefit." Brookhart vowed, "the Senate had better send the Bernard Baruchs, the (Wesley) Mitchells, and the (Robert) Lamonts back to their business" and "pass a real bolshevik bill in the interest of the people of the United States."(15)

Congress, meanwhile, debated several crucial measures assisting organized labor. In 1931 the House passed an immigration bill excluding 376,000 persons over a two-year period and sharply curtailing the European, Canadian, and Mexican quotas. Labor unions enthusiastically greeted the immigration legislation because hordes of foreigners between 1880 and 1920 had taken jobs away from native American workers by toiling for lower wages. Congress in 1932 overwhelmingly approved the Norris-La Guardia Act forbidding injunctions against certain outlawed union practices, guaranteeing jury trials by violators, and making yellow-dog contracts unenforceable in federal courts. During debate o the Revenue Act of 1932, the House crushed an amendment to levy a one yearr sales tax on articles of wide use and distribution by all socio-economic classes. Organized labor, which advocated increasing either graduated income of property levies, denounced the sales tax because it did not alleviate the plight of poor workers.(16)

With economic motivations again paramount, the Immigration Restriction Bill of 1931 and the Norris-La Guardia Act of 1932 were endorsed unanimously by te Iowa Congressional delegation. (Tables 2, 3) Alarmed over the chronic national unemployment rate, Iowa Senators and Representatives argued that foreigners often had stolen jobs from American workers by accepting subsistence wages. "To add 150,000 to our unemployed, by admitting that many employment seekers from foreign lands," Representative Cole warned, "might create a more serious situation than is being created by increasing the loans to former service men." According to Congressman Thurston, "If those in public life during the ten years preceding 1921 had .

. . been able to see the ultimate folly of our
too-liberal immigration policy, there would be no
unemployment today."(17) In addition, the Iowa
delegation charged that immigrants disrupted the
stability and order in American life. "We would
have," Cole feared, "a land teeming with mobs, riots,
communism and anarchy." Cole even declared "our
restrictive immigration law has been our best
enactment in recent years, if not since the
Declaration of Independence."(18) The Norris-La
Guardia Act, several Iowa Congressmen asserted, would
obliterate economic discrimination against organized
labor and guarantee workers more protection.
Representative Haugen stressed "judging by the votes
received, and the sentiment generally expressed by
practicing attorneys, legislation along the line
seemed necessary." A dedicated defender of labor
causes, Congressman Campbell charged that "human
rights had been interfered with under the present
method of granting injunctions."(19)

Unlike the immigration and Norris-La Guardia
measures, however, the sales tax question fragmented
the Iowa Congressional delegation. Five Iowa
Congressmen, along with Senator Dickinson deserted
organized labor this time, lauding the one year sales
tax method for raising federal revenue. (Tables 2, 3)
They claimed that the levy would not only expedite
balancing of the budget, but argued that it would not
hurt ordinary workers. Representative Swanson
proclaimed, "The important matter for consideration
under all circumstances is the balancing of the
budget." Congressman Cole insisted, "The tax is so
light that it is not believed that any one will be
seriously affected."(20)

On the other hand, six Iowa Representatives and
Senator Brookhart warned about the economic dangers of
the sales tax. (Tables 2, 3) Adamant defenders of
organized labor, they protested that the sales tax
discriminated against the downtrodden working classes.
Representative Campbell deplored the sales levy for
"the unfairness it represents," while Senator
Brookhart maintained that "this is a tax directly upon
the people, who are not able to pay for it." In lieu
of a sales tax, they campaigned for increasing
graduated income and property levies. "During times
like these," Campbell retorted, "the rich should
assume the greater portion of the taxation. Surely
these men can far better assume heavy taxes."
Likewise, Brookhart argued that these income and

property levies would be better methods to
"redistribute some of the amassed wealth of the
country" and "build a solid foundation for
prosperity."(21)

By contrast, Iowa Congressmen usually repudiated
federal unemployment relief measures. In June, 1932,
all Iowa Representatives except Democrat Jacobsen
rejected the controversial Garner Relief Bill. (Table
2) This legislation, approved by the House, would
have authorized over two billion dollars for building
construction, flood control projects, and rivers and
harbors improvements. A month later, three
Republicans joined Jacobsen in ratifying the
conference report largely containing the Garner
version.(22)

In the Senate, Brookhart clashed with Dickinson
on federal work relief legislation. During 1932,
Brookhart vigorously favored and Dickinson rejected,
the La Follette-Costigan and Wagner Bills and the
conference report. (Table 3) The La-Follette-Costigan
measure, crushed in February by the Senate, would have
provided direct grants of 375 million dollars to
states for unemployment and public works projects.
The less comprehensive Wagner bill, adopted by the
Senate four months later, would have permitted
Reconstruction Finance Corporation loans totalling 300
million dollars to states and authorized the federal
government to spend 500 million dollars for local
public works projects.(23)

Political and economic connotations of direct
national work relief upset most members of the Iowa
Congressional delegation. Above all, they feared that
such measures would grant the federal government too
much power and authority over the American people.
Senator Dickinson brusquely accused the relief
proposals of being "dangerous in future existence of
government itself," while Congressman Cole attacked
the Garner bill as "hysteria in the nth power,"
"demagogism in the superlative degree," and "bribery
on a national scale."(24) Deploring federal
assistance, they recommended instead that states and
local communities furnish unemployment relief.
Otherwise, critics feared that federal taxes would
skyrocket. Representative Swanson attacked "the
unsound and uneconomic policy of the construction of
public buildings in any section of the country in
times like these when our people are overburdened with
taxes and are themselves in financial distress."

249.

Similarly, Congressman Haugen implored that "drastic reduction in expenditures must be made, not only in local and state expenditures, but with the Federal Government as well."(25) In addition, most Iowa Representatives charged that the Garner measure discriminated economically against the midwestern states. Besides denouncing the Garner proposal as the "biggest pork barrel ever devised," Cole repudiated it as "a form of bribery or corruption, of pollution, and everything else that is bad." In a similar vein, Haugen protested that the measure meant spending "enormous" sums to construct southern projects and claimed that a few northern buildings were included "as a bait to catch the vote from the North."(26)

Economic factors prevailed among the minority defending federal work relief. Alarmed at the ten million jobless rate, they stressed that extensive public works projects would help alleviate the chronic national situation. "If you crowd your poor-houses," Congressman Campbell warned, "it only means additional taxes on the owners of the home and property." Along with charging that "Congress fails all the time to do its duties," Senator Brookhart asserted that work relief was only "one-tenth of what it ought to be." Federal intervention on behalf of the jobless, defenders argued, would help equalize the distribution of income. According to Brookhart, the relief appropriations were largely collected off of large incomes and big estates and not a direct burden on ordinary people."(27)

Between 1929 and 1933, Congress also disagreed over the expansion of federal competition with private enterprise. In April, 1930, the Senate approved the Norris bill permitting the federal government to own and operate power facilities on the Tennessee River at Muscle Shoals, Alabama and construct Cove Creek Dam on the Clinch River in Tennessee. The House, however, discarded the measure, opting instead to lease the government properties at Muscle Shoals to private industry. Nine months later, the House consented to a conference report largely restoring the original Norris version.(28)

For a combination of political and economic reasons, the Iowa Congressional delegation resoundingly remonstrated against the expansion of federal controls over Muscle Schoals. Most Iowa Representatives dissented on the original Norris version, while five even urged leasing the government

properties at Muscle Shoals to private industry. In
February, 1931, eight Iowa Congressmen refused to
accept the ultimate conference report.(29) (Table 2)
As critics of the burgeoning federal bureaucracy, they
charged that the Norris bill would allow the national
government to have an unfair advantage over private
power companies. Representative Cole brusquely
denounced the federal operation of power plants as
"somewhat Russian "and retorted "the more the
government keeps its hands out of business the better
for both business and the government." The Muscle
Shoals project, Congressman Thurston charged, would
"furnish cheap power that might be disastrous to the
coal industry on which my own district is so strongly
dependent. Some may call this a narrow-minded view
but I believe no congressman should acknowledge
leadership other than the sentiment of his
constituents."(30) As on the Garner relief bill, they
complained that the Muscle Shoals measure would
benefit the South at the expense of the Middle West
and other geographical regions. "So far as Iowa is
concerned," Cole contended, "Muscle Shoals is about as
important as the man in the moon. Southern
politicians who still believe that a federal
government owes them something for Civil War losses
are trying to maneuver the United States into a
position of furnishing their planters with
fertilizers made at government expense." Heavy
financial burdens on the American taxpayer, critics
feared, would accrue from the federal operation of
power facilities. "No cheap fertilizer can be made at
the Shoals," Cole claimed, "unless the federal
treasury is looted to do so."(31)

Economic arguments prevailed among the few Iowa
Congressmen defending the Muscle Shoals public power
concept. From the outset, Senators Brookhart and
Steck and Representative Campbell strongly favored the
Norris bill letting the goverment operate the power
facilities. After abstaining originally, Congressmen
Dowell and Dickinson joined Campbell in endorsing the
conference report. (Tables 2, 3) Since private power
companies might ignore the public interest in
developing the Muscle Schoals region, these members
argued that federal government operation of the
facilities would better guarantee consumer protection.
Representative Dickinson warned, "if we cannot
regulate power trusts, we will not be successful in
either owning them or operating them as a Government.
A definite effort should be made to devise a joint
state and Government supervisory policy whereby the

251.

public interest would be protected against the power organizations of the country."(32)

Although almost exclusively Republican, the Iowa delegation ranged from progressive to conservative on the above economic issues. (Tables 2, 3). Representatives Campbell and Gilchrist, along with Senator Brookhart, boldly backed progressivism, aligning with organized labor against big business, demanding massive federal relief for the jobless, and welcoming government competition with private enterprise. Congressman Dowell, a moderate progressive, representing Des Moines, backed organized labor except on the sales tax and defended both work relief and federal operation of the Muscle Shoals facilities. In the moderate camp, Representatives Dickinson, Haugen, and Kopp supported measures aiding business and organized labor and resisted federal unemployment relief., By contrast, Congressmen Cole, Letts, Ramseyer, and Swanson usually aligned with conservatives on Capitol Hill. They not only defended big business over organized labor, but attacked direct federal work relief programs and expanding federal competition with private industry.

The Iowa Congressional delegation largely echoed President Hoover's sentiments on legislation aiding business. An advocate of very limited federal government intervention in the economy, Hoover endorsed both the Smoot-Hawley and Reconstruction Finance Corporation Acts. Nine Iowa Congressmen agreed with the President on both issues, while Senator Brookhart alone consistently repudiated the President's views. Representative Campbell, who split with Hoover over the tariff, admitted, "It is not any easy matter to vote against the leadership and the rest of the delegation. I refuse to be a rubber stamp politician for any group or any organization. I've been sent to Washington to do what I can for the northwestern Iowa district and I'm going to do it."(33)

On the other hand, the Iowa Congressional delegation responded more enthusiastically than Hoover toward legislation helping organized labor. Although favoring the Immigration Restriction Bill of 1931, the President almost vetoed the Norris-La Guardia Act and assiduously defended the anti-labor sales tax. Hoover feared that the Norris-La Guardia Act might make labor unions too powerful and argued that graduated income and property taxes discriminated against wealthier

economic classes. Senator Brookhart and
Representatives Campbell, Dowell, Gilchrist, Haugen,
Kopp, and Thurston aligned more often than the
President with organized labor. They not only
welcomed the Norris-La Guardia Act, but strenuously
objected to the sales tax. Congressman Campbell
lauded labor unions as "the life blood which brings us
the American Standard of Living" rescuing "from the
dark doors of industrial slavery many men and
women."(34) By contrast, Senator Dickinson and
Representatives Cole, Ramseyer, Robinson, and Swanson
were the only members of the Iowa delegation sharing
Hoover's more conservative views on labor legislation.
Cole, who represented the district Hoover was born in,
adamantly defended the President. According to Cole,
"no man has ever done a greater or better work in such
a high office than Mr. Hoover has been doing. Some
day, when we are further along on the way to recovery,
the world over, we will realize what he has been doing
and praise and honor him for it."(35)

On federal work relief measures, the Iowa
Congressional delegation largely concurred with
Hoover. The President despised both the La
Follette-Costigan and Garner bills, demanding instead
the individuals, private organizations, communities,
and states coordinate unemployment relief programs.
In July, 1932, Hoover vetoed the conference report and
particularly attacked the Garner "pork barrel"
provisions.(36) On these controversial issues,
Senator Dickinson and Representatives Cole, Haugen,
Kopp, Ramseyer, Robinson, Swanson, and Thurston
rallied behind the President. Hoover, however, did
not win the support of Congressmen Campbell,
Dowell,and Gilchrist and especially Senator Brookhart,
all of whom demanded an extensive infusion of federal
assistance for the jobless

Similarly, the Muscle Shoals controversy saw a
majority of the Iowa Congressional delegation in
accord with the President. A defender of private
enterprise and voluntarism, Hoover boldly denounced
the direct federal ownership and operation of the
Muscle Shoals properties. In July, 1931, Hoover
issued a stinging veto of the final conference report
containing the Norris version. "This is not
liberalism," Hoover declared, "it is degeneration."
Eight Iowa Representatives sided with the President in
remonstrating against federal operation of the Muscle
Shoals plant, while Senators Brookhart and Steck and
Representatives Campbell, Dickinson, and Dowell

demanded public control.(37)

The Iowa Congressional delegation, to a surprising extent, mirrored national legislative sentiment. Although serving rural constituents primarily and comprising relatively few Democrats, Iowa Senators and Representatives reacted in a more progressive manner than anticipated to national economic problems. Iowa Congressmen surpassed the House as a whole in the degree of enthusiastic support for legislation aiding business and organized labor. (Table 4) By contrast, Iowa Representatives lagged behind national sentiment only on the unemployment relief and public power questions.

Several conclusions might be drawn. During the Hoover era, Iowa Senators and Representatives zealously defended federal assistance to business and organized labor. On the other hand, it rejected aid to the jobless by the federal government and public operation of the Muscle Shoals power facilities. Bloc voting normally occurred on business or labor measures, most notably on the Reconstruction Finance Corporation and Norris-La Guardia Acts and the Immigration Restriction bill. Iowa Representatives, though, split sharply on the sales tax and lacked consensus on the work relief and Muscle Shoals issues. The attitudes of individual members fluctuated considerably, ranging from the rabid progressivism of Brookhart, Campbell, and Gilchrist to the marked conservatism of Cole, Letts, Ramseyer, and Swanson.

Economic factors usually overshadowed political considerations as voting determinants among the Iowa Congressional delegation. Spirited advocates of business and labor legislation, Iowa Senators and Representatives sought to revive economic prosperity across the nation and especially for farmers from the Middle West. Iowa farmers, already suffering serious economic difficulties in the 1920's, continued to experience a drastic decline in prices for their products. Business revival and tariff increases, the Iowa delegation argued, would spark agricultural recovery. Iowa Senators and Representatives backed legislation aiding urban workers in hopes that organized labor would reciprocate on agricultural measures. Political and economic determinants both affected the voting behavior of the Iowa Congressional delegation on then work relief and Muscle Shoals questions. Fearful that these measures would increase taxes, Iowa Congressmen also charged that the federal

government would seize too much power and warned that
other geographical sections would derive greater
benefits than the Middle West.

Finally, the Iowa Congressional delegation
exhibited more progressive attitudes than Hoover on
these crucial economic issues. Progressive sentiments
of Iowa Senators and Representatives flourished most
readily on labor legislation, but several members also
were more receptive than the President to federal work
relief and government operation of the Muscle Shoals
power facilities. Business measures, however, saw
widespread cooperation between the Iowa Congressional
delegation and Hoover.

Table 1
Members of Iowa Delegation, 1929-1933

Member/Hometown	Party	Chamber	Years
Smith W. Brookhart Washington	Repl.	Senate	1922-1925 1927-1933
Ed. H. Campbell Battle Creek	Repl.	House	1929-1933
Cyrenus Cole Cedar Rapids	Repl.	House	1921-1933
Lester J. Dickinson Algona	Repl.	House Senate	1919-1931 1931-1937
Cassius C. Dowell Des Moines	Repl.	House	1915-1935 1937-1940
Fred C. Gilchrist Laurens	Repl.	House	1931-1945
Gilbert N. Haugen Northwood	Repl.	House	1899-1933
Bernhard M.Jaconbson Clinton	Demo.	House	1931-1936
William F. Kopp Mt. Pleasant	Repl.	House	1921-1933
Fred D. Letts Davenport	Repl.	House	1925-1931
C. Wm. Ramseyer Bloomfield	Repl.	House	1915-1933
Thos. J.B. Robinson Hampton	Repl.	House	1923-1933
Daniel F. Steck Ottumwa	Demo.	Senate	1926-1931
Chas. E. Swanson Council Bluffs	Repl.	House	1929-1933
Lloyd Thurston Osceola	Repl.	House	1925-1939

Table 2
House Roll Calls

Member	Campbell	Cole	Dickinson	Dowell	Haugen	Kopp	Letts	Ramseyer	Robinson	Swanson	Thurston	Gilchrist	Jacobsen
ROLL CALL/DATE													
Smoot-Hawley Tariff Act (6/14/30)	N	Y	Y	Y	Y	Y	Y	Y	Y	Y	Y		
Reconstr. Fin. Corp. Act. (1/15/32)	Y	Y		Y	Y	Y		Y	Y	Y	Ab	Y	Y
Immigr. Recon. Bill (3/2/31)	Y	Y	Y	Y	Y	Y	Y	Y	Y	Y	Y	Y	
Norris-LaGuardia Act (3/8/32)	Y	Y		Y	Y	Y		Y	Y	Y	Y	N	Y
Sales Tax Rev. Act (4/1/32)	N	Y		N	Y	N		Y	Y	Y	N	N	N
Garner Bill (6/7/32)	N	N		Ab	N	N		N	N	N	N	Y	Y
Work Relief Conf. (7/7/32)	Y	N		Y	N	N		N	N	N	N		Y
Muscle Shoals Bill (5/28/30)	N	Y	Ab	Ab	Ab	Ab	Y	Y	Ab	Y	Y		
Muscle Shoals Conf. (2/18/31)	Y	N	Y	Y	N	N	N	N	N	N	N		

Y=Yes Vote   N=No Vote   Ab=Abstain or absent

TABLE 3
Senate Roll Calls

Roll Call and Date	Brookhart	Steck	Dickinson
Smoot-Hawley Tariff Act (6/13/30)	N	N	
Reconstr. Fin. Corp. Act (1/11/32)	N		Ab
Norris-La Guardia Act (3/1/32)	Y		Y
LaFollette-Costigan Bill (2/16/32)	Y		N
Wagner Bill (6/10/32)	Y		Ab
Work Relief Conference (7/9/32)	Y		Ab
Muscle Shoals Bill (4/4/30)	Y	N	
Muscle Shoals Conf. (2/21/31)	Y	Y	

Y=Yes Vote   N=No Vote   Ab=Abstain or Absent

The Senate did not vote on Immigration Restriction Bill of 1931 or Sales Tax provision of Revenue Act of 1932.

TABLE 4
House Roll Call Votes on Economic Issues

Issue/Date	Percentage Iowa Delegation For	Percentage Entire House For
Smoot Hawley Tariff 6/14/30	91	59
Reconstr. Fin. Corp. 1/15/32	100	86
Immigr. Restr. 3/2/31	100	78
Norris-LaGuardia 3/18/32	100	96
Sales Tax 4/1/32	45	40
Garner Relief 6/7/32	10	54
Work Relief (Confer.) 7/7/32	36	56
Muscle Shoals (initial) 5/28/30	83	63
Muscle Shoals (Confer.) 2/18/31	27	59

Bibliographical Essay

This essay is based largely on Congressional collections. At the State Historical Society of Iowa, the voluminous Gilbert N. Haugen Papers have significant material on the tariff and organized labor. Although much smaller, the Cyrenus Cole Papers contain several invaluable scrapbooks of weekly newsletters describing economic legislative issues. The Lloyd Thurston Papers are of less value, but contain newspaper clippings of his speeches and his unpublished autobiography. At the University of Iowa, there are several pertinent manuscript collections. The C. William Ramseyer Papers has much correspondence on legislation affecting business, while the Fred D. Letts Papers and particularly the Ed Hoyt Campbell Papers are helpful on elections and tariffs. The Lester J. Dickinson Papers and the Thomas J. B. Robinson Papers contain little pertinent material, although the former is abundant in anti-New Deal speeches. At the Hoover Library, the Presidential and Post-Presidential Papers include candid letters from Dickinson and Thurston to Hoover. The President, despite being a native of Iowa, corresponded surprisingly little with the Republican dominated Congressional delegation.

Government publications, along with newspapers and journals, illuminate economic issues in the 1929-1933 period. Besides listing roll call votes made by each member, the Congressional Record reveals the legislative attitudes of Smith W. Brookhart, Cassius C. Dowell, William F. Kopp, Daniel F. Steck, and others. The New York Times and the Washington Post provide excellent legislative histories of economic issues, while the Des Moines Register and the Cedar Rapids Gazette are indispensable on both Congressional elections and the attitudes of Iowa Senators and Representatives on several vital measures. For an excellent analysis of trade issues, see "Iowa Senators and Congressmen Discuss Tariff," The Iowa Homestead (May 16, 1929), 5-6.

Unfortunately there are few published studies of the Iowa Congressional delegation in the Hoover era. Sketchy biographical information appears in Mildred Throne, "Iowans in Congress, 1847-1953," Iowa Journal of History, 51 (1953), 329-368 and Biographical Directory of the American Congress 1774-1971 (Washington: U.S.Government Printing Office, 1971). Cyrenus Cole, I Remember, I Remember; A Book of

Recollections (Iowa City: State Historical Society of
Iowa, 1936) is a spicy anecdotal memoir highlighting
his Congressional career. Brookhart, the most
flamboyant member of the Iowa delegation, captures the
most attention of individual members, being the
subject of several unpublished graduate school studies
and of a forthcoming biography by George W. McDaniel.
For the Senator's often controversial election
campaigns, see Jerry Alvin Neprash, The Brookhart
Campaigns in Iowa, 1920-1926: a Study in the
Motivations of Political Attitudes (New York: Columbia
University Press, 1932). Reinhard H. Luthin, "Smith
Wildman Brookhart of Iowa: Insurgent Agrarian
Politician," Agricultural History, XXV (October,
1951), 187-197 ably summarizes Brookhart's dynamic
career. On Brookhart's early years, consult George W.
McDaniel, "Prohibition Debate in Washington County,
1890-1894: Smith Wildman Brookhart's Introduction to
Politics," The Annals of Iowa, 45 (Winter, 1981),
519-536. Peter T. Harstad and Bonnie Michael are
preparing a biography of Haugen, but there are
unfortunately no published biographies of Dickinson,
Dowell, Kopp, or Ramseyer. Philip A.Grant, Jr., "Iowa
Congressional Leaders, 1921-1932," Annals of Iowa, 42
(Fall, 1974), 430-442 gives very helpful background
information on Dickinson, Dowell, Haugen, and Kopp.
David L. Porter, "Ramseyer's Battle for Monetary
Reform," Books at Iowa, 34 (April, 1981), 15-28
concentrates on the economic role of a crucial member
of the Ways and Means Committee.

    Several books are indispensible on economic
issues during the Hoover presidency. The best
Congressional study is Jordan A. Schwarz, The
Interregnum of Despair: Hoover, Congress, and the
Depression (Urbana: University of Illinois Press,
1970). Ellis W. Hawley, The Great War and the Search
for a Modern Order: A History of the American People
and Their Institutions, 1917-1933 (New York: St.
Martin's Press, 1979); James S. Olson, Herbert Hoover
and the Reconstruction Finance Corporation, 1931-1933
(Ames: Iowa State University Press, 1977); Susan
Estabrook Kennedy, The Banking Crisis of 1933
(Lexington: University Press of Kentucky, 1973); and
Robert Himmelberg, The Origins of the National
Recovery Administration (New York: Fordham University
Press, 1976) ably illuminate important business issues
confronting the Hoover administration. On labor
legislation, the best sources are Irving Bernstein,
The Lean Years: A History of the American Worker,
1920-1933 (Boston: Houghton Mifflin, 1960) and J.

Joseph Huthmacher, Senator Robert F. Wagner and the
Rise of Urban Liberalism (New York: Atheneum, 1968).
Work relief issues are perceptively surveyed in John
A. Garraty, Unemployment in History: Economic Thought
and Public Policy (New York: Harper & Row, 1978), and
Patrick J. Maney, 'Young Bob' La Follette: A Biography
of Robert M. La Follette, Jr., 1895-1953 (Columbia:
University of Missouri Press, 1978). Preston J.
Hubbard, Origins of the TVA: Ths Muscle Shoals
Controversy, 1920-1932 (New York: W. W. Norton, 1961)
and Richard Lowitt, George W. Norris: The Persistence
of a Progressive 1913-1933 (Urbana: University of
Illinois Press, 1971) illuminate the public power
question.

        Several other books have significant background
information on the Hoover era. Joan Hoff Wilson,
Herbert Hoover: Forgotten Progressive (Boston: Little,
Brown, 1975); David Burner, Herbert Hoover: A Public
Life (New York: Alfred A, Knopf, 1978); Martin L.
Fausold and George T. Mazuzan, eds., The Hoover
Presidency: A Reappraisal (Albany: State University of
New York Press, 1974); and J. Joseph Huthmacher and
Warren I. Sussman, eds., Herbert Hoover and the Crisis
of American Capitalism (Cambridge, Mass.: Schenkman
Publishing Company, 1973) describe the 1929-1933
period, utilizing extensively the Hoover Papers.
Albert U. Romasco, The Poverty of Abundance: Hoover,
the Nation, the Depression (New York: Oxford
University Press, 1965) and Harris G. Warren, Herbert
Hoover and the Great Depression (New York: Oxford
University Press, 1959) are informative earlier
accounts of the Hoover era. For the transition from
Hoover to Franklin D. Roosevelt, see the excellent
Frank Freidel, Franklin D. Roosevelt: Launching the
New Deal (Boston: Little, Brown, 1973) and Arthur M.
Schlesinger, Jr., The Age of Roosevelt: The Crisis of
the Old Order 1919-1933 (Boston: Houghton Mifflin,
1960).

FOOTNOTES

1. I am indebted to the National Endowment for the
   Humanities for financial assistance in
   researching this topic at the Hoover Library, the
   University of Iowa Library, and the State
   Historical Society of Iowa. James T. Patterson,
   The New Deal and the States: Federalism in
   Transition (Princeton: Princeton University
   Press, 1969) and Paul E. Mertz, New Deal Policy
   and Southern Rural Poverty (Baton Rouge:
   Louisiana State University Press, 1978) discuss
   the response to national reform programs at the
   state and local levels during the Great
   Depression.

2. Business measures examined are the Smoot-Hawley
   Tariff Act of 1930 and the Reconstruction Finance
   Corporation Act of 1932, while the labor
   legislation studied includes the Immigration
   Restriction Bill of 1931, the Norris-La Guardia
   Act of 1932, and the sales tax provision of the
   Revenue Act of 1932. The La Follette-Costigan,
   Garner, and Wagner Bills of 1932 are the federal
   unemployment relief measures examined, while the
   Muscle Shoals Bill of 1930 is the principal
   legislation enhancing federal competition with
   private industry. For background on Hoover
   and/or Congress, see David Burner, Herbert
   Hoover: A Public Life (New York: Alfred A. Knopf,
   1978); Joan Hoff Wilson, Herbert Hoover: A
   Forgotten Progressive (Boston: Little, Brown,
   1975); Jordan A. Schwarz, The Interregnum of
   Despair: Hoover, Congress and the Depression
   (Urbana: University of Illinois Press, 1970);
   Ellis W. Hawley, The Great War and the Search for
   a Modern Order: A History of the American People
   and Their Institutions, 1917-1933 (New York: St.
   Martin's Press, 1979); Martin L. Fausold and
   George T. Mazuzan (eds.), The Hoover Presidency:
   A Reappraisal (Albany: State University of New
   York Press, 1974); J. Joseph Huthmacher and
   Warren I. Sussman (eds.), Herbert Hoover and the
   Crisis of American Capitalism (Cambridge, Mass.:
   Schenkman, 1973); Albert U. Romasco, The Poverty
   of Abundance: Hoover, the Nation, and the
   Depression (New York: Oxford University Press,
   1965); and Harris G. Warren, Herbert Hoover and
   the Great Depression (New York: Oxford
   University Pres, 1959).

3. Mildred Throne, "Iowans in Congress, 1847-1953,"
    Iowa Journal of History, 51 (1953), 329-368;
    Biographical Directory of the American Congress
    1774-1971 (Washington: U. S. Government Printing
    Office, 1971); Philip A. Grant, Jr., "Iowa
    Congressional Leaders, 1921-1932," Annals of
    Iowa, 42 (Fall, 1974), 430-442.

4. For a pertinent memoir, see Cyrenus Cole, I
    Remember I Remember: A Book of Recollections
    (Iowa City: The State Historical Society of Iowa,
    1936). There unfortunately are no published
    biographies of Iowa Senators and Representatives
    from the Hoover era, but George W. McDaniel is
    preparing one of Smith Wildman Brookhart and
    Peter T. Harstad and Bonnie Michael are
    collaborating on one of Gilbert N. Haugen. There
    are numerous unpublished studies of Senator
    Brookhart, including Ray S. Johnston, "Smith
    Wildman Brookhart: Iowa's Last Populist" (M.A.
    thesis, Iowa State Teachers' College, 1964);
    George W. McDaniel, "Over Here: The Mobilization
    of the Republican Service League to Defeat Smith
    Wildman Brookhart" (M.A. essay, University of
    Iowa, 1977); C   D. Cornell, "Smith W.
    Brookhart and Agrarian Discontent in Iowa" (M.A.
    thesis, University of Iowa, 1946); Barry A.
    Russell, "The Changing Concept of Iowa
    Progressivism: Smith W. Brookhart vs. Albert B. C
    [sic] s, 1920-1926" (M.A. thesis, University of
    North Carolina, 1973); Cornelius Holland ull
    III, "Smith Wildman Brookhart -- Neither God nor
    Little Fish" (Senior thesis, Princeton
    University, 1950). For published works on
    Brookhart, see Rei   Luth   Smith Wildman
    Brookhart of Iowa: Insurgent Agrarian
    Politician," A [sic] (October, 1951), 187-197;
    George W. McDaniel, "Prohibition Debate in
    Washington County, 1890-1894: Smith Wildman
    Brookhart's Introduction to Politics," The Annals
    of Iowa, 45 (Winter, 1981), 519-536; Jerry
    Neprash, The Brookhart Campaigns in Iowa,
    1920-1926 (New York: Columbia University Press,
    1932).

5. For Smoot-Hawley Act of 1930, see Frank W.
    Taussig, The Tariff History of the United States,
    8th ed. (New York: G. P. Putnam's Sons, 1931) and
    Joseph M. Jones, Jr., Tariff Retaliation
    (Philadelphia: University of Pennsylvania Press,
    1934).

6. Congressional Record, 71 Cong., 2 Sess., June 14,
    1930, p. 10789;   Cyrenus Cole Washington
    Newsletter, January 2, 1930.   Cyrenus Cole
    Papers, State Historical Society of Iowa,
    Scrapbook 7 (hereafter CC, SSHI);   Cyrenus Cole
    to Walter H. Newton, June 9, 1930, "Tariff
    Commission," Presidential Papers, Herbert Hoover
    Library, Box 281 (hereafter HHPL).

7. Gilbert N. Haugen, "Campaign Remarks," 1930,
    Gilbert N. Haugen Papers, SHSI, Box 129
    (hereafter GNH, SHSI);   "Iowa Senators and
    Congressmen Discuss Tariff," The Iowa Homestead
    (May 16, 1929) in Fred D. Letts Papers,
    University of Iowa Libraries, Scrapbook 9
    (hereafter FDL, UIL).

8. Thomas J. B. Robinson, "Tariff," 1930, Thomas J.
    B. Robinson Papers, UIL, Speeches (hereafter
    TJBR, UIL);   North Iowa Times, October 6, 1932 in
    GNH Papers, SHSI, Box 129.

9. "Congressman Ramseyer Talks About the Tariff,"
    Des Moines Register, August 2, 1929, "Ramseyer,"
    Presidential Papers, HHPL, Box 686.

10. Congressional Record, 71 Cong., 2 Sess., June 13,
    1930, p. 10635;   Smith W. Brookhart, Radio
    Address, March 19, 1932, in Congressional Record,
    72 Cong., 1 Sess., March 21, 1932, p. 6786.

11. Ed H. Campbell, N.B.C. Radio Address, Washington,
    D. C., March 19, 1930, Ed H. Campbell Papers,
    UIL, Box 11 (hereafter EHC, UIL);   Ed H. Campbell
    to Lewis L. Robbins, June 19, 1930, EHC Paper,
    UIL, Box 10;   Iowa Homestead, May 16, 1929.

12. Congressional Record, 72 Cong., 1 Sess., January
    15, 1932, p. 2081;   January 11, 1932, p. 1705.
    James S. Olson, Herbert Hoover and the
    Reconstruction Finance Corporation, 1931-1933
    (Ames: Iowa State University Press, 1977), and
    Gerald D. Nash, "Herbert Hoover and the Origins
    of the Reconstruction Finance Corporation,"
    Mississippi Valley Historical Review, 46
    (December, 1959), 455-468 describe the
    Reconstruction Finance Corporation.

13. Ed H. Campbell, Speech, undated, EHC Papers, UIL,
    Box 11, Speeches.

14. Gilbert N. Haugen to F. K. Runner, February 1, 1932, GNH Papers, SHSI, Box 37; Gilbert N. Haugen to O. T. Knudtson, January 11, 1932, GNH Papers, SHSI, Box 37; Cyrenus Cole Washington Newsletter, January 18, 1932, CC Papers, SHSI, Scrapbook 7.

15. Congressional Record, 72 Cong., 1 Sess., January 8, 1932, pp. 1493, 1496-97; January 7, 1932, p. 1436.

16. For labor measures in the Hoover era, see Schwarz, Interregnum of Despair; Irving Bernstein, The Lean Years: A History of the American Worker, 1920-1933 (Boston: Houghton Mifflin, 1960); Richard Lowitt, George W. Norris: The Persistence of a Progressive, 1913-1933 (Urbana: University of Illinois Press, 1971); Howard Zinn, La Guardia in Congress (Ithaca: Cornell University Press, 1959); and J. Joseph Huthmacher, Senator Robert F. Wagner and the Rise of Urban Liberalism (New York: Athenaum, 1968).

17. Congressional Record, 71 Cong., 3 Sess., March 2, 1931, pp. 6744, 6721; 72 Cong., 1 Sess., March 8, 1932, p. 5511; March 1, 1932, p. 5019; Cyrenus Cole Washington Newsletter, February 18, 1931, CC Papers, SHSI, Scrapbook 7; Lloyd Thurston, Speech, Derby Fair, 1932, Lloyd Thurston Papers, SHSI, Box 4, Newspaper Clippings (hereafter LT, SHSI).

18. Cyrenus Cole Washington Newsletter, March 1, 1928, CC Papers, SHSI, Scrapbook 6.

19. Gilbert N. Haugen to Leo Hufschmidt, March 25, 1932, GNH Papers, SHSI, Box 37; Ed H. Campbell to George T. Hatley, March 28, 1932, EHC Papers, UIL, Box 11.

20. Congressional Record, 72 Cong., 1 Sess., April 1, 1932, . 7329; May 31, 1932, p.11666; March 16, 1932, p. 6264; Cyrenus Cole Washington Newsletter, March 19, 1932, CC Papers, SHSI, Scrapbook 7. House rejection of the sales tax approach dismayed the anti-labor forces within the Iowa delegation. "The debacle," Cole declared, "was the most expensive piece of legislative cowardice and bungling that I have

seen since I have been in Congress." Cyrenus
Cole Washington Newsletter, June 4, 1932. CC
Papers, SHSI, Scrapbook 7; Cole, I Remember, p.
515.

21. Sioux City News Release, January 25, 1932, EHC
Papers, UIL, Box 4; Brookhart, Radio Address,
March 19, 1932.

22. Congressional Record, 72 Cong., 1 Sess., June 7,
1932, p. 12244; July 7, 1932, p. 14820. For
work relief measures, see the books listed in
footnote 16.

23. Congressional Record, 72 Cong., 1 Sess., February
16, 1932, p. 4052; June 10, 1932, p. 12549;
July 9, 1932, p. 14957.

24. Cyrenus Cole Washington Newsletter, May 28, 1932,
CC Papers, SSHI, Scrapbook 7.

25. Congressional Record, 72 Cong., 1 Sess., June 7,
1932, p. 12249; Gilbert N. Haugen to C. A.
Hammer, April 9, 1932, CNH Papers, SHSI, Box 37.

26. Cole Newsletter, May 28, 1932; Gilbert N.
Haugen, Speech, 1932, GNH Papers, SHSI, Box 129.

27. Ed H. Campbell, Speech, undated, EHC Papers, UIL,
Box 11; Congressional Record, 72 Cong., 1 Sess.,
June 10, 1932, 12536.

28. Congressional Record, 71 Cong., 2 Sess., April 4,
1930, p. 6511; May 28, 1930, p. 9767; 71 Cong.,
3 Sess., February 1 , 1931, pp. 5570-71;
February 21, 1931, p. 5716. In May, 1930,
Representatives Dickinson, Dowell, Haugen, Kopp,
and Robinson abstained on the Muscle Shoals Bill.
For the Muscle Shoals controversy, see Lowitt,
Norris: Persistence of a Progressive, pp.
457-463; Preston J. Hubbard, Origins of the TVA:
The Muscle Shoals Controversy, 1920-1932 (New
York: W.W.Norton, 1961).

29. Congressional Record, 71 Cong., 2 Sess., May 28,
1930, p. 9767; 71 Cong., 3 Sess., February 18,
1931, pp. 5570-71.

30. Cyrenus Cole Washington Newsletter, April 3,
1930, CC Papers, SHSI, Scrapbook 7; Lloyd
Thurston Speech, Monroe County, Iowa, 1934, LT

Papers, SHSI, Box 4.

31. Cyrenus Cole Washington Newsletter, January 14, 1931, CC Papers, SHSI, Scrapbook 7.

32. Congressional Record, 71 Cong., 2 Sess., April 4, 1930, p. 6511; May 28, 1930, p. 9767; 71 Cong., 3 Sess., February 18, 1931, pp. 5570-71; February 21, 1931, p. 5716; Lester J. Dickinson, C.B.S. Radio Speech, Washington, D. C., March 31, 1931, "Dickinson," Presidential Papers, HHPL, Box 530.

33. Spencer News Herald, July 4, 1932; Campbell to Robbins, June 19, 1930.

34. Ed H. Campbell, Speech, September 1, 1930, EHC Papers, UIL, Box 11.

35. Cyrenus Cole Washington Newsletter, January 7, 1931, CC Papers, SHSI, Scrapbook 7. Other Iowa Representatives defended Hoover's performance as chief executive. See Fred D. Letts to Constituents, October 31, 1930, FDL Papers, UIL, Scrapbook 2; Lester J. Dickinson, Speech, Donnelson, Iowa, September 27, 1930, GNH Papers, SHSI, Box 140.

36. Schwarz,. Interregnum of Despair, pp. 162-172; Warren, Hoover and Great Depression, pp. 205-07.

37. Lowitt, Norris: Persistence of a Progressive, pp. 463-64; Congressional Record, 71 Cong., 3 Sess., February 21, 1931, p. 5716.